Cases on Crimes, Investigations, and Media Coverage

Liam James Leonard
University of Winchester, UK

A volume in the Advances in Criminology, Criminal Justice, and Penology (ACCJP) Book Series

IGI Global
PUBLISHER of TIMELY KNOWLEDGE

Published in the United States of America by
IGI Global
Information Science Reference (an imprint of IGI Global)
701 E. Chocolate Avenue
Hershey PA, USA 17033
Tel: 717-533-8845
Fax: 717-533-8661
E-mail: cust@igi-global.com
Web site: http://www.igi-global.com

Library of Congress Cataloging-in-Publication Data

Names: Leonard, Liam James, 1965- editor.
Title: Cases on crimes, investigations, and media coverage / Liam Leonard, editor.
Description: Hershey, PA : Information Science Reference, [2023] | Includes bibliographical references and index. | Summary: "This book examines a series of case studies on key crimes and the subsequent media coverage of those crimes, including films, television, social media and podcasts to add to our current understandings of the impact of serious crimes but also the media coverage of such crimes, including movies, television, documentaries, social media, podcasts etc"-- Provided by publisher.
Identifiers: LCCN 2022027227 (print) | LCCN 2022027228 (ebook) | ISBN 9781799896685 (hardcover) | ISBN 9781799896692 (paperback) | ISBN 9781799896708 (ebook)
Subjects: LCSH: Crime--Case studies. | Crime--Press coverage. | Mass media and crime.
Classification: LCC HV6025 .C3544 2023 (print) | LCC HV6025 (ebook) | DDC 364--dc23/eng/20220902
LC record available at https://lccn.loc.gov/2022027227
LC ebook record available at https://lccn.loc.gov/2022027228

This book is published in the IGI Global book series Advances in Criminology, Criminal Justice, and Penology (ACCJP) (ISSN: pending; eISSN: pending)

British Cataloguing in Publication Data
A Cataloguing in Publication record for this book is available from the British Library.

All work contributed to this book is new, previously-unpublished material.
The views expressed in this book are those of the authors, but not necessarily of the publisher.

For electronic access to this publication, please contact: eresources@igi-global.com.

Advances in Criminology, Criminal Justice, and Penology (ACCJP) Book Series

ISSN:pending
EISSN:pending

Editor-in-Chief: Liam J. Leonard Winchester University, UK

MISSION

Criminology has never been more relevant. Violence, serial murder, crime and victimization continue to remain an unfortunate staple of society. Crime is a key issue globally, nationally, and regionally. Law enforcement personnel within the criminal justice system must keep pace with ever changing modes of crime. As officials work to predict and prevent crimes, as well as apprehend offenders, they will need to devise new tools and strategies to preserve the safety of society and ensure proper justice is served.

The **Advances in Criminology, Criminal Justice, and Penology (ACCJP)** Book Series explores emerging research behind crime control strategies, crime motivation, new methods and the utilization of technology for committing illegal acts, criminal justice and reform strategies, and the effects of crime on society and its victims. The publications contained within this series are valuable resources for government officials, law enforcement officers, corrections officers, prison management, criminologists, sociologists, psychologists, forensic scientists, security specialists, academicians, researchers, and students seeking current research on international crime.

COVERAGE

- Criminology
- Victimology
- Policing
- Penal System
- Criminal Psychology
- Criminal Justice Systems
- Drug Trafficking
- Hacking
- Human Trafficking
- Serial Killers

IGI Global is currently accepting manuscripts for publication within this series. To submit a proposal for a volume in this series, please contact our Acquisition Editors at Acquisitions@igi-global.com or visit: http://www.igi-global.com/publish/.

The Advances in Criminology, Criminal Justice, and Penology (ACCJP) Book Series (ISSN pending) is published by IGI Global, 701 E. Chocolate Avenue, Hershey, PA 17033-1240, USA, www.igi-global.com. This series is composed of titles available for purchase individually; each title is edited to be contextually exclusive from any other title within the series. For pricing and ordering information please visit http://www.igi-global.com/book-series/advances-criminology-criminal-justice-penology/212650. Postmaster: Send all address changes to above address.

Titles in this Series

For a list of additional titles in this series, please visit:
www.igi-global.com/book-series/advances-criminology-criminal-justice-penology/212650

Paths to the Prevention and Detection of Human Trafficking
Sharon K. Andrews (University of Houston-Clear Lake, USA) and Caroline M. Crawford (University of Houston-Clear Lake USA)
Information Science Reference • © 2022 • 422pp • H/C (ISBN: 9781668439265) • US $215.00

Comparative Criminology Across Western and African Perspectives
Simeon P. Sungi (United States International University-Africa, Kenya) and Nabil Ouassini (Prairie View A&M University USA)
Information Science Reference • © 2022 • 322pp • H/C (ISBN: 9781799828563) • US $250.00

Handbook of Research on Present and Future Paradigms in Human Trafficking
Essien D. Essien (University of Uyo, Nigeria)
Information Science Reference • © 2022 • 488pp • H/C (ISBN: 9781799892823) • US $295.00

Global Perspectives on Reforming the Criminal Justice System
Michael Pittaro (American Military University, USA)
Information Science Reference • © 2021 • 380pp • H/C (ISBN: 9781799868842) • US $215.00

Interventions, Training, and Technologies for Improved Police Well-Being and Performance
Eamonn Patrick Arble (Department of Psychology, Eastern Michigan University, USA) and Bengt B. Arnetz (College of Human Medicine, Michigan State University, USA)
Information Science Reference • © 2021 • 278pp • H/C (ISBN: 9781799868200) • US $215.00

Invisible Victims and the Pursuit of Justice Analyzing Frequently Victimized Yet Rarely Discussed Populations
Raleigh Blasdell (North Central College, USA) Laura Krieger-Sample (Southeast Missouri State University, USA) and Michelle Kilburn (Southeast Missouri State University, USA)
Information Science Reference • © 2021 • 474pp • H/C (ISBN: 9781799873488) • US $215.00

IGI Global
PUBLISHER of TIMELY KNOWLEDGE

701 East Chocolate Avenue, Hershey, PA 17033, USA
Tel: 717-533-8845 x100 • Fax: 717-533-8661
E-Mail: cust@igi-global.com • www.igi-global.com

Table of Contents

Preface...xiii

Acknowledgment...xviii

Chapter 1
Introduction: Cases on Crime and Media 1
Liam James Leonard, University of Winchester, UK

Chapter 2
The Making of a Monster: UK Press Coverage of Myra Hindley 11
Mark Pettigrew, University of Bolton, UK

Chapter 3
Levi Bellfield: The Bus Stop Stalker 30
Shannon DeBlasio, Arden University, UK

Chapter 4
Fake It Until You Make It! The Crimes and Trial of Anna Sorokin (Delvey).....52
Angelo Kevin Brown, Arkansas State University, USA

Chapter 5
The Murder of Sophie Toscan du Plantier and Its Implications for the Study of Media and Crime: A Case Study in West Cork 68
Shane O'Mahony, University of Hertfordshire, UK

Chapter 6
Trayvon Martin: A Black Boy Who Made an Impact..94
Michelle Eliasson, University of Florida, USA

Chapter 7
Crime in Perugia: The Murder of Meredith Kercher 117
Beatrice Ugolini, University "N. Cusano", Rome, Italy & British Society of Criminology, UK

Chapter 8
Corpus Delicti? Forensic Dimensions of the No-Body Murder 133
Anna Chaussée, University of Winchester, UK

Chapter 9
An Analysis of Biases in US Policing and Subsequent Media Coverage in Response to the Ferguson Shooting of 2014 169
Liam James Leonard, University of Winchester, UK

Chapter 10
The Aileen Wuornos Case: Bending the Criminal Binary of Monsters and Martyrs 192
Christine Bussey, Judson College, USA

Chapter 11
A Rural Community's Mobilization and Media Strategies in Response to a Contested Infrastructural Project 201
Liam James Leonard, Arden University Manchester, UK

Chapter 12
A Penchant for Murder: The Case Study of John Wayne Gacy 221
Gianna M. Strube, Independent Researcher, USA

Compilation of References 227

About the Contributors 248

Index 251

Detailed Table of Contents

Preface..xiii

Acknowledgment..xviii

Chapter 1
Introduction: Cases on Crime and Media 1
Liam James Leonard, University of Winchester, UK

The link between crime and the media is a longstanding one. Indeed, crime is one of the mainstays of traditional and contemporary media, alongside politics and sports. This volume of the Advances in Criminology, Criminal Justice, and Penology series includes a series of contributions that examine a number of crimes, which include cases that are both notorious and interesting. The volume has contributions from a number of eminent criminologists, who have a combined expertise in the field which lends itself to a collection of both depth and variety of discussion and analysis. As criminology has become more popular, it is now a topic that engenders a great deal of media coverage, with films, documentaries, podcasts, and even whole channels dedicated to famous and infamous cases. While this increase in popularity is welcome, it also necessitates a greater level of expertise and analysis.

Chapter 2
The Making of a Monster: UK Press Coverage of Myra Hindley 11
Mark Pettigrew, University of Bolton, UK

Occurring between 1963 and 1965, the murders committed by Myra Hindley and Ian Brady are notorious in British criminal history. Whilst the crimes were callous and coldblooded, their infamy is largely the result of the media's enduring and relentless preoccupation with Hindley herself. Although it has been nearly 20 years since her death, Hindley continues to appear as a news story even in 2022. This chapter will critically analyse the media discourses that surrounded Hindley from her trial, through the years of her imprisonment, to the time of her death. Particularly, it will assess the detriment of press coverage to her bids for freedom in the context of public opinion and its effect upon politicians who were responsible for the setting and review of her life tariff.

Chapter 3
Levi Bellfield: The Bus Stop Stalker 30
Shannon DeBlasio, Arden University, UK

Levi Bellfield, now known as Yusuf Rahim, was the first person within the UK to be handed a life sentence whilst already serving a whole life sentence within Her Majesty's Prison. He was convicted in 2008 of the murders of Marsha McDonnell and Amelie Delgrange as well as the attempted murder of Kate Sheedy. Then in 2011 he was further convicted for the murder of Milly Dowler. The UK press coverage of Bellfield's crimes has been monumental, with the media serving as both a help and a hinderance during the police investigation and years to follow. This chapter provides a detailed overview of Bellfield's crimes, an insight into the complex police investigation, and a glimpse at how the media impacted events which unfolded. Finally, Bellfield's motivations will be explored through the criminal narrative framework, offering a theoretical overview of his likely personal story.

Chapter 4
Fake It Until You Make It! The Crimes and Trial of Anna Sorokin (Delvey).....52
Angelo Kevin Brown, Arkansas State University, USA

The chapter will provide an overview of the life, crimes, and trial of Anna Sorokin better known as Anna Delvey. Anna had invented a false persona and life so that people would think she was a rich German heiress instead of her real identity of a woman from a working-class Russian family. Anna used her false identity to defraud banks, hotels, and friends for about $275,000. Anna's life became internationally known with her story being published in major news and media articles including podcasts, 60 Minutes, HBO, a $300,000 book deal to her former friend Rachel Williams, and a $320,000 Netflix deal for Anna. Anna was arrested and convicted in 2019 and was sentenced to four to 12 years in New York State. After her release from prison, she was arrested again by U.S. Immigration and Customs Enforcement and held for overstaying her visa.

Chapter 5
The Murder of Sophie Toscan du Plantier and Its Implications for the Study of Media and Crime: A Case Study in West Cork 68
Shane O'Mahony, University of Hertfordshire, UK

Criminologists have often highlighted how the news media tends to disseminate simplified and stigmatised narratives to represent violence against women. Furthermore, these narratives often interweave with class-based fears, sensationalism, and mythology. However, recently, several authors have begun to examine the potential of new media sources (podcasts, documentary series, social media) to subvert these narratives. Drawing on a case study examining the murder of Sophie Toscan du Plantier in West Cork, Ireland (December 1996), the current chapter examines the ways in which three recent new media examinations of the case subvert and reinforce these narratives. The chapter demonstrates that while the new media sources foreground the victim's biography and background, give voice to her family, and situate the case within broader social and political contexts, they also reinforce class-based stereotypes relating to deserving and undeserving victims and problematically focus on the mythical elements of the case for entertainment purposes.

Chapter 6
Trayvon Martin: A Black Boy Who Made an Impact..94
Michelle Eliasson, University of Florida, USA

In 2012, while returning from a visit at a local convenience store, 17-year-old Trayvon Martin was fatally shot by George Zimmerman, a community watch group member, in Sanford, Florida. Zimmerman stated that he was being attacked by Martin and shot him in self-defense, and in 2013 Zimmerman was acquitted of the death of Martin. There was a significant public reaction to Martin's death and the subsequent acquittal of Zimmerman. This chapter will describe Martin's death, the news media and social media coverage of the case, and the implications Martin's death brought on the discussion of racial profiling, implicit bias, and police conduct and practices. The chapter highlights the various roles Martin's death and news media and social media coverage played in the mobilization for social movement and activism highlighting racial justice in the United States.

Chapter 7
Crime in Perugia: The Murder of Meredith Kercher..117
Beatrice Ugolini, University "N. Cusano", Rome, Italy & British Society of Criminology, UK

On the night between 1st and 2nd November 2007, a 21-year-old English student called Meredith Kercher was killed in Perugia, Italy. After a long and controversial court case, the American, Amanda Knox, and the Italian, Raffaele Sollecito, after initially being found guilty, were acquitted of the crime. The only convict remains the Ivorian Rudi Guede. The case aroused unexpected media attention and international outcries. Many questions on the whole affair remain unresolved, which has contributed to adding conspiracy-like theories to standard criminological analysis. This chapter intends to provide a reconstruction of the events, highlighting the reasons that explain the case's great media attention.

Chapter 8
Corpus Delicti? Forensic Dimensions of the No-Body Murder 133
Anna Chaussée, University of Winchester, UK

Corpus delicti, or body of evidence, is a fundamental to criminal prosecutions. This contribution takes a more literal perspective by exploring the 'no-body murder'. Body disposal is not a single event; it is a complex process that dynamically responds to social and environmental circumstances. This contribution explores the legislative response to no-body murders through the Prisoners Act 2020 and presents six dimensions explaining non-disclosure of location of victim remains. Four high-profile no-body cases are presented, demonstrating the complexities inherent in searching for the long-term missing, presumed dead. This chapter focuses on the offender deposition strategy, the operational response, and environmental dimensions that explain prisoner non-disclosure and the failures to detect clandestine depositions.

Chapter 9
An Analysis of Biases in US Policing and Subsequent Media Coverage in Response to the Ferguson Shooting of 2014 169
Liam James Leonard, University of Winchester, UK

This chapter will examine the biases in the policing and subsequent media coverage in response to the shooting of Michael Brown in Ferguson, Missouri, a suburb of St Louis, in 2014. This shooting has become a landmark case that highlight these biases that can have fatal consequences for young African-Americans. The list of cases of police shootings of African-Americans in controversial circumstances is a long and disturbing one and includes victims such as young Tamir Rice, and 12-year-old child shot by police while playing in the playground by his home, also in 2014. The chapter presents an analysis of issues in criminal justice, policing, the courts, and the media which occurred in this case. The shooting of Michael Brown can also be placed alongside the killing of George Floyd in Minneapolis in 2020 as an example of biases in policing, which can have a fatal outcome for African-Americans in the United States.

Chapter 10
The Aileen Wuornos Case: Bending the Criminal Binary of Monsters and Martyrs 192
Christine Bussey, Judson College, USA

During an era in which serial killers simultaneously terrified and titillated the American public, Aileen Wuornos stood out in what had largely been, and continues to be, a boys' club. However, unlike her male counterparts, Wuornos incited revulsion rather than enthrallment. Indeed, even feminist advocacy groups, which had championed the right of abused women to defend themselves, were silent when it came to

Wuornos's prosecution, incarceration, and execution. To understand this abdication requires consideration of the ways in which understandings of crime, specifically those involving women, are dichotomized. Two decades after the execution of Aileen Carol Wuornos, have these same binaries been bent?

Chapter 11
A Rural Community's Mobilization and Media Strategies in Response to a Contested Infrastructural Project 201
Liam James Leonard, Arden University Manchester, UK

The chapter will examine the mobilization and social media response of a rural community in Ireland to the imposition of a gas pipeline on their farms, in the western coastal region of that jurisdiction. This analysis will include a discussion of the concept of 'rural sentiment' as a factor in the mobilization of community campaigns against infrastructural projects which are perceived as a threat to existing ways of life in regional areas. The chapter will also explore key theoretical concepts for this community-based responses to environmental degradation in rural areas, including critical criminology, green criminology rural criminology and resource curse theory and ask whether the campaign was ecopopulist, with issues of social and environmental justice at its core. The 'crime' here was in relation to the disruption of nature and community life in a rural area by a corporate entity, backed by the state. The case analysis will be achieved through a case study approach.

Chapter 12
A Penchant for Murder: The Case Study of John Wayne Gacy 221
Gianna M. Strube, Independent Researcher, USA

John Wayne Gacy is a name that lives in infamy in the study of American serial killers. His fiendish means of murder and his countless victims make Gacy a fascinating subject when attempting to understand the pathology of a serial killer. This chapter will examine contextual factors encompassing Gacy's murders and the psychological factors that may have contributed to his offending, including paraphilia. Certain theoretical principles of homicide will be used to analyze John Wayne Gacy's murder motivations such as the frustration-aggression theory, psychosexual aggression, and the social control theory. This chapter will also include information from the media, courts, character involvement, and general case notes. Media analysis is important because many serial killers reach out to the media and want that recognition and the attention they so crave. Although the media attention can also cause more problems by creating broadcasts and giving away secrets about the investigation, putting it in the hands of the killer.

Compilation of References 227

About the Contributors 248

Index 251

Preface

This book had its origins during my time teaching at California State University, Los Angeles. At that time, I wanted to look at the number of famous crimes associated with that city. In time, as I moved to the UK, the remit of the book was extended, and we now have an international discussion of crimes which have occurred across the world. This provides us with a very interesting volume, one which should be of interest to academics, criminal justice practitioners and the wider public. In recent years, true crime has become a fascination with the public, and criminologists and criminal justice practitioners find themselves and their work more and more in the spotlight.

This volume of the Advances in Criminology, Criminal Justice, and Penology book series with IGI Global should address this growing interest from all sectors, including researchers, practitioners, media and the wider public. As such, it provides an insight into the latest in criminological inquiry into historical crimes. This research has been undertaken by a collection of contributors who excel in their field, and the collection reflects their dedication and commitment to their subject.

Chapter 1 introduces the link between crime and the media is a longstanding one. Indeed, crime is one of the mainstays of traditional and contemporary media, alongside politics and sports. This volume of the Advances in Criminology, Criminal Justice and Penology series includes a series of contributions which examine a number of crimes, which include cases that are both notorious and interesting. The volume has contributions from a number of eminent Criminologists, who have a combined expertise in the field which lends itself to a collection of both depth and variety of discussion and analysis. As Criminology has become more popular, it is now a topic which engenders a great deal of media coverage, with films, documentaries, podcasts and even whole channels dedicated to famous and infamous cases. While this increase in popularity is welcome, it also necessitates a greater level of expertise and analysis. This is the focus of our volume, and I am very pleased with the collection of authors and chapters contained within the covers of this book.

Chapter 2 focuses on the grisly murders occurring between 1963 and 1965 committed by Myra Hindley and Ian Brady. These murders are notorious in British criminal history. Whilst the crimes were callous and coldblooded, their infamy is largely the result of the media's enduring and relentless preoccupation with Hindley herself. Although it has been nearly twenty years since her death, Hindley continues to appear as a news story even in 2022. This chapter will critically analyse the media discourses that surrounded Hindley from her trial, through the years of her imprisonment, to the time of her death. Particularly, it will assess the detriment of press coverage to her bids for freedom in the context of public opinion and its effect upon politicians who were responsible for the setting and review of her life tariff.

Chapter 3 in based upon Levi Bellfield, now known as Yusuf Rahim, who was the first person within the UK to be handed a life sentence, whilst already serving a whole life sentence within Her Majesty's Prison. He was convicted in 2008 of the murders of Marsha McDonnell and Amelie Delgrange, as well as the attempted murder of Kate Sheedy, then in 2011 he was further convicted for the murder of Milly Dowler. The UK press coverage of Bellfield's crimes has been monumental, with the media serving as both a help, and a hinderance during the police investigation and years to follow. This chapter provides a detailed overview of Bellfield's crimes, an insight into the complex police investigation and a glimpse at how the media impacted events which unfolded. Finally, Bellfield's motivations will be explored through the criminal narrative framework, offering a theoretical overview of his likely personal story.

Chapter 4 will provide an overview of the life, crimes, and trial of Anna Sorokin better known as Anna Delvey. Anna had invented a false persona and life so that people would think she was a rich German Heiress instead of her real identity of a woman from a working-class Russian family. Anna used her false identity to defraud banks, hotels, and friends for about $275,000. Anna's life became internationally known with her story being published in major news and media articles including podcasts, 60 Minutes, HBO, a $300,000 book deal to her former friend Rachel Williams, and a $320,000 Netflix deal for Anna. Anna was arrested and convicted in 2019 and was sentenced to four to 12 years in New York State. After her release from prison, she was arrested again by U.S. Immigration and Customs Enforcement and held for overstaying her visa.

Criminologists have often highlighted how the news media tends to disseminate simplified and stigmatised narratives to represent violence against women. Furthermore, these narratives often interweave with class-based fears, sensationalism, and mythology. However, recently several authors have begun to examine the potential of new media sources (podcasts, documentary series, social media) to subvert these narratives. Chapter 5 reiterates that concept by drawing on a case study examining the murder of Sophie Toscan du Plantier in West Cork, Ireland (December 1996), the current chapter examines the ways in which three recent new media examinations of the case subvert and reinforce these narratives. The chapter demonstrates that while the new media sources foreground the victim's biography and background, give voice to her family, and situate the case within broader social and political contexts, they also reinforce class-based stereotypes relating to deserving and undeserving victims, and problematically focus on the mythical elements of the case for entertainment purposes.

Chapter 6 covers the murder of Trayvon Martin. In 2012, while returning from a visit at a local convenience store, 17-year-old Trayvon Martin was fatally shot by George Zimmerman, a community watch group member, in Sanford, Florida. Zimmerman stated that he was being attacked by Martin and shot him in self-defense and in 2013 Zimmerman was acquitted of the death of Martin. There was a significant public reaction to Martin's death and the subsequent acquittal of Zimmerman. This chapter will describe Martin's death, the news media and social media coverage of the case, the implications Martin's death brought on the discussion of racial profiling, implicit bias, and police conduct and practices. The chapters highlight the various roles Martin's death and news media and social media coverage played in the mobilization for social movement and activism highlighting racial justice in the United States.

On the night between 1st and 2nd November 2007, a 21-year-old English student called Meredith Kercher was killed in Perugia, Italy. After a long and controversial court case, the American, Amanda Knox, and the Italian, Raffaele Sollecito, after initially been found guilty, were acquitted of the crime. The only convict, "in concerted action with unknown persons", remains the Ivorian Rudi Guede. The case aroused unexpected media attention and international outcries. Many questions on the whole affair remain unresolved, which has contributed to adding conspiracy-like theories to standard criminological analysis. Chapter 7 intends to provide a reconstruction of the events, highlighting the reasons that explain the case's great media attention.

Corpus Delicti, or body of evidence, is a fundamental to criminal prosecutions. This contribution takes a more literal perspective by exploring the 'no-body murder'. Body disposal is not a single event; it is a complex process that dynamically responds to social and environmental circumstances. This contribution explores the legislative response to no-body murders through the Prisoners Act 2020 and presents six dimensions explaining non-disclosure of location of victim remains. Four high-profile no-body cases are presented, demonstrating the complexities inherent in searching for the long-term missing, presumed dead. Chapter 8 focuses on the offender deposition strategy, the operational response, and environmental dimensions that explain prisoner non-disclosure and the failures to detect clandestine depositions.

Chapter 9 examines the biases in the policing and subsequent media coverage in responses to the shooting of Michael Brown in Ferguson, Missouri, a suburb of St Louis, in 2014. This shooting has become a landmark case which highlight these biases, which can have fatal consequences for young African-Americans. The list of cases of police shootings of African-Americans in controversial circumstances is a long and disturbing one, and includes victims such as young Tamir Rice, and twelve year old child shot by police while playing in the playground by his home, also in 2014. The chapter presents an analysis of issues in criminal justice, policing, the courts and the media which occurred in this case. The shooting of Michael Brown can also be placed alongside the killing of George Floyd in Minneapolis in 2020, as an example of biases in policing which can have a fatal outcome for African-Americans in the United States.

Chapter 10 focuses on Aileen Wuornos. During an era in which serial killers simultaneously terrified and titillated the American public, Aileen Wuornos stood out in what had largely been, and continues to be, primarily a boys' club. However, unlike her male counterparts, Wuornos incited revulsion rather than enthrallment. Indeed, even feminist advocacy groups, which had championed the right of abused women to defend themselves, were silent when it came to Wuornos' prosecution, incarceration, and execution. To understand this abdication requires consideration of the ways in which understandings of crime, specifically those involving women, are dichotomized. Two decades after the execution of Aileen Carol Wuornos, have these same binaries been bent?

Chapter 11 examines the mobilization and social media response of a rural community in Ireland to the imposition of a gas pipeline on their farms, in the western coastal region of that juristiction. This analysis will include a discussion of the concept of 'rural sentiment' as a factor in the mobilization of community campaigns against infrastructural projects which are perceived as a threat to existing ways of life in regional areas. The chapter will also explore key theoretical concepts for this community-based responses to environmental degradation in rural areas, including critical criminology, green criminology rural criminology and resource curse theory and ask whether the campaign was ecopopulist, with issues of social and environmental justice at its core. The 'crime' here was in relation to the disruption of nature and community life in a rural area by a corporate entity, backed by the state. The case analysis will be achieved through a case study approach.

John Wayne Gacy is a name that lives in infamy in the study of American serial killers. His fiendish means of murder and his countless victims make Gacy a fascinating subject when attempting to understand the pathology of a serial killer. Chapter 12 examines contextual factors encompassing Gacy's murders and the psychological factors that may have contributed to his offending, including paraphilia. Certain theoretical principles of homicide will be used to analyze John Wayne Gacy's murder motivations such as the frustration-aggression theory, psychosexual aggression, and the social control theory. This chapter will also include information from the media, courts, character involvement, and general case notes. Media analysis is important because many serial killers reach out to the media and want that recognition and the attention they so crave. Although the media attention can also cause more problems by creating broadcasts and giving away secrets about the investigation, putting it in the hands of the killer.

Liam James Leonard
University of Winchester, UK

Acknowledgment

I am pleased with this volume of the series, and would like the following people for their personal and professional assistance and support during the development of this book, from a concept when I was teaching at California State University, Los Angeles through to my time in Arizona, Ireland, and both Manchester and the University of Winchester in the United Kingdom. Firstly, I would like to thank my family, particularly Shane and Trina for their support. In addition, there is a number of people to thank, including Paula Kenny, Gianna Strube, Shannon De Blasio, and Anna Chaussee for their assistance, contributions and reviews, alongside all the contributors to this volume. I also want to thank many students, colleagues, and friends for everything, including Ruzena Salakvardova, Jaie Hart, Melissia Lawson and Siobhan Hartigan Hehir, who lent their support to me throughout the duration of this project. I also want to thank IGI Global's Commissioning Editors for their assistance. I am grateful to all for their contribution and support.

Chapter 1
Introduction:
Cases on Crime and Media

Liam James Leonard
University of Winchester, UK

EXECUTIVE SUMMARY

The link between crime and the media is a longstanding one. Indeed, crime is one of the mainstays of traditional and contemporary media, alongside politics and sports. This volume of the Advances in Criminology, Criminal Justice, and Penology series includes a series of contributions that examine a number of crimes, which include cases that are both notorious and interesting. The volume has contributions from a number of eminent criminologists, who have a combined expertise in the field which lends itself to a collection of both depth and variety of discussion and analysis. As criminology has become more popular, it is now a topic that engenders a great deal of media coverage, with films, documentaries, podcasts, and even whole channels dedicated to famous and infamous cases. While this increase in popularity is welcome, it also necessitates a greater level of expertise and analysis.

INTRODUCTION

Cases on Crime and Media

The link between crime and the media is a longstanding one. Indeed, crime is one of the mainstays of traditional and contemporary media, alongside politics and sports. This volume of the *Advances in Criminology, Criminal Justice and Penology* series includes a series of contributions which examine a number of crimes, which include cases that are both notorious and interesting. The volumes have contributions from

DOI: 10.4018/978-1-7998-9668-5.ch001

a number of eminent Criminologists, who have a combined expertise in the field which lends itself to a collection of both depth and variety of discussion and analysis. As Criminology has become more popular, it is now a topic which engenders a great deal of media coverage, with films, documentaries, podcasts, and even whole channels dedicated to famous and infamous cases. While this increase in popularity is welcome, it also necessitates a greater level of expertise and analysis. This is the focus of our volume, and I am very pleased with the collection of authors and chapters contained within the covers of this book.

Ever since Victorian times, with the onset of the 'Jack the Ripper' case in late 1800s London, the link between the popular press and serious crime in both the United States and the United States has been extensive. Serious crime, and in particular murder, has provided a prurient and sensationalist focus for the tabloid media in those both jurisdictions and globally, ever since. The thread between murder and media is interwoven in the public's mind, with a link between both being a key focus of society's agenda which combines fear and fascination, security and sensationalism, and moral panic with public populism. Famous murders have become part of national and global contemporary culture, from the Black Dahlia case through to Moors Murders, while major trials have also become the focus of the media and public alike, from the OJ Simpson related media sensationalism through to the recent fascination with Johnny Depp/Amber Heard trial. This volume includes a range of cases and crimes from various countries, across Europe, America and Africa. This provides the book with a cross section of cases, with a diversity of crimes, investigations, trials and outcomes.

Furthermore, the chapters provide a good insight into the challenges faced my those who work in the criminal justice system, when dealing with the demands of the media, and increasingly, with the expectations and sometimes misconceptions of a public which commands a media generated 'expertise' on crimes, investigations, forensics, and trails, which has been derived from a media which has advertisers and ratings in mind as much as criminological accuracy and veracity. This issue has become an increasing aspect of the criminal justice system, with even policy makers and law makers becoming influenced by populist media trends and demands. As a result, the demands on professionals in the field of policing, forensics, and the courts, which have always been substantial, are now complicated by both a sensationalist media and a voyeuristic public. While this increased interest in criminal justice issues can be positive, it can lead to a populist pressure which isn't helpful in the already challenging arena which pits law enforcement against an increasingly organized and ruthless criminal sector.

In this context, it is the role of the criminologist to examine cases and provide a requisite degree of understanding to the cultural contest that surrounds major crimes. As such the 'case study' method provides us with an excellent way to unpack the major issues which were features of criminal activity and law enforcement detection, investigation and prosecution. The background to the Case Study Method evolved alongside the development of the social sciences. Its origins in medical case studies- developed to trace histories of patient and illness. Through the era of social science development in the 1900s through to the 1930s, the 'case study' became associated with the 'Chicago School' of enquiry emanating from Chicago University. Studies focused on 'Issues of poverty, unemployment, and other conditions deriving from immigration were ideally suited to the case study methodology'. In some ways, this was in response to assertions about migrant populations, providing instead more positive science and evidence-based approaches to social science research.

Through the Chicago School approach, subjects were 'given voice' through the case study, enhancing validity and avoiding 'elitist perspectives' when studying marginal groups. As disagreements emerged in social science between case driven 'qualitative' and data driven 'quantitative' methods, the Chicago School method held that studies require elements of both, creating 'Grounded Theory' to increase understandings of 'social processes' through the case's coded material. Moving forward, a Case Study Method allows the use of local evidence to support the development of global findings:

This ensures the transformation from the local to the global for explanation. characterized such singularity as a concentration of the global in the local (Hamel et al, 1993).

Moreover, this leads to an increased salience for Case Study in era of globalization, but which also supports local perspectives. This is also significant in order to recognize diverse perspectives within the target research group. A Case Study method can 'satisfy the three tenets of the qualitative method: describing, understanding, and explaining'. General understandings emerge from these tenets, supported by rigorous findings derived from the focus on individual cases. Different types of cases can benefit from differing theoretical approaches. Exploratory case studies, fieldwork, and data collection may be undertaken before research questions and hypotheses, but the framework of the study must be in place. Selecting appropriate cases can be a difficult process. However, this offers the opportunity to maximize what can be learned.

Explanatory case studies are suitable for doing causal studies. Case outcomes can be explained by three different theories: a knowledge-driven theory, a problem-solving theory, and a social-interaction theory. Knowledge-driven theory means that ideas and discoveries from basic research eventually become commercial products. Problem-solving theory follows the same path, but originates not with a researcher, but with an external source identifying a problem. The social-interaction theory claims that researchers and users belong to overlapping professional networks and are in frequent communication.

Descriptive cases require that the investigator begin with a descriptive theory. This facilitates comparative studies, 'active learning', and cause-effect relationships. The descriptive theory must cover the depth and scope of the case study.

The Unit of Analysis is central to the case study, usually being a system or process rather than individual crimes. This approach allows the study to be developed into wider comparative research, building on local detail and applying data to national or global cases. For instance, a local case study can be based on relevant systems of detection, trial and sentencing. This is then applied analysis of these systems to wider range of crime cases. This may be applied in future studies to global law enforcement systems-important in facilitating global crimes such as cyber-crime. The sociologist Andrew Szasz (1994) employs an interesting methodology called an 'issue history'. It requires the trans-disciplinary use of theory, criminal justice, criminology, psychology, history, sociology and political science. Szasz (1994) utilizes sources from the government, the media, surveys and law enforcement, in addition to theories of political economy and medicine, to analyze various interrelated facets of the main criminal justice issue. In addition, Szasz (1994) remarks that 'things become conceptionally interesting exactly when action transcends the boundaries of any one discipline' and that the idea is to better 'understand the conditions under which issues jump' from discipline to discipline.

Case studies can provide multi-perspective analyses. This means that the researcher considers not just the voice and perspective of the actors, but also going wider to consider relevant groups of actors and the interaction between them. This one aspect is a salient point in the characteristic that case studies possess. Another part of the case study method is known as a 'triangulated' research strategy. We can assert that triangulation can occur with data, investigators, theories, and even methodologies. In this way, the researcher can argue that the measurements that are used to ensure accuracy and alternative explanations are provided through this triangulation. This need for triangulation arises from the ethical need to confirm the validity. In case studies, this is done by using and confirming multiple sources of data.

Denzin identified four types of triangulations. Data source triangulation, when the researcher looks for the data to remain the same in different contexts; Investigator triangulation, when several investigators examine the same phenomenon; Theory triangulation, when investigators with different viewpoints interpret the same results; and Methodological triangulation, when one approach is followed by another, to increase confidence in the interpretation. A Case Study Research Design might ask the following: 'What questions to study', 'What data are relevant' 'What data to collect' and 'How to analyze that data'. Yin (2008) proposes 3 ways to construct validity: 'Using multiple sources of evidence', 'Establishing a chain of evidence', and

'Having the case study reviewed'. Yin suggested 'using multiple sources of evidence as the way to ensure construct validity. This would include survey instruments, interviews, and documents'. As well as archives, newspapers, official papers. Case Studies can therefore be used to confirm or challenge theory, or to represent a unique or extreme case (Yin, 2008).

So, how have our contributors presented and analyzed their case studies in crime?

Yin (2008) suggests that every investigation should have a general analytic strategy, so as to guide the decision regarding what will be analyzed, and for what reason. He presented some possible analytic techniques, such as 'pattern-matching', 'explanation-building', and 'time-series analysis'. This final analysis of evidence may demonstrate that the analysis relied on all the relevant evidence, include all major rival interpretations in the analysis including strengths & weaknesses address the most significant aspect of the case study and use the researcher's prior, expertise professional knowledge to further the analysis.

In relation to the media, it has been argued that the increased frequency of dramatic moral narratives in the mass-media over the past two decades is partly a response to the increased pressures of market competition, but is also a key means by which the at-risk character of modern society is magnified and is particularly inclined to take the form of moral panics in modern society due to factors such as the loss of authority of traditional institutions and elites, with anxieties about national identity in the face of increasing external influences and internal diversity increasing. Arguably the real power of contemporary media lies in the way each of these forces neutralize one another – rendering audiences almost helpless before the endless flow of mediated misery encountered in their daily lives.

It has even been noted that the most profound moral demand television makes on spectators is to place us as witnesses of human suffering, without giving us the option to act directly on it (Ellis, 2000). Political spin doctors, global media corporations and tabloid celebrity marketing have replaced monarchs, church and nobility as the patrons and sponsors of much mass communication. However, there are many ways spectators respond to and actively involve themselves with what they see on screen, read in newspapers, or browse online. The discourses produced by mediated moral panics should be understood as rhetoric of indignant denunciation – these are typically directed at the scapegoats, but the persecutors could also find themselves angrily accused of prejudice.

In his account of how modern media use images and language to render distant suffering not only intelligible but also morally acceptable to the spectator, Boltanski and Thevenot (1999) identify three rhetorical 'topics' with which audiences engage with mediated misfortune. The distinctive argument is that ever since the end of the eighteenth century, when pity became central to politics, the topics of 'denunciation', 'sentiment' and 'aesthetics' have become the ethically proper ways of responding to the disturbing spectacles of distant suffering such as murder cases. Mediatized events can, at times, unleash great social change, while, at others, produce little more than banal indifference among media audiences. Each involve competing ways of organizing emotions and, by extension, the norms that govern the ethics of cosmopolitan citizenship.

As global corporations compete for the hearts and wallets of consumers who not only buy their products but willingly advertise them from head to toe—witness today's schoolbooks, superstores, sporting arenas, and brand-name synergy—a new generation has begun to battle consumerism with its own best weapons.

In this provocative, well-written study, a front-line report on that battle, we learn how the Nike swoosh has changed from an athletic status-symbol to a metaphor for sweatshop labor, how teenaged McDonald's workers are risking their jobs to join unions and get a minimum wage, and how "culture jammers" utilize spray paint, computer-hacking acumen, and anti-propagandist wordplay to undercut the slogans and meanings of billboard ads through graffiti. The worry is that by transforming politics into entertainment, the difficulties surrounding development issues are submerged beneath the banalities of celebrity lifestyle, brand identity and show business.

The third possibility of engaged spectatorship arises from criticism of the first two. It consists of being moved by neither indignation nor sentimentalism, but instead by rising above it all to the point where 'suffering is looked at in the face and confronted in its truth, as unacceptable' (Boltanski and Thevenot, 1999). The complaint here, however, is that to aestheticize tragedy will ultimately anaesthetize the feelings of those who witness suffering and injustice across society. Indeed, Boltanski and Thevenot conclude with a discussion of the contemporary 'crisis of pity' rendered by the mass media and the 'spectacle' effects they produce. Susan Sontag has made a similar point:

Imagery that would have had an audience cringing and recoiling in disgust forty years ago is watched without so much as a blink by every teenager in the multiplex. Indeed, mayhem is entertaining rather than shocking to many people in most cultures. (Sontag, 2004)

It is significant that Cohen (2002) has himself moved from an early interest in over-reaction (moral panic) to under-reaction (public denial) in his later work – the 'ways we are manipulated into taking some things too seriously and other things not seriously enough'. Internet pornography, reality television, performance art and campus humiliation rituals are among the sources said to have inspired the brutality and at the same time domesticating it well within the terms of US popular entertainment. Indeed, there is much evidence to suggest that these violations of humanity scarcely trouble consciences – a view borne out by the banal response to the cruelty in so many sections of American public opinion (Carrabine, 2011). To understand how these processes operate necessitates examining how media organizations and institutionalized practice produce news stories, the textual conventions and meanings embedded in them and the diverse ways in which audiences respond.

Moreover, it requires a normative commitment to not simply exposing the socially constructed nature of reality but rather a reopening up of important epistemological questions over the sociology of knowledge and rival ways of knowing the world. Yet it is also important to note that the distinction between what is and what ought to be is often integral to news reporting. The 'new journalism' of the late nineteenth century sought to expose hidden realities, by revealing the secrets of the rich and prompting sympathy for the poor through 'human interest' stories. It is also significant that new media technologies themselves have generated distinctive anxieties, which should not be simply reduced to a fear of the new, but rather that a certain paranoid disposition structures much of the debate. It is one that has been described as a 'hermeneutics of paranoia' that arises in 'a particular context of self to technology and the visual' (Fuery, 2017), and thereby governs much of the mistrust, threat and uncertainty surrounding new technology. This is especially evident in how the mainstream media have tended to depict the Internet, which has been through the 'rhetoric of moral panic' where digital culture is depicted in 'negative terms' where threats like viruses, spam, fraud, stalking and various other media threats are prevalent.

Of course, Western society is fascinated with crime and justice. From films, books, newspapers, magazines, television broadcasts, to everyday conversations, we are constantly engaging in crime 'talk'. The mass media play an important role in the construction of criminality and the criminal justice system. Furthermore, the public's perception of victims, criminals, deviants, and law enforcement officials is largely determined by their portrayal in the mass media. Criminological research indicates that the majority of public knowledge about crime and justice is derived from the media (Surette, 1998). Therefore, it is imperative to examine the effects that the mass media have on attitudes toward crime and justice. The purpose of this talk is to examine how the media influences audience perceptions of police effectiveness and to examine whether media consumption is related to fear of crime and punitive justice attitudes.

Research on the effect that the media has on the public revolves around two interconnected issues. Does coverage of sensationalistic and violent crime create fear among the general public and does this fear influence criminal justice policy attitudes? Research indicates that there are mixed results regarding the influence of the news media on creating an attitude of fear among the general public (Surette, 1998). In an earlier study, Gerbner and Gross (1976) hypothesized that heavy viewing of television violence leads to fear rather than aggression. That study found that individuals who watch a large amount of television are more likely to feel a greater threat from crime, believe crime is more prevalent than statistics indicate, and take more precautions against crime. They find that crime portrayed on television is significantly more violent, random, and dangerous than crime in the "real" world. Researchers argue that viewers internalize these images and develop a "mean world view" or a scary image of reality. This view is characterized by "mistrust, cynicism, alienation, and perceptions of higher-than-average levels of threat of crime in society" (Surette, 1998). Further studies on the relationship between fear and television viewing indicate a direct and strong relationship.

Criminologists find that the relationship between media presentations and crime is dependent on characteristics of the message and the audience. Presentation of large amounts of local crime news engenders increased fear among the larger public, while the presentation of large amounts of non-local crime news has the opposite effect by making the local viewers feel safe in comparison to other areas (Liska and Baccaglini, 1990). In addition, researchers find that local and national news are related to fear of crime. The effect of local news on fear of crime is stronger for residents in high crime areas and those who experienced victimization. In terms of audience effects, fear of victimization will depend on who is viewing the crime stories. Research indicates that residents in high crime urban areas who watch a large amount of television are more likely to be afraid of crime. Another important factor is whether audience members have direct victim experience or share characteristics that make them crime vulnerable.

The National Opinion on Crime and Justice (NOCJS) finds that local media attention to crime was significantly related to fear of sexual assault; getting mugged, beaten up, knifed or shot; and being burglarized while at home. Fear of crime was not significantly related to fear of carjacking, being murdered, or being burglarized while not at home. Moreover, they did not find the source of crime news to be a factor in fear of crime. For example, those who received their crime news from radio, newspapers or television had similar levels of worry about crime. In addition, their findings indicate that crime show viewers were more likely to worry about being sexually assaulted; getting beaten up, knifed, or shot; and getting killed. However, crime-drama viewing is not related to fear of carjacking, mugging, or burglary. Researchers argue that public fear and anxiety is inextricably connected with public pressure for solutions to crime problems.

A number of research studies focus on whether media depictions of crime influence public attitudes towards criminal justice policy. They find that presentations of crime news increase public pressure for more effective policing and more punitive responses to crime. Furthermore, Surette claims that the news media feature agents of crime control as negatively ineffective and incompetent which results in support for more police, more prisons, and more money for the criminal justice system.

Other research finds that for white males, crime show viewing is related to high levels of aggression towards those who break the law, and low levels against those who defend it.

CONCLUSION

Studies also found that fear of victimization and fear of victimization based on real life experiences did not have a mediating effect on the relationship. In addition, Oliver and Armstrong (1995) find that frequent viewing and greater enjoyment of reality-based crime shows are related to holding punitive attitudes. However, frequent viewing and greater enjoyment of fictional crime shows are not related to holding punitive attitudes. For example, researchers claim that docu-dramas and news tabloid programs represent the police as heroes that fight evil, yet print and broadcast news personify the police as ineffective and incompetent. Likewise, the general public evaluates police performance more favorably compared with courts and correction. Nevertheless, he also states that the media provides little information to judge police and that the news media focus on negative criticism rather than positive or successful crime prevention efforts. In essence, most media crime is punished, but policemen are rarely portrayed the heroes.

REFERENCES

Boltanski, L., & Thevenot, L. (1999). The Sociology of Critical Capacity. *European Journal of Social Theory*, *2*(3), 359–377. doi:10.1177/136843199002003010

Carrabine, E. (2011). Images of torture: Culture, politics and power. *Crime, Media, Culture*, *7*(1), 5–30. doi:10.1177/1741659011404418

Cohen, S. (2002). *Folk Devils and Moral-Panics* (3rd ed.). Routledge.

Elliza, J. (2000). *Seeing Things: Television in the Age of Uncertainty*. I.B. Tauris. doi:10.5040/9780755604784

Fuery, K. (2017). *New media: Culture and image*. Bloomsbury Publishing.

Gerbner, G. & Gross, L. (1976). Living With Television: The Violence Profile. *Journal of Communication, 26*(2), 172-194.

Hamel, J., Dufour, S., & Fortin, D. (1993). *Case Study Methods*. Sage Publications. doi:10.4135/9781412983587

Liska, E., & Baccaglini, W. (1990, August). Feeling Safe by Comparison: Crime in the Newspapers. *Social Problems*, *37*(3), 360–37. doi:10.2307/800748

Oliver, M. B., & Armstrong, G. B. (1995). Predictors of viewing and enjoyment of reality-based and fictional crime shows. *Journalism & Mass Communication Quarterly*, *72*(3), 559–570. doi:10.1177/107769909507200307

Sontag, S. (2004). *Regarding the Pain of Others*. Picador.

Surette, R. (1998). *Media, crime, and criminal justice: Images and realities* (1st ed.). Wadsworth Publishing.

Szasz, A. (1994). *EcoPopulism: Toxic Waste and the Movement for Environmental Justice*. University of Minnesota Press.

Yin, K. R. (2008). Case Study Research: Design and Methods (4th ed.). Sage Publications Incorporated.

ADDITIONAL READING

Feagin, J. R., Orum, A. M., & Sjoberg, G. (Eds.). (1991). *A case for the case study*. UNC Press Books.

Flanagan, T. J., & Longmire, D. R. (1997). Americans view crime and justice: A national public opinion survey. *Journal of Criminal Justice*, *25*(2), 173–174. doi:10.1016/S0047-2352(97)83747-6

Glaser, B. G., & Strauss, A. L. (1967). *The Discovery of Grounded Theory: Strategies for Qualitative Research*. Aldine Publishing Company.

Leonard, L. (Ed.). (2011). *Community Campaigns for Sustainable Living: Health, Waste & Protest in Civil Society*. Emerald. doi:10.1108/S2041-806X(2011)7

Stake, R. (1995). *The Art of Case Study Research*. Sage.

Tellis, W. (1997). Application of a case study methodology. *Qualitative Report*. Advance online publication. doi:10.46743/2160-3715/1997.2015

Yin, K. R. (1993). *Application of Case Study Research*. Sage Publication.

Chapter 2
The Making of a Monster:
UK Press Coverage of Myra Hindley

Mark Pettigrew
https://orcid.org/0000-0001-7241-8244
University of Bolton, UK

EXECUTIVE SUMMARY

Occurring between 1963 and 1965, the murders committed by Myra Hindley and Ian Brady are notorious in British criminal history. Whilst the crimes were callous and coldblooded, their infamy is largely the result of the media's enduring and relentless preoccupation with Hindley herself. Although it has been nearly 20 years since her death, Hindley continues to appear as a news story even in 2022. This chapter will critically analyse the media discourses that surrounded Hindley from her trial, through the years of her imprisonment, to the time of her death. Particularly, it will assess the detriment of press coverage to her bids for freedom in the context of public opinion and its effect upon politicians who were responsible for the setting and review of her life tariff.

Like the image of the Medusa, this photograph has acquired the attributes of myth, the stony gaze of Britain's longest-serving woman prisoner striking terror, mingled with fascination, in those who look upon it (Birch, 1993, p.32).

DOI: 10.4018/978-1-7998-9668-5.ch002

Figure 1. Mugshot of Myra Hindley taken at the time of her arrest. Courtesy of BBC News (2000)

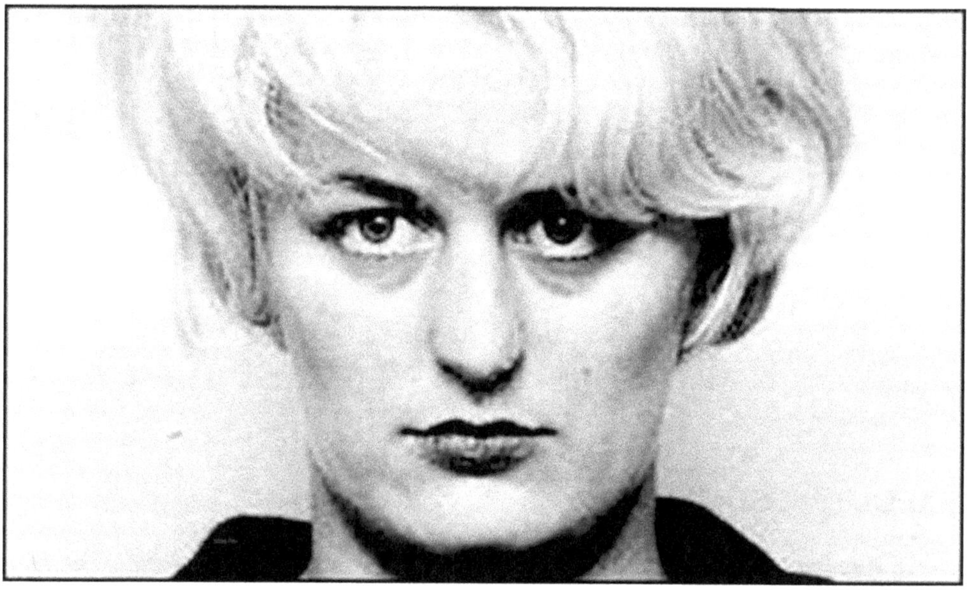

INTRODUCTION

At 8am on the 13th of August 1964, Peter Allen was hanged at Walton prison in Liverpool whilst Gwyn Evans was, simultaneously, hanged at Strangeways prison in Manchester; the last executions to take place in the United Kingdom. Eleven miles away from the execution site of Evans, Ian Brady and Myra Hindley lived, for all outward appearances, as an unremarkable young and in love couple, in the home of Hindley's grandmother. They had met three years earlier when Hindley began work as a typist at a wholesale chemical distribution company where Ian Brady held a clerical position. After a period of infatuation for Hindley, the two became romantically involved. At the time Peter Allen and Gwyn Evans were hanged the couple had abducted, sexually assaulted, and murdered three local children; they would go on to kill, in total, at least five before they were apprehended.

For Hindley and Brady, after their trial and conviction in 1966, a life sentence was to have a literal meaning, even though a true-life sentence did not exist in England at the time they were sentenced. Hindley died in prison in November 2002. Brady also died whilst incarcerated, in a secure psychiatric hospital, in May 2017. More so than Brady, who never sought release, Hindley would become an enduring fascination for tabloid newspapers over the course of her life, and after her death, continuing to appear with some regularity even in recent years (see for example, Towers, 2021; Bellotti, 2021; Hume, 2022). The most hated and reviled woman in Britain (Stanford, 2002), Hindley's legacy would not only be of a cultural phenomenon, a subverted icon of femininity, warped and perverted, but the creation of the whole of life tariff in England & Wales designed, primarily, to assuage public opinion and to keep Hindley detained for the remainder of her life. In that regard, Hindley, through repeated public appeals for release that featured so predominantly in her press coverage, was the architect of her own eventual sentence, and of those who followed her. As Schone notes,

It is no exaggeration to say that [Myra] Hindley is popularly considered to be the embodiment of evil ... this single 'hard case' has had an irrevocable effect on penal policy in the United Kingdom (Schone, 2000, p.273).

The first section of this chapter will provide an overview of the murders committed by Brady and Hindley. The second section will provide a chronological analysis of newspaper coverage of Hindley and her successive pleas for parole consideration. The chapter will conclude with a discussion of the manner in which Hindley was treated in press coverage and its consequent effect upon criminal justice politics and policy in England & Wales.

MURDERS

Myra Hindley and Ian Brady were not tried, or convicted, for two of the murders they committed and would, in fact, deny any knowledge of them for twenty years after their arrest. The first of those two victims, 16-year-old Pauline Reade, was lured into a car by Hindley in July 1963. On the pretence of helping her retrieve a lost glove, Hindley drove the teenager to the moors outside the city of Manchester; Brady followed on his motorcycle. The events that took place after Brady arrived on the moor remain disputed. Hindley claimed she did not actively participate in the victim's death (Topping, 1989) whilst Brady claimed that she played a full role in both the victim's sexual assault and murder (Keightley, 2017). The victim was buried in a shallow grave and would not be found until 1987.

On the evening of November 23, 1963, the second victim, a 12-year-old boy, John Kilbride, was picked up by Hindley and Brady when they offered him a lift home. Once again, using the pretence of looking for a lost glove, they drove the victim to the moors. Once there, Brady sexually assaulted, killed him, and buried him in a shallow grave. Photographs of Hindley kneeling on the grave, looking at the ground, were subsequently recovered by detectives after their arrest.

The following summer, in June 1964, Hindley asked a young boy, 12-year-old Keith Bennett, if he would help her carry some boxes. After driving to collect Brady, the story of a lost glove was once again given as an excuse for driving to the moor. The accounts of Brady and Hindley, as to what happened when they arrived on the moor, contradict each other. On Hindley's account, after walking approximately three miles onto the moorland, she stopped and acted as a lookout whilst Brady and the victim continued to walk out of sight; Brady returned alone after approximately thirty minutes. On Brady's account, Hindley pinioned the boy's legs whilst Brady sexually assaulted and then strangled him. He then took photographs of the body after which Hindley helped bury the victim in a shallow grave (Keightley, 2017). The body remains undiscovered.

Whilst Hindley claimed that Brady was with her when she lured the fourth victim, ten-year-old Lesley Ann Downey, into her car, Brady claimed the victim was already in the car when Hindley picked him up. Whether Hindley or Brady are to be believed, the outcome was the same. On December 26, 1964, the victim was taken to their home and forced to pose for pornographic pictures. In what would be particularly damning for Hindley, and her future protestations of innocence and pleas for parole, the photographic session was recorded. Whilst it remains debated whether the audio recording occurred just before the photographs were taken or immediately after (Keightley, 2017) its content ensured that Hindley would be unable to claim that she was not there when the sexual assault took place. In the seventeen-minute recording, the child begs to be allowed to go home, calling Hindley and Brady 'mummy' and 'daddy', and repeatedly asks them to stop what they are doing. Hindley can be heard threatening the child into compliance, telling her to keep a gag in her mouth. When questioned about the tape at trial Hindley claimed, "I wouldn't have hit her much" (Keightley, 2017, p.231). With regards to the child's murder, once again Hindley's and Brady's subsequent accounts differed: Hindley claimed Brady had strangled her, Brady claims that Hindley strangled the child (Keightley, 2017). The body was taken to the moors and, as with previous victims, buried in a shallow grave.

The final victim, 17-year-old Edward Evans, was picked up by Brady at a local train station in October 1965. Hindley drove them home claiming to be Brady's sister. On Brady's instruction, after they arrived, Hindley left and walked to her sister's house to collect her brother-in-law. When they arrived back home Evans was in the living room sitting on the couch. Approaching him from behind, Brady hit the victim in the head with a small hatchet; after a struggle and the infliction of numerous blows to the victim, Brady strangled him with some electric flex. After the three cleaned the scene and stowed the body in an upstairs bedroom, Hindley's brother-in-law left; he called the police. Just hours after Edward Evans had been killed, police arrived at the property and, finding the body upstairs, arrested Brady;

Hindley was not arrested until five days later. Hindley insisted that she had not been in the room when the murder took place and had only assisted in mopping up blood, after the fact. Upon examination, however, blood was found on Hindley's shoes, not smears that may corroborate her version of events but arterial spray, indicating she was very close when the victim died. Hindley claimed she had not been wearing any shoes at the time; there was no blood found inside the shoes however, indicating that someone had been wearing them when the victim was killed.

After being charged in connection with three murders, that the police were aware of, Hindley and Brady were kept on remand awaiting trial. Their case was tried in April 1966. On May 6, 1966, Brady was found guilty of three counts of murder and Hindley was found guilty of two counts of murder and one of harbouring an offender (Brady). At the end of a trial which lasted fourteen days, in which the jury spent just two hours and fourteen minutes in their deliberations, Brady and Hindley were each sentenced to life imprisonment. The death penalty having been formally abolished whilst they on remand awaiting trial, a life sentence was the only sentence then permitted by law upon conviction of murder. The trial judge did not set a tariff for Hindley, the recommended amount of time to be served before consideration for parole, but he did remark,

Though I believe that Brady is wicked beyond belief without hope of redemption (short of a miracle), I cannot feel the same is necessarily true of Hindley once she is removed from his influence (quoted by Lord Bingham CJ in R v Secretary of State for the Home Department; Exparte Hindley [1998] at 760).

Press Coverage

Initial newspaper reports of the arrest and charge of Hindley and Brady were short and factual. When held on remand and making their first court appearances, for committal to the Crown Court, Hindley was simply described as, "...aged 23, shorthand-typist" ('Clerk Accused of Three Murders,' 1965, p.17). Even when further details were released to the public and the case was heard in the Crown Court in 1966, newspaper coverage largely remained factual. Under the headline 'Attorney General says, 'Perverted Sexual Element' was Involved in the Moors Killings' Hindley was again simply described as "...aged 23, shorthand-typist" (1966, p.10). Other newspapers reported even less about the defendants choosing, instead, to factually document the case. Under the headline 'Moors Trial: Recording Played in Court', in which the recordings of the sexual abuse and torture of a ten-year-old victim were reported, Hindley is described only as "23" (1966, p.4). Such objective and restrained reporting, however, was in stark contrast to the scenes that occurred on a daily basis outside the local magistrate's court, when Hindley and Brady were remanded in custody, and outside the Crown Court when their trial was eventually heard. Such was the perceived strength of public feeling and the consequent risk to conducting the trial safely, bullet proof glass was erected around the Crown Court dock (De Lucia, 2016). At both sites, hundreds of spectators gathered to see the defendants, to try and attack them, and to publicly protest for the restoration of the death penalty (Associated Press, 1966; Ritchie, 1988; De Lucia, 2016).

Less than two weeks after conviction, Hindley gave notice of her intention to appeal; the start of decades of publicly proclaiming her innocence and desire to be freed. On October 17, 1966, the Court of Appeal heard Hindley's case, it was dismissed the same day. This is a key time juncture in Hindley's timeline, a year earlier and the only subsequent news reports of her or Brady would concern their execution, after which they would likely have become mere footnotes in the history of British capital punishment (Birch, 1993).

Over the following years, after her conviction, Hindley would become a recurring newspaper story. In January 1968 Hindley was temporarily moved from HMP Holloway, where she was detained upon conviction, to Risley remand centre, on compassionate grounds to see her ailing grandmother. The move, and its associated costs, was labelled as damnable ('Protest Over Hindley's Transfer Cost'). Public outrage was stoked once again in 1972 when Hindley was escorted by the Governor of HMP Holloway on a walk to a local park, as the governor had previously done with other prisoners. The reaction to this walk, and this prisoner, however, was universally condemnatory and the prison Governor was publicly rebuked by the Home Secretary. In an analysis of the condemnation from the tabloid press which precipitated the involvement of the Home Secretary, the unique nature of Hindley's case was illuminated,

The Home Secretary's public rebuke to the Governor.... was capitulation to the worst kind of hysteria. Frankly, my sympathies for Myra Hindley, whose crimes were particularly hideous, are strictly limited (though I suspect if a dog was denied a walk in the sun after being shut up six years there would be as great a protest as over Miss Hindley's walk – and probably from the same people) (Wilson, 1972, p.8).

Reaction to the brief excursion convinced Hindley that she would not be paroled in the foreseeable future and, as such, she became involved in a prison escape plot. When the escape plot was revealed so too was Hindley's romantic relationship with a female prison officer; her sexual escapades whilst incarcerated eclipsed details of the escape plot which was advanced in its preparation. Headlines such as 'Hindley's Gaol Love for Former Nun' would cement Hindley's 'otherness'; her sexual activity during her incarceration used as further evidence of her depravity and ability to manipulate those around her.

In the mid-1970s, after serving longer than the average prisoner without consideration for parole, the prospect of freedom for Hindley became a national talking point. In July 1977 the BBC aired a televised discussion of the prospect of release in which Hindley herself made a written submission,

If I'd been charged only with what I was guilty of I'd have got about seven years. I've done more than that and I think I've served my time, but I haven't even been considered for parole yet and I don't think that is fair. I was guilty only of being in the room when the photographs of Lesley Ann Downey were taken and of being an accessory after the fact in the Evans case. I know it is only public opinion that's keeping me in prison. I can't show remorse for things I haven't done (Brass Tacks, 1977).

Overwhelmingly, the public and the popular press were appalled at the prospect of freedom for Myra Hindley. The day after the television programme aired the Daily Mirror ran a story under the headline, 'The Case Against: Never Free a Monster'. Emotive headlines continued into 1978, 'Angry Plea of a Tortured Mother: Don't Free Hindley', and 'Myra is too Evil to Free'. Hindley's cause was not helped by her co-defendant, Brady, who made it clear that he would never seek parole. Quoting Brady, the Daily Mirror ran a front-page story in January 1978 'Myra and I Must Die in Jail'. Successive tabloid opinion polls demonstrated public agreement with Brady, from the 1970s onwards such polls were consistent in demonstrating strong opposition to any prospect of release for Hindley (Greaves, 1985; Campbell, 1997).

The 1980's

As early as May 1980 the Daily Mirror ran a story under the headline 'Don't Pity These Evil Women'; Hindley was prominent. Yet, after more than fifteen years in prison, Hindley anticipated freedom by the early 1980s and so did many legal observers. Although routinely described in prison reports of her progress as manipulative and cunning, Hindley was, simultaneously, frequently described as a model inmate and, pertinently, at a very low risk of reoffending if released (Pettigrew, 2016a). By the 1980s, Hindley had been incarcerated longer than other prisoners serving 'life' sentences, and, in prospect of her parole, the tabloid newspapers launched a campaign to prevent her release. In 1984 the Daily Mirror ran a story under the headline of 'The Wild Boasts of Mad Myra', claiming she had been boasting to fellow inmates that she would be imminently released. Regional newspapers followed suit, conducting opinion polls on the meaning of life sentences, placing Hindley at the centre of that debate: 'Should Life Mean Life?' was one such article, published by the Liverpool Echo in March 1985. Even the more liberal sections of the news media recognised that, by the mid-1980s, Hindley had become "a bogey figure in a class of her own" (The Myra Hindley Conundrum, 1985). A 1985 poll conducted by The Times found 83% of people believed Hindley should remain in prison (Greaves, 1985). The collective tabloid campaign worked and in 1985 Hindley, and Brady, were told that they were not eligible for parole at that point. Headlines such as that in the Daily Mirror, May 1985, 'Hindley on Brink of Breakdown' demonstrated the delight of tabloids in their apparent success in wounding Hindley herself. At the time Hindley and Brady were told neither would be considered for parole at that point, Brady had been transferred to a high security psychiatric hospital: "at least [he] had the decency to go mad" remarked the mother of one victim (Birch, 1995). With a psychiatric diagnosis somewhat absolving Brady of responsibility (Storrs 2004), Hindley was left as the sole competent and rationale participant in the murders, her repeated pleas for release only hardening public opposition to her and used as proof of her lack of remorse (Storrs 2004). Indeed, whilst Brady remained in relative obscurity, public feeling towards Hindley worsened over time, spurred on by repetitive tabloid stories describing Hindley as not mad, but evil (see for example, Kay & Gay, 1985; Barnes, 1990; Saxty, 1999; Kay, Saxty & Hartley, 2000).

Rumours of further victims had circulated around the case, and around Brady and Hindley, since their arrest. Detectives even visited both in prison within a year of their conviction in an attempt to secure information relating to additional murders. Indeed, as early as 1970, detectives undertook another cursory search of the moors in the hope of finding additional victims. Yet, it was not until December 1985 that Hindley's co-defendant was featured on the front page of the Daily Mirror, 'Brady: Now Will He Tell Truth About Secret Murders?' Brady would drip-feed hints to various newspapers that there were additional murder victims to be found on the moors. Hindley would, at first, offer to help detectives by showing them places she and Brady had visited as a couple whilst denying any knowledge or involvement in other crimes. Later, however, she was forced to make a full confession before Brady could implicate her and provide evidence of her guilt; there were additional victims and she had played a fuller part in the murders that she had been charged with than she had earlier admitted. Throughout, reaction to Hindley was universally condemnatory. 'At Last Myra Finds Tears to Weep' (Liverpool Echo); 'Myra: Heartless' (Daily Mirror); 'Moors Murderers Evil' (Irish Independent); 'Call a Halt to the Evil Myra Circus' (Liverpool Echo); 'The Macabre Myra' (Irish Independent).

If a full confession, and a public declaration to help find the bodies of additional victims to, as she claimed, end the anguish of grieving families, was intended to help Hindley's attempts at parole, it did not work. Headlines continued to stoke public hostility throughout the remainder of the 1980s: 'Free Myra Plea Fury' (Reading Evening Post); 'Top Cop Slams Free Myra Call' (Liverpool Echo); 'That Bitch Hindley Wrecked my Life' (Daily Mirror); 'Lying Myra's Crocodile Tears'

(Daily Mirror); 'Trapped by her own Cunning' (Sunday Mirror); 'Moors Monster' (Daily Mirror). Opposition to Hindley continued into the 1990s when, once again, the meaning of a life sentence would be debated, not only in tabloid newspapers but in the courts.

The 1990's

Hindley was a news story as early as January 2nd in 1990 but, rarely, owing to an impassioned plea from one of her few supporters.

To the tabloid press Myra Hindley is a monster, to be publicly vilified. A quarter of a century on, the witch hunt is still in full cry... the story is chiefly kept alive by the extravagance of the language used. The woman is usually referred to as 'evil' or 'monster' or 'moors monster' and is ritually abused in the most unrestrained terms, as if she had lost her human status... the fact that the verbal tormenting of this woman today has sold mountains of newspapers, with far more success than any other form of entertainment they could find, suggests that the high excitement of witch-hunting is as infectious today as yesterday... It is hard to believe that the Government's treatment of a prisoner is controlled by fear of the tabloid press but there is no other explanation (Astor, 1990).

As the 1990s progressed, tabloid newspapers continued their negative coverage of Hindley and her desire for freedom. 'Let her Suffer the Hell of her Victims' (Daily Mirror, May 1993); 'Death to Myra' (Daily Mirror, June 1993); 'Hypnotic Hindley is the Devil who Lied to me' (Kensington Post, February 1994); 'Storm at Myra Parole Hopes' (Sandwell Evening Mail, March 1994); 'Hindley Must not be Freed' (Staffordshire Sentinel, March 1994); 'Evil Myra Sells her Life Story' (Daily Mirror, July 1995); 'Moaning Myra' (Daily Mirror, December 1995); 'Just Zip it Myra' (Daily Mirror, December 1995). Overwhelmingly, the public mood was not one of forgiveness but of determination to keep Hindley imprisoned. Indeed, the dominant narrative of Hindley was only seldom punctuated by her core supporters,

She is a political prisoner. She is [in prison] because the government of either party are frightened of unpopularity if they release her. She is living out a cruel fate imposed on her by cowardly politicians (Lord Longford cited in Ford 1994).

As the prospect of release was once again discussed in the mid-1990s, the focus was upon the Home Secretary and his powers to keep Hindley detained. Yet, he did "not want to go down as the man who released a Moors Murderer" (Sympathy for a She-Devil?' 1994). It was in 1994 that the decision to increase Hindley's tariff to a whole life term was communicated to her.

Whilst Hindley pursued legal relief from the political decision made by the Home Secretary, to keep her imprisoned for the remainder of her life, the tabloid press showed no sympathy for her plight,

Myra Hindley has an unerring instinct for self-pity. She also has the unfailing talent to make the British public feel sick. Her open letter claiming it is politics, not justice, that keeps her behind bars is a nonsense... Hindley should realise she is lucky to live out her days in prison. If there was true justice, she would have swung from the end of a rope (Beyond Pity, 1997).

Even the more liberal quarters of the news media offered little sympathy to Hindley, although in less sensationalised term than their tabloid counterparts: "I have read nothing to suggest that she has spent her time in prison considering anyone other than herself and her own grievances" (Grant, 1997). Nor would Hindley receive any help or sympathy from the political establishment, the Home Secretary, in 1997, echoing his predecessor, "I will not be the Home Secretary who sets her free" (Kavanagh, 1997). Hindley's supporters knew of the difficult situation those charged with deciding the fate of Hindley were placed in as a result of vitriolic public opinion, opinion that was provided a platform, and simultaneously encouraged by, the tabloid press.

I am not surprised that people in this House and elsewhere say to me, 'I agree with you, my dear chap. Of course, after all these years she ought to come out. But you can't imagine any Home Secretary having the guts to let her out, can you? Think what would happen to him. Think what the tabloids would do to him' (Lord Longford cited in Schone, 2000, p.288).

Even relatively early in her term of imprisonment Hindley was aware of the predicament created for politicians by the tabloid newspapers,

The whole area of neglect and inhumanity pervading my case stems, from what I interpret to be public opinion, but someday, someone has to have the courage to stand up to this so-called public opinion.... Is society going to be compensated for being thwarted of the rope by my perpetual imprisonment? (Hindley, 1980).

Myra Hindley died in November 2002 and the tone of newspaper coverage was as uniform in her death as it had been during her life. 'The Devil: At last Myra is where she belongs... HELL' (The Sun); 'Myra Hindley's young victims died screaming...

The final injustice: she died peacefully' (The Mail); 'Go to Hell' (The Express); 'Gone but not forgiven' (The Mirror). So contaminated by the strength of public opinion and repeated assertions of her evil in the popular press, several undertakers refused to take Hindley's corpse for cremation. To date, the final resting place of her ashes remains undisclosed.

DISCUSSION

The media's preoccupation with Hindley was undoubtedly, at its core, because she was a woman. That is not to say that preoccupation with, and hatred of, Hindley was not augmented by the sadistic nature of the crimes themselves, Hindley's inconsistent account of her involvement, and her persistent appeals for release but, even now, the question persists: how could a woman be involved in such crimes against children? Indeed, the use of Judeo-Christian concepts of good and evil, of heaven and hell, in describing Hindley are the last recourse in explaining her and her actions. Forever memorialised on the audio recording of the torture of 10-year-old Lesley Ann Downey, it is only Hindley's voice that can be heard threatening the child, behaviour beyond comprehension at the time, and still even now. As such, abstract religious concepts became the last bastion of hope to explain Hindley. The culturally familiar, idealised role of women became the antonym to Hindley and her involvement in the torture, sexual assault, and murder of children. As Wilde notes,

Women are perceived to be the softer sex, biologically programmed to be good mothers, to love and nurture children, to be kind and gentle (cited in Cummins, Foley, & King, 2019, p.137).

The crimes of Hindley and Brady have, unfortunately, been surpassed in their depravity and callousness since they were first known to the public, but Hindley was the first, the archetype against which others, other women in particular, are measured. Such comparison was aided in no small part by the now infamous photograph of Hindley (figure 1), taken upon her arrest, in which various commentators throughout the years have sought to draw from it evidence of evil etched in her steely composure. No other picture of Hindley, or indeed of any female murderer since Hindley, has dislodged its status as a piece of cultural iconography, of femininity perverted (Birch, 1993). As Burn has questioned,

Is it possible to discern evil, as many have supposed, in the cavernous upturned eyes, the pasty planes, the heavy bones, the holed head of bleached blonde fringe, the fondant of deep shadow… As usual Hindley looks like a composite, an identikit, a media emanation, a hypothetical who never existed in the flesh (cited in Cummins, Foley & King, 2019, p.135).

Hindley's media image was in no small way aided by that of her co-offender, Ian Brady. Whilst unrepentant, Brady did not court the ire of the public in the way that Hindley managed. Indeed, his silence counterpointed by her protestations of repentance, of minimised involvement, only cemented her place in the public consciousness as the more culpable of the two. Whilst Brady faded into relevant obscurity, his occasional media appearances displayed the image of a broken and pathetic individual. In 1985, he was transferred under the 1983 Mental Health Act from the main prison estate to Ashworth high security hospital; he was confirmed as suffering from paranoid schizophrenia. In contrast, whilst Brady "at least had the decency to go mad", (Birch, 1995), Hindley remained, seemingly, untouched by her crimes, determined and resolute in her pursuit of freedom. Against the image of a mentally unwell Brady, in 1989 Hindley was awarded a degree in humanities from the Open University, a woman confirmed as in full control of her mental faculties (Odell & Gregg, 2006). Hindley wanted to become more than a murderess, more than a mugshot, more than a monster, in the public eye she wanted to appear reformed, to be humanised. Her attempts failed. A relative of one victim, upon newspaper coverage of Hindley receiving her degree, remarked, 'Satan in satin is still Satan' (Birch, 1993, p.55).

The irony of Hindley's imprisonment was that she was one of the relatively few who could be considered a prison success story. Hindley gained favourable reports regarding her conduct, commitment to academic study, and her low-level risk of reoffending yet, as Stanford notes,

She was a woman whom jail had provided an opportunity to make herself a better person... the more that convincing evidence was presented of her transformation, the more the myth grew, in response, that she was a manipulative schemer, prepared to trick anyone to be free (Stanford, 2002).

The 'myth' of Myra Hindley was, on the objective view of some, much larger than the reality and would become that against which her crimes and prospects for release would be measured,

...even a summary examination of other whole lifers reveals that the evilness of Hindley's crime is not, in fact, unique. There are many examples of gross and shocking cruelty amongst those serving life sentences for murder, against whom Hindley looks decidedly ordinary (Gurnham, 2003, p.618).

It was not until the 1980s that the term 'serial killer' was cemented in everyday parlance in Great Britain, coinciding with the time at which legal observers asserted that changes to the tariff setting system would need to occur if Hindley, and other such killers, were to be kept imprisoned. Increased awareness and publicity of serial killing occurring in the United States, Richard Ramirez, Jeffrey Dahmer, and Henry Lee Lucas, for example, verified that Ted Bundy, offending in the 1970s, was not an aberration. That recognition coincided with the explicit, dedicated study and creation of typologies of such offenders by the FBI (Ressler et al., 1986). Domestically, Peter Sutcliffe and Dennis Nilsen confirmed that serial killing was not just an American phenomenon. Retrospectively, Hindley and Brady were each given the moniker of serial killer; Hindley's repeated appearance in the popular press ensured that the term was easily applied. Within that context, the press coverage of Hindley was increasingly damning. Against the backdrop of vitriolic, incessant reporting, in 1985, after a recommendation of a 25-year tariff minimum was issued by the Lord Chief Justice in 1982, the then Home Secretary set a higher tariff of thirty years.

The coalescence of Hindley's gender, her role in sexualised violence, child victims, and repeated public appeals for sympathy placed her beyond the realm of comprehensibility, aided in no small part by the repetition of the 'evil' Hindley narrative that was so dominant in newspaper coverage of her and the 'Moors Murders' case (Pettigrew, 2016b). Despite her prominence in the news media, Hindley could not be fathomed so, instead, she was condemned. Indeed, Hindley became a cause around which the general public could rally, a collective resistance to any prospect of her reform or release. As Katz states,

The reading of crime news is a collective, ritual experience. Read daily by a large proportion of the population, crime news generates emotional experiences in individual readers, experiences which each reader can assume are shared by many others (Katz, 1987, p.64).

As Bates argues, with reference to serial killers generally, but with a particular resonance in the case of Myra Hindley, media focus is not solely upon how serial killers operate but how they do so, undetected,

[They] command vast coverage within the media and focus on the gruesome details of the offences and the seemingly ordinary backgrounds of the offenders to portray to its audience the fact that a person next door could go undetected and unsuspected for serial crime whilst giving the impression that they lead a normal life (Bates, 1999, p.23).

Hindley was the girl next door who held a respectable job, who lived at home taking care of her elderly grandmother she was not, pivotally, recognisable as an 'outsider'. As such the collective effort of media portrayals was to cast Hindley in the more comforting and familiar role of the outsider, of the criminal 'other', as a recognisable threat. Newspaper articles frequently referred to Hindley's infamous mugshot, from which they could discern evil in her hardened look and peroxide blonde hair. Much was made of her lesbian love affairs whilst in prison and even now, 20 years after her death, under headlines such as 'Myra Hindley, the Former Nun and their Lesbian Trysts in Prison after Table Tennis' (Brooke, 2013) and 'How Twisted Serial Killers Myra Hindley and Rose West Became Lesbian Lovers in Jail' (Mcfadden, 2020). Column inches were devoted to anyone who had encountered Hindley and could attest to her manipulative nature and remorseless disposition. Simultaneously, regarding those who would come to Hindley's defence, they were portrayed across press coverage as dupes of Hindley, under her spell, thus affirming, subconsciously, notions of her evil and otherness.

That Hindley continues to feature across British media, and in newspaper tabloids particularly, confirms the assertion of Schlesinger (1977) that the newspaper industry is a 'time machine'. Even now she can be called upon as a familiar figure to remind contemporary audiences of what feminine evil looks like,

Hindley remained a hate figure, even among those too young to remember her trial. To reflect such prejudices – and, some argued, to inflame them – her name was only ever used in tabloid newspapers with the qualifying adjective "evil". That Medusa-like snapshot, taken in 1966, with peroxide hair swept up and back and a fixed, almost defiant, look in the eyes, became an icon of crime (Stanford, 2002).

A victim of timing, from a criminal justice perspective Hindley was the test case of what was to be done with those offenders, murderers, who would have previously been hanged. In formulating a policy response to that conundrum, the popular press, as a voice of 'common sense' penal populism, was pivotal. Had Hindley been executed it is unlikely that Hindley would remain the hate figure she remains today, there would not have been the repeated press coverage that plagued her life. Hindley herself made the same observation,

I knew I was a selfish coward, but I could not bear the thought of being hanged. Although over the years I wish I had been. It would have solved so many problems. The family of the victims would have derived some peace of mind and the tabloids would not have been able to manipulate them as they do to this day. I would have made a total confession to the priest before I hanged and would not still be half crippled by the burden of guilt that will not go away. But I didn't hang (BBC News, 2000).

That observation is echoed in academic analysis of the moor's murders case and of Hindley herself,

Had the couple been hanged, it is unlikely that they would have continued to haunt the public consciousness a quarter of a century later. As it is, they, and Hindley in particular, remain the subjects of constant surveillance, scrutinized for visible signs of badness or madness... (Birch, 1993, p.43).

It is a common misconception that life imprisonment was to have a literal meaning as a replacement for capital punishment (Blom-Cooper and Morris, 1999; Kandelia, 2011). Prophetically though, when abolition of the death penalty was debated, the Home Secretary of the time did suggest that some prisoners may have to be detained for a full life term if they remained a risk (Kandelia, 2011); Myra Hindley, however, was not judged on the risk of her reoffending. Instead, her case settled the appropriateness and domestic legality of imposing a whole life tariff for purely retributive purposes (R v Secretary of State for the Home Department; Ex Parte Hindley [2000]) a point settled by Hindley but since extended to others also serving whole life terms (Pettigrew, 2016b).

Pertinently, Valier questions how figures such as Hindley can ever have their basic rights restored to them when they become media and newspaper commodities,

[C]an the principles of universal human rights be upheld given the national contexts in which notorious criminals are represented in the mass media as monstrous figures who can never be punished enough? (Valier, 2002, p.15).

The media coverage of Hindley was not without consequence. The tabloids in particular become a battleground upon which Hindley's nature, and thus her future, would be decided. The dominant narrative of Hindley as unrepentant, evil, and in need of lifelong incarceration won decisively,

...this woman has become a pawn, serving the self-interest of so many parties. The tabloids need her to boost their sales. Their readers need her to satisfy their demand for a national scapegoat. Governments need her, to enable them to be seen to be enforcing their "tough stance" on crime and criminals, thus increasing their appeal to the electorate. In a real sense Myra Hindley has become a political prisoner, serving the interests of successive Home Secretaries, who have placed political expediency and, effectively, a lynch-mob rationale, before the dictates of justice and basic human rights (White, 1997, p.15).

The legacy of Myra Hindley is a life without parole sentence, Hindley the point of transition from the death penalty. The sentence was built around her as newspaper coverage fed off populist sentiment, and vice versa, and held the Home Secretary, responsible for tariff setting at the time, to account in the court of public opinion. Since that time, with the general public reassured that, for those deemed 'the worst of the worst', those who would have hanged half a century ago, life will indeed mean life, the tabloid, populist press has not created a mythical monster like Hindley, with that position settled they have not had to.

REFERENCES

Associated Press. (1966). *CAN757: File Footage of Moors Murder Case Pre Trial.* https://www.youtube.com/watch?v=wrt2dJXb9Q

Astor, D. (1990, Jan. 2). Why the Moors Murders are Kept Alive. *The Guardian*, p. 15.

Attorney General says 'Perverted Sexual Element' was Involved in the Moors Killings. (1966, Apr. 21). *The Times,* p. 10.

Barnes, G. (1990, February 2). Brady's a Liar Says Evil Myra. *The Mirror (Stafford, Tex.).*

Bates, A. (1999). The Newsworthiness of Crime. *British Journal of Forensic Practice, 1*(2), 22–27. doi:10.1108/14636646199900012

BBC News. (2000). *Hindley: I Wish I'd Been Hanged.* https://www.news.bbc.co.uk/1/hi/uk/661139.stm

Bellotti, A. (2021, July 6). Vile Criminals who Bonded Behind Bars – Including Rose West and Myra Hindley's Love Affair. *The Mirror (Stafford, Tex.).*

Beyond Pity. (1997, Feb. 6). *The Sun*, p. 6.

Birch, H. (1993). If looks could kill: Myra Hindley and the iconography of evil. *Moving targets: Women, murder and representation*, 32-61.

Birch, H. (1995). A special kind of evil. *The Independent, 23.*

Blom-Cooper, L., & Morris, T. (1999). Life until death: Interpretations of section 1 (1) of the Murder (Abolition of the Death Penalty) Act 1965. *Criminal Law Review (London, England)*, 899–905.

Brooke, C. (2013, July 20). Myra Hindley, the Former Nun and their Lesbian Trysts in Prison after Table Tennis. *Daily Mail*. https://www.pressreader.com/uk/scottish-daily-mail/20130720/282329677548152

Campbell, D. (1997, Oct. 29). 83pc Oppose Hindley's Release. *The Guardian*, p. 9.

Clerk Accused of Three Murders. (1965, Dec. 3). *The Times*, p. 17.

Cummins, I., Foley, M., & King, M. (2019). *Serial killers and the media: The Moors Murders legacy*. Springer. doi:10.1007/978-3-030-04876-1

De Lucia, C. (2016, April 19). How the Chester Chronicle Covered the Infamous Moors Murders Trial. *Chester Chronicle*. Retrieved from https://www.cheshire-live.co.uk/news/history/how-chester-chronicle-covered-infamous-11209509

Ford, R. (1994, Dec. 8). Hindley asks for mercy after 28 years in prison. *The Times*, p. 9.

Grant, L. (1997, May 28). The Time for Atonement. *The Guardian*, p. A11.

Greaves, S. (1985, May 29). Hindley Decision Backed by Poll. *The Times*, p. 12.

Gurnham, D. (2003). The moral narrative of criminal responsibility and the principled justification of tariffs for murder: Myra Hindley and Thompson and Venables. *Legal Studies*, *23*(4), 605–623. doi:10.1111/j.1748-121X.2003.tb00230.x

Hindley, M. (1980). *Petition to the Home Secretary*. Academic Press.

Hindley's Gaol Love for Former Nun. (1972, Apr. 2). *The Guardian*, p. 7.

Hume, H. (2022, Jan. 22). Infamous Moors murderer Myra Hindley's final days spent rotting in a Suffolk prison. *Suffolk Live*.

Kandelia, S. (2011). Life meaning life: Is there any hope of release for prisoners serving whole life orders? *Journal of Criminal Law*, *75*(1), 70–87. doi:10.1350/jcla.2011.75.1.684

Katz, J. (1987). What makes crimenews'? *Media Culture & Society*, *9*(1), 47–75. doi:10.1177/016344387009001004

Kavanagh, T. (1997, May 22). Straw: I'll Never Let Evil Myra Walk Free. *The Sun*, p. 25.

Kay, J., & Gay, M. (1985, Mar. 2). 15 Years More for Evil Myra. *The Sun*.

Kay, J., Saxty, G., & Hartley, C. (2000, Mar. 31) Uniquely Evil Myra. *The Sun*.

Keightley, A. (2017). *Ian Brady: The Untold Story of the Moors Murders*. Robson Books.

Mcfadden, B. (2020, Sept. 21). How Twisted Serial Killers Myra Hindley and Rose West Became Lesbian Lovers in Jail. *Daily Star*.

Moors Trial: Recording Played in Court. (1966, Apr. 27). *The Guardian*, p. 4.

Myra Hindley and Thompson and Venables. (n.d.). *Legal Studies*, *23*(4), 605–623.

Odell, R., & Gregg, W. (2006). *Murderers' Row: An International Murderers' Who's Who*. The History Press.

Pettigrew, M. (2016a). Public, Politicians, and the Law: The Long Shadow and Modern Thrall of Myra Hindley. *Current Issues in Criminal Justice*, *28*(1), 51–66. doi:10.1080/10345329.2016.12036056

Pettigrew, M. (2016b). Myra Hindley: Murderer, Prisoner, Policy Architect. The Development of Whole Life Prison Terms in England & Wales. *International Journal of Law, Crime and Justice*, *47*, 97–105. doi:10.1016/j.ijlcj.2016.09.001

Pleasance, H. (2011). Lost Children, the Moors & Evil Monsters: The photographic story of the Moors murders. *Image & Narrative*, *12*(4), 18–38.

Protest Over Hindley's Transfer Cost. (1968, Feb. 3). *The Guardian*, p. 3.

R v Secretary of State for the Home Department; Ex Parte Hindley [1998]

R v Secretary of State for the Home Department; Ex Parte Hindley [2000]

Ressler, R. K., Burgess, A. W., Douglas, J. E., Hartman, C. R., & D'Agostino, R. B. (1986). Sexual killers and their victims: Identifying patterns through crime scene analysis. *Journal of Interpersonal Violence*, *1*(3), 288–308. doi:10.1177/088626086001003003

Ritchie, J. (1988). *Myra Hindley: Inside the Mind of a Murderess*. Angus & Robertson Publishers.

Saxty, D. (1998, Nov. 6). Myra One Step Closer to Hell. *The Sun*, p. 17.

Saxty, D. (1999, Feb. 10). Never Forget Evil of Myra. *The Sun*.

Schlesinger, P. (1977). Newsmen and their Time-Machine. *The British Journal of Sociology*, *28*(3), 336–350. doi:10.2307/589998

Schone, J. M. (2000). The Hardest Case of All: Myra Hindley, Life Sentences, and the Rule of Law. *International Journal of the Sociology of Law*, *28*(4), 273–289. doi:10.1006/ijsl.1999.0125

Stanford, P. (2002, Nov. 16). Myra Hindley. *The Guardian*.

Storrs, E. (2004). Our Scapegoat: An Exploration of Media Representations of Myra Hindley and Rosemary West. *Theology and Sexuality*, *11*(1), 9–28. doi:10.1177/135583580401100103

Sympathy for a She-Devil? (1994, Dec. 11). *The Observer*, p. 20.

Tacks, B. (1977). *Freedom for Myra Hindley?* S.1. E.1. (*Roger Casstles, Dir.). BBC.*

The Myra Hindley Conundrum. (1985, Feb. 7). *The Guardian*, p. 12.

Topping, P. (1989). *Topping: The Autobiography of the Police Chief in the Moors Murders Case*. Angus & Robertson Publishers.

Towers, T. (2021, May 6). Moors Murderers Ian Brady and Myra Hindley's Chilling Links to Occult and Devil Worship. *Daily Star.*

Valier, C. (2002, June). Cruel Britania. *Counsel*, 14–15.

White, B. (1997, Dec. 6). Myra Hindley as Scapegoat. *The Tablet*, p. 15.

Wilson, D. (1972, Sept. 17). Myra Hindley and her Walk. *The Observer*, p. 8.

Chapter 3
Levi Bellfield:
The Bus Stop Stalker

Shannon DeBlasio
https://orcid.org/0000-0003-4873-9683
Arden University, UK

EXECUTIVE SUMMARY

Levi Bellfield, now known as Yusuf Rahim, was the first person within the UK to be handed a life sentence whilst already serving a whole life sentence within Her Majesty's Prison. He was convicted in 2008 of the murders of Marsha McDonnell and Amelie Delgrange as well as the attempted murder of Kate Sheedy. Then in 2011 he was further convicted for the murder of Milly Dowler. The UK press coverage of Bellfield's crimes has been monumental, with the media serving as both a help and a hinderance during the police investigation and years to follow. This chapter provides a detailed overview of Bellfield's crimes, an insight into the complex police investigation, and a glimpse at how the media impacted events which unfolded. Finally, Bellfield's motivations will be explored through the criminal narrative framework, offering a theoretical overview of his likely personal story.

INTRODUCTION

In February 2008 Levi Bellfield, who has since changed his name to 'Yusuf Rahim', was found guilty of the murders of Marsha McDonnell and Amelie Delgrange, as well as the attempted murder of Kate Sheedy. Bellfield was sentenced to life imprisonment (BBC, 2008). On 23rd June 2011, more than three years later, Bellfield was found guilty of an additional murder, that of Milly Dowler (BBC, 2011). This additional conviction means that Bellfield is the only prisoner within the United

DOI: 10.4018/978-1-7998-9668-5.ch003

Kingdom who is serving two whole life orders. Bellfield will never be released from custody or eligible for a parole hearing (Lavender, 2020).

Since his convictions, the case of Bellfield has been subject to mass media coverage. The crimes that Bellfield committed rocked the nation, credited in part to the period of time in which Bellfield remained undetected, as well as the accused failings of the police during each of the investigations. Various books have documented the unfolding events, and a three-part television series '*Manhunt*', dramatised the criminal investigation that proceeded Bellfield's arrest (Mangan, 2019).

Bellfield had a relatively normal start to life; he was born in London in 1968 to parents of Romani descent, and he is one of five siblings who attended mainstream school in southwest London. In 1978, Bellfield's father died from a heart attack, and it was here that Bellfield appeared to embark on his criminal career. Aged just 13, Bellfield picked up his first conviction for burglary, and by 2002 Bellfield had racked up nine convictions and a short-term custodial stay (Edwards, 2008). It is not known when Bellfield's involvement in sexual offending began, but the earliest proven offence is that of 13-year-old Milly Dowler, who was reported missing on 21st March 2002 (Bird, 2010). There have been rumours surrounding Bellfield's involvement in crime against women from as early as 1980, including the death of an ex-girlfriend, Patsy Morris (HeraldScotland, 2008), however these have remained speculation.

In response to the three murders and one attempted murder, Bellfield has shown little remorse. He failed to appear in court on several occasions during the hearings and provided 'no comment' responses to police during their investigations (Lavender, 2020). Surprisingly, Bellfield did admit to the lone involvement in the Milly Dowler case to Surrey Police in 2016, however he retracted his statement a short time later and issued a denial (Rawlinson, 2016).

Levi Bellfield – A Short Background

Levi Bellfield was born at West Middlesex Hospital, in Isleworth, London on 17th May 1968. His parents, Jean and Joseph Rabetts, were of Romani decent, and Levi was one of five siblings (two brothers and two sisters). The Rabetts' (nee Bellfield) resided as a nuclear family on a council state in southwest London until his father's death in 1978. Journalist's report that Joseph died from a heart attack whilst battling with Leukaemia, and following his father's death, Bellfield was cared for predominantly by his mother, Jean (Bird, 2008).

Each of the five children attended mainstream school, and it wasn't until 1981 (when Levi was 13) that he was brought to the attention of police. This encounter led Bellfield to his first conviction, which was for burglary (Edwards, 2008). Following this, it is reported that Bellfield gathered a string of convictions in quick succession, for theft, assaulting a police officer and driving/motor offences. By 2002, it is reported that Bellfield had nine convictions, and had already spent almost a year in custody (Edwards, 2008).

It is not known when Bellfield's involvement in sexual offending began, but the earliest proven offence is that of 13-year-old Milly Dowler, who was reported missing on 21st March 2002 (Bird, 2010). There have been rumours surrounding Bellfield's first involvement in crimes against women from as early as 1980 (including the death of an ex-girlfriend, Patsy Morris [HeraldScotland, 2008]), however these have remained speculation. As a result, it is concluded that Bellfield did not embark on his endeavour as a serial killer and sexual offender until 2002.

Crimes Against Women

In sum, Bellfield has been convicted of the murder, and attempted murder, of four females: Milly Dowler (Murdered March 2002), Marsha McDonnell (Murdered February 2003), Kate Sheedy (Attempted Murder April 2004), and Amelie Delagrange (Murdered August 2004). Despite these crimes taking place between March 2002 and August 2004, Bellfield was not tried, nor convicted of these offences until 2008 (Marsha McDonnell, Kate Sheedy, and Amelie Delagrange) and 2011 (Milly Dowler).

Milly Dowler

On 21st March 2002, 13-year-old Milly Dowler (formally Amanda Dowler) was making her journey home from Heathside School, Weybridge, when she was abducted from a bus stop in Walton-on-Thames. On the day of the abduction, Milly had departed her train ride a stop early, so she could meet with a friend at a café. However, at 16:05, the girls left the café and went in separate directions. It was during this walk home that Milly was kidnapped. A large police investigation and media frenzy followed Milly's disappearance, but it wasn't until six months later, that her body was finally discovered Yateley Heath Woods, near Fleet in Hampshire (BBC News, 2008).

Marsha McDonnell

Less than 12 months after Milly's disappearance, Marsha McDonnell was attacked at a bus stop in Sunbury-on-Thames (BBC News, 2008). It is reported that on the night of 5th February 2003, Marsha McDonnell (DOB 14/10/1983) had just got off the bus after a night out with friends, when she was hit 3 times in the back of the head with a lump hammer (BBC News, 2008). Nearby residents heard Marsha's screams and came to her aid, however Marsha died in hospital some 30 hours later.

Kate Sheedy

In 2004, 14 months after the murder of Marsh McDonnell, 18-year-old Kate Sheedy was also attacked at a bus stop in Isleworth. Kate had been socialising with friends, after finishing her last day at Gumley House School. Kate reported that during a walk from the bus stop to her home address, she was struck by a white car, which was later identified as a white Toyota Previa. It was later revealed that the offender drove towards Kate Sheedy at speed, before reversing back over her body. Luckily, Kate recovered from the injuries sustained in the attack.

Amelie Delagrange

That same year, 22-year-old Amelie Delagrange was struck with a blunt object, after she left a bus stop in Twickenham Green (20th August 2004) (BBC News, 2008). It is believed that Amelie had been out with friends earlier in the evening, before taking a short bus ride home (Sutton, 2019). Amelie allegedly missed her stop, and as a result, she had a brief walk back to her home address. However, before she could make it across the green near her address, Amelie was hit over the head by a blunt object. She was taken to hospital by police, after being discovered lying in a pool of blood by a passing male. Unfortunately, Amelie later died in hospital as a result of the injuries she sustained in the attack (BBC News, 2008).

Aside from these four convictions, Bellfield has also been tried in court for various other crimes against women.

Anna-Maria Rennie was 17 when Bellfield allegedly approached her at a bus stop in Twickenham and attempted to kidnap her (14th October 2001). She was making her way home after an argument with her boyfriend, when Bellfield's car is suggested to have pulled up behind her. Anna-Maria reported that two men got out of the vehicle, but it was Bellfield who grabbed her by the arms and tried to bundle her into the dark-blue Ford Mondeo. Anna-Maria reported how she 'struck back' at Bellfield and a violent struggle pursued. After breaking free, Anna-Maria ran home, where she made the decision to report this incident to the police. Anna-Maria was successful in identifying Bellfield at an identification parade in March 2005 (Sutton, 2019), however at the 2008 trial, the jury could not agree verdicts on charges of kidnap and false imprisonment (BBC News, 2008).

On 20th March 2002 (the day before Milly Dowlers abduction), 11-year-old Rachel Cowles was walking home from school in Shepperton when she was approached by an unknown male. Allegedly the victim was approached by a man, who claimed to be her neighbour, and asked if she wanted a lift home. Rachel described the offender to be fat, short with dark hair and a squeaky voice, and to be driving a red hatchback vehicle which had two car seats in the rear (Davies, 2011; Sutton, 2019).

The red hatchback was hypothesised to be a vehicle Bellfield was known to use, as he shared usage with his ex-partner, and mother of his children (1x young boy and 1x young girl, hence the car seats). The attempted abduction reported by Rachel's father was described to have occurred just 3 miles from what was to be the site of Milly's abduction, and during the trial of Bellfield, the media reported on Rachel's 'uncanny' resemblance to Milly (Davies, 2011). Nevertheless, due to 'an avalanche of adverse publicity' Old Bailey judge, Mr Justice Wilkie, decided to abandon the trial of already convicted serial killer Levi Bellfield (Greenslade, 2011). This decision sparked a media outcry given Bellfield's earlier 'no verdict' cases.

Similar to the murder of Marsha McDonnell, Irma Dragoshi (age 36 at the time of the attack), was hit over the head with a blunt instrument whilst she waited at a bus stop in Longford, West Drayton (16th December 2003) (BBC News, 2008). It is alleged Bellfield got out of a nearby vehicle, ran over and attacked Irma whilst she was on the phone to her husband, Astri. It was Bellfield's associate, Sunil Gharu, who disclosed Bellfield's involvement in the attack, however, the jury could not reach a verdict on whether Bellfield was guilty of this attack during the hearing in 2008. This was despite Gharu reporting that he heard him say "Watch this" before getting out and attacking Irma (BBC News, 2008).

At the time of the investigation into the murders, attempted murder, kidnap/false imprisonment and assault of Marsha, Amelie, Kate, Anna-Marie and Irma, a string of reports was made against Bellfield for violent and sexual crimes. A number of these were made by young females, between the ages of thirteen and seventeen, who accused Bellfield of similar crimes – drugging them and subjecting them to rapes. However, due to the complexity of the case against Bellfield in regard to the murders, and the lack of evidence supporting the associations, these cases were never brought against Bellfield. Victims were supported by Family Liaison Officers and coaching towards '*her justice is my justice*'[1] coping (Sutton, 2019, p.214).

The Police Investigation

Within 24-hours of Amelie Delagrange's death, the Metropolitan police were able to link the characteristics of the offence, to the murder of Marsha McDonnell. This case was also grouped with the attacks of Jesse Wilson and Edel Harbison, under the Operation name 'Upwey' (Sutton, 2019). The only saving grace for both Jesse and Edel, is that they survived their attacks, whereas Marsha McDonnell died some 30 hours after her attack took place. Operation Upwey was subsequently responsible for investigating the three attacks congruently, due to the similarity in injuries (several blows to the back of the head by a blunt object), location (south-west London) and victim profiles (young females). However, it was when Detective Chief Inspector Colin Sutton took over the murder investigation of Amelie Delagrange, that Operation

Upwey, became linked with Operation Yeaddiss (Sutton, 2019). In his terms, the '*linked investigative series*' was appropriate to describe the four crimes, as the established description of 'linked series' relied on physical evidence to link the crimes, which was not true for this case (Sutton, 2019). Sutton also chose to label these crimes as a 'linked investigative series' to reassure the public that a '*randomly striking killer [was not] on the loose*' (Sutton, 2019, pp.54-55).

Investigation of Amelie Delagrange's Murder

Within the first day of Amelie's murder investigation, Senior Investigating Officer Colin Sutton had been assigned 70 members of staff to his task force. Two of these personal, had worked on cases under Operation Upwey. DI Richard Ambrose had been the Officer Manager for the Marsha McDonnell murder, and Clive Grace served as the liaison officer for Edel Harbison. Having first-hand knowledge and experience of the other cases, these staff members provided immense support to Sutton during the investigation (Sutton, 2019). According to Sutton (2019), the first few days of Amelie Delagrange's investigation were spent searching Twickenham green for evidence, trawling CCTV for sightings of vehicles and searching the River Thames for Amelie's belongings. Successfully, her purse and keys were retrieved, but her mobile phone and bag was not. Alongside this, the Met police drip fed the media with snippets of information regarding the murder, including the victim's profile, its suspected link with Marsha McDonnell and the nature of the attack. During a press conference on Friday 20th August, Detective Chief Superintendent Andy Murphy was asked if there was also a link between Amelie Delagrange's murder, and that of Milly Dowler, which had occurred two years prior. Due to the dissimilarities between the ages of victims (Milly was a young teen) and injuries (Milly was subject to various assaults, and was kidnapped before her murder), the link was considered 'unhelpful' and was shot down by Murphy during the talks (Sutton, 2019).

As the investigation developed, staff begun to tire. Sutton (2019) reports in his book, 'Manhunt', that by mid-September he was averaging 70 hour working weeks, and overtime had exceeded the budget. The media were starting to put pressure on the police, as their lines of enquiry had so far proven unhelpful. However, on 24th September, CCTV identified a small white van which had been parked on Hampton Road between 10 and 10.08pm (the suspected time of Amelie's attack). Sutton pursued this sighting as a priority, and the identification of the driver became priority. Meanwhile, reports had come in from members of the public, with 'Single Suggestions'[2] of who the killer was. One of these reports came from a Johanna Collings. She reported that an ex-partner of hers 'hated women' and had a particular dislike for blonde women. She described finding a copy of *Cosmopolitan* magazine among her ex-partners belongings, and all images of blonde females had had their faces 'stabbed'. Johanna also described the areas which her ex-partner frequented, and informed police that he drove a white van. She described his occupation as a 'bouncer' and 'wheel clamper' and Johanna also suggested he was currently on bail for GBH and Fraud – he had attacked a male with a hammer. Johanna Collings named her ex-partner as Levi Bellfield. This Single Suggestion was of interest to officers, as a previous inquiry at a local garage triggered the reporting of a courier van registration P610 XCN, to have been recently sold to a 'gypsy who gave the name Levi'. The pieces of the puzzle were starting to come together, and officers had two snippets of intelligence that linked Levi Bellfield, to a white Ford courier van, which he is known to drive around the area of Twickenham Green and Walton on Thames.

Intelligence Analysts were tasked to build a subject profile, gathering all known information on Bellfield into a concise report. They explored intelligence databases, police interviews, PNC files and other records for any known information on the individual. Two things were immediately considered to be 'of interest'; the first – Levi Bellfield's mobile number was registered on a Met Police database, and this was the same mobile number left at the garage where he was believed to have purchased the white Ford courier van, and the second, before owning the white van in question, Levi Bellfield was known to be the registered keeper of a Toyota Previa, which had blacked out windows – this description 'fitted the bill' of a people carrier used in an attack on Kate Sheedy in 2004. Further investigation confirmed that the Previa owned by Bellfield was in fact white, as Kate Sheedy had described during her victim statement in April 2004. This led to the attack on Kate Sheedy (Operation Zenda) to be linked in series, to the crimes within Operation Yeaddiss (Sutton, 2019).

THE ARREST OF LEVI BELLFIELD

During the time between establishing the above crime series linkage, and the arrest of Levi Bellfield on Monday 24th November 2004, officers were hard at work behind the scenes. They were offering 24/7 surveillance of Bellfield, establishing links between him, and known associates (who happened to be known murderers, rapists, and paedophiles), and obtaining confirmation legally, that an arrest could lead to charges. Those charges were in part, pinned on Sonia Salvetierra confirming it was Levi Bellfield who attacked her three months prior to Marsha McDonnell's death[3]. On the day of his arrest (24/11/2004), whilst Levi Bellfield was being questioned at a police station in Heathrow, Sonia was engaging with the Identification Parade. Unfortunately, Sonia was unable to make a positive identification – She did not rule

Levi Bellfield's image out, but she could not confirm it was him who attacked her. Despite this blow to the investigation, officers who were conducting the search on Bellfield's home address, had become increasingly concerned about the presentation of his partner, Emma Mills. Emma was described by officers as being shy, well spoken, and bright, but was reluctant to work with the police. Officers believed that for some reason, she was scared of Bellfield, as she alluded to the possible consequences of speaking with the police. This fear is what ultimately led Emma Mills to report Levi Bellfield for a catalogue of offences, including rapes, assaults, kidnaps, imprisonment, and psychological abuse (Sutton, 2019). Emma had taken the opportunity presented to her as a means of escape, she made a statement outlining her experiences, and confirmed that she knew he had behaved towards his ex-partners in the same way. He was, according to Emma Mills, a serial abuser.

The victim statements provided by Emma Mills, Johanna Collings and Rebecca Wilkinson were almost identical. They described how Bellfield had exerted physical violence, psychological control, and sexual abuse over the course of their relationship and had 'lured' them in with his superficial charm and generosity (Sutton, 2019). It was apparent that this grooming behaviour was simply a profession for Bellfield – he knew what to do and exactly how to execute it. Bellfield had shown no remorse to any of his ex-partners and had isolated them from family and friends to evade detection. The statements were enough to warrant a charge against Bellfield, remanding him in custody, but the final nail in the coffin emerged when Emma Mills described a set of circumstances that would lead to the allegation that it was in fact Levi Bellfield that kidnapped and murdered Millie Dowler. These statements were sent over to Surrey Police, who, like the Met Police, were confident they had caught their offender.

Preparing the Case for Court

Between 2004 and 2008, the Met Police prepared the case which was to be heard at The Old Bailey during February 2008. The charges to be heard at the trial related to the murder of Marsha McDonnell in 2003, the murder of Amelie Delagrange in 2004, the attempted murder of Kate Sheedy in 2004, the kidnap and false imprisonment of Anna-Maria Rennie in 2001, and the assault on Irma Dragoshi in 2003. The Met had secured enough evidence to link the 5 crimes to Bellfield, but it would be ultimately down to the jury to determine his guilt.

The trial opened on 2nd October 2007 at 10.35am (Sutton, 2019), and one of the first to speak was William Boyce, QC, who asked for a restriction on the publishing of Bellfield's image in the press, or link to Milly's case, to prevent possible jury bias. This request was granted, and the decision to not print Bellfield's image in the media was made. The jury was also selected, on the premise of meeting set criteria including: no former knowledge of Bellfield and his victims, not residents of the London Boroughs of Richmond, Hounslow, or Hillingdon, or in Surrey or Middlesex, and not affiliated to Met or Surrey Police. This further ensured the jury members had no prior knowledge of the ongoing connection between the Bellfield standing trial, and Bellfield's involvement in the Milly Dowler case.

Despite the careful selection of jurors, and the restriction of printing Bellfield's image within the press, complaints regarding the media was regularly put in front of the judge. On several occasions William Boyce (acting on behalf of Bellfield) made claims that media reporting could undoubtably be having an adverse effect on the impartiality of the jury. Complaints were also made by Bellfield regarding the use of 'screens' to restrict the view of the victim/witnesses and defendant, contributing to prejudices against him. However, as Sutton describes, both Kate Sheedy and Emma Mills articulated with courage and bravery what had happened to them both at the hands of Bellfield, and no doubt provided evidence which would result in a favourable outcome, despite his attempts to intimidate.

On 25th February 2008, Bellfield was found guilty of murdering Marsha McDonnell and Amelie Delagrange, as well as the attempted murder of Kate Sheedy. Unfortunately, the cases against Bellfield concerning Anna-Maria Rennie and Irma Dragoshi were dismissed due to unfair media coverage, however, Bellfield was handed three whole-life sentences with the denial of opportunity for parole and 'justice was served' (Sutton, 2019).

Operation Ruby

The first link to Milly and 'Operation Ruby', was identified by Sutton during the early investigations into Bellfield. In November 2004 a phone call was made to Surrey Police, where Sutton outlined what they knew about Bellfield. However, it wasn't until 2005 that Sutton and colleagues were able to link the red Daewood Nexia that Bellfield was known to have been driving, to the CCTV footage at the time of Milly's disappearance. Disappointingly though, Surrey Police had only saved 20 minutes worth of footage from the day of Milly's disappearance, and therefore there was no evidence to confirm that it was Bellfield driving the vehicle. This failing was what led the Crown Prosecution Service (CPS) to deal with the cases (Op Ruby and Op Yeaddiss) as separate entities. The reasoning for this was that the case of Milly Dowler was 'piecemeal' due to the 'holes and avenues of escape' – ultimately the CPS did not want the flaws of Operation Ruby to jeopardise the successfulness of Operation Yeaddiss (Sutton, 2019, p.217).

As a result, Surrey Police embarked on their own investigation in parallel to the work being done under Operation Yeaddiss (headed by Colin Sutton). Despite Bellfield being named as a prime suspect in connection with Milly's murder in the immediate aftermath of his first trial (in 2008) I took a further 2 years for Surrey

Police to gather enough evidence to charge Bellfield for his involvement in the abduction and murder of Milly Dowler.

On 6th October 2010, Bellfield appeared in court via video link and was formally charged with one count each of: attempted abduction, (actual) abduction, disposal of evidence, and murder regarding the case of Milly Dowler, and one count of attempted abduction of Rachel Cowles.

A Second Trial

Bellfield's second trial began at the Old Bailey on 10th May 2011. Bellfield was tried for the attempted abduction of Rachel Cowles, abduction of Milly Dowler, and subsequent murder of Milly Dowler. On 23rd June the jury reached a guilty verdict for his role in Milly Dowler's death (both the kidnap and murder) and overnight, the media went into a frenzy. As a result, the outstanding verdict on the Rachel Cowles case was dismissed, history almost repeating itself as a mirror of circumstances which led to an unresolved outcome concerning Anna-Maria Rennie and Irma Dragoshi in 2008.

During the second trial, it was well document that the family of Milly Dowler were subjected to gruelling cross examination, and the presentation of Bellfield was ever as evil as it was during the first trial. Whilst the court case itself did not last as long as the first (1 month vs 5), the media interest in reporting on the case 'live' was significantly greater. This impacted the jury's ability to provide conclusion on Rachel's case, but thankfully, did not impede on the conviction for Milly's death.

As with his previous murder convictions, Bellfield received a life sentence for his crimes against Milly Dowler. As a result of Bellfield receiving a life sentence, whilst serving life sentences, he is named as the only prisoner to have been sentenced to two separate whole-life orders for two separate crimes in the UK, and as a result of this he will never leave custody.

Media Reporting

In the case of Levi Bellfield, the media were described as both a help, as well as a hinderance. They supported with several appeals, requests for information and public attention, but also ran stories which impeded court cases, treated the victims of Bellfield's crime with disrespect, and continue to provide Bellfield with a spotlight for fame. This has maintained Bellfield's name as a frequent edition within newspaper reporting.

From the offset, the media were keen to provide commentary to the crimes committed by Bellfield. Within the book 'My Sister Milly', Gemma Dowler (2018) reports her experiences with journalists and reporters at her home address from the day of Milly's disappearance. She reports feeling 'judged and unprotected', by those seeking an update for the press. Gemma also reports how her parents were the target of media attention, with some articles pointing suspicion at their father, along with defamatory comments about Milly herself. Gemma Dowler described the media's attention as an 'obsession' and has spoke publicly about her challenges dealing not only with the trauma of her sister's death, but also the way in which her life changed as a result of the media attention.

The biggest failing on behalf of the media, was an alleged hack of Milly's phone by the News of the World (NoW). Reporting on the hacking, the BBC News (2011) shared how an investigator working for the NoW had hacked into the voicemail of Milly whilst she was missing. The Guardian (2011) further claimed that News of the World were able to intercept messages which were left by family and friends and even allege that NoW were able to mark some as 'read' and 'delete' messages, which gave false hope that Milly had had contact with the phone. This sparked a media frenzy in 2011 and brought the crimes of Bellfield back into the spotlight, after what had been a quite few years post sentencing.

Good Cop Bad Cop

Around the time of Marsha McDonnell and Amelie Delagrange's murders (2003/2004), the media had begun to report on the likelihood that a 'serial' killer was terrorising the streets of Surrey. They had suspected that the murders of Marsha and Amelie were connected to the attack on Kate Sheedy, along with a number of other incidents within the area, and momentum once again quickened, as the police ramped up their efforts to identify the killer.

Whilst the media hypothesised who the suspected serial killer could be, in February 2005, *Crimewatch* agreed to run an appeal for new information regarding Kate Sheedy's attack. The report was carefully planned and executed alongside officers who worked closely on the case. They could not mention the case of Amelie Delagrange, as they had already made an arrest, and this could infringe the Human Rights of the suspect. Subsequently, the appeal for information was cunningly pitched, as officers revealed the make and model of the car to viewers, in the hope they could gather more intelligence on the owner, Levi Bellfield. It was not a '*fishing expedition*' as Sutton describes, it was a '*realisation that their worst fears about this man they thought they knew was actually true*' (Sutton, 2019, p.154). This demonstrates the willingness the media had on assisting with the enquiries of the police.

Within hours of the Crimewatch broadcast, witness statements began to flood in. Those who were once afraid to provide evidence against Bellfield, became passionate in bringing the killer to justice (Sutton, 2019). Within his book 'Manhunt' Sutton describes an 'excellent relationship with the media during operation Yeaddiss'

(Sutton, 2019, p.74). This was a stark contrast to the way they had jeopardised the case and handling of Milly Dowler's murder in 2002. From there on it, the media played close attention to the evolving case of the 'Bus Stop Stalker'.

Reporting on the Trial

During the time of Bellfield's first trial in 2007/8, news outlets were reporting internationally as events unfolded within the Old Bailey.

As discussed in the previous chapter, 'The Police Investigation', William Boyce QC, asked the judge during the first day of the trial, for a restriction on the publishing of Bellfield's image in the press or link to Milly's case. Concerns were raised by Bellfield's defence that the naming and publishing of images could result in possible jury bias. This request was granted, and the decision to not print Bellfield's image in the media was made. Whilst the trial continued into early 2008, William Boyce (acting on behalf of Bellfield) made claims that media reporting was undoubtably having an adverse effect on the impartiality of the jury. Unfortunately, on the day of verdict (25th February 2008) Bellfield was acquitted of the cases concerning Anna-Maria Rennie and Irma Dragoshi, due to unfair media coverage. He was, however, found guilty of murdering Marsha McDonnell and Amelie Delagrange, as well as the attempted murder of Kate Sheedy.

On Monday 25th February 2008, The BBC News summarised their commentary of the trial with an interactive map, and overview of each of the crimes Bellfield was accused of. The maps listed the murders and attempted murder of Marsha McDonnell, Amelie Delgrange, and Kate Sheedy, and also linked Bellfield to 2 'no verdict' charges (Anna-Maria Rennie and Irma Dragoshi), and the suspected involvement in an ongoing murder case, 13-year-old Milly Dowler. The webpage plotted on an interactive map the whereabouts of each attack and provided detail on the proximity to Bellfield home address.

Later that same day, the BBC post another article on their website, titled, 'Stalker guilty of student murders'. The article again, summarises the details of each of the 3 cases which Bellfield was found guilty of as well as detailing those which the Jury returned no verdict on. As with the previous article, the later linked the ongoing court case with a pending investigation into the murder of Milly Dowler.

The following day, the BBC updated their website to report on the outcome of Bellfield's hearing. Titled, 'Bellfield given 'whole life' term', the article summarises the previous days court proceedings, comments made by the judge and families, and sentencing implications. The article once again, commented on the ongoing case involving the abduction and murder of Milly Dowler.

The three articles outlined above demonstrate the scale of reporting that was evident around the time of Bellfield's first trial. Not only was the BBC producing a high volume of articles (with some less than two hours apart), but it had a space dedicated in the margin of their site linking all articles relating to the trial. Alongside this, there were hundreds of other sites who were exploiting the case for their own gains, and by the end of February 2008, most news pages had tabs dedicated to Bellfield's crimes and trial.

Bellfield's Second Trial

In 2011, Bellfield was back in court for the trail concerning Milly Dowler's abduction and murder, and also the attempted abduction of Rachel Cowles.

As with the first trial in 2008, the media intensely reported on daily activity within the court room. Alongside this, the media had the advantage of prior knowledge gained of Bellfield from the 2008 trial, so the eruption of reports came thick and fast detailing Bellfield's background, prior crimes, and involvement in offences similar to those he was previously convicted of. The media were also keen to feature images and snippets of information on the Dowler's, given their involvement in the trail itself. On 16th May 2011, Milly Dowler's father Rob Dowler, broke down in tears following a string of defence questioning which painted him and his wife as negligent parents, who did not know their own daughter. Again, the media reported tirelessly on this, and snippets of evidence gathered by the police within the early days, which suggested Rob Dowler was a 'suspect', were detailed within newspaper articles.

The defence's ultimate goal was to provide a narrative that Milly Dowler was a run-away teen, who was unhappy at home. The subsequent lines of questioning attempted to question Rob and Sally's parenting, however, when it was Bellfield's time to answer questions, he refused. On 6th June 2011, Levi Bellfield declined his right to provide evidence at court, and informed judge Mr Justice Wilkie that he would not be speaking in his defence (BBC News, 2011b).

On 24th June 2011, the case involving the attempted abduction of Rachel Cowles was discharged, due to an 'avalanche of adverse media reporting' and 'bad character' reporting on Bellfield. The BBC shared a 42 second clip outside court, of Rachel describing her hurt and anger at the decision. The BBC titled the article 'Rachel Cowles angry at Bellfield case collapse' and provided a 4-line summary of the statement. Concluding, they wrote Ms Cowles said she was "hurt and angry" by what she called media coverage which had "robbed her of justice" but welcomed the conclusion of the Dowler case (BBC News, 2011c). This was yet another example of media reporting which had had a negative effect on desired outcomes against Bellfield, however this time, repercussions were faced by the media outlets.

On 18th July 2012, The Attorney General's Office and The Rt Hon Dominic Grieve QC published findings from a hearing that concluded articles published by newspapers around the time of the second trial, had adversely affected outcomes in court. Summarising, the article reads '*Mirror Group Newspapers Ltd and Associated Newspapers Ltd were both found guilty of contempt of court for publishing potentially prejudicial material whilst the jury was considering its verdict in relation to Rachel Cowles' alleged abduction by Levi Bellfield*'. The articles concerned were published by the Daily Mirror and the Daily Mail on 24th June 2011, shortly after the jury had returned the guilty verdict in relation the charges involving Milly Dowler. Despite not having a retuned verdict on Rachel Cowles case, the newspapers ran articles which went 'way beyond' what the jury had been told within court. This resulted in the case being discharged, and both companies fined (Attorney General's Office and The Rt Hon Dominic Grieve QC, 2012).

Recent Media Attention

Since Bellfield's most recent trial, there have been numerous reports, documentaries and podcasts concerned with the police's handing of the cases, Bellfield early life and criminal career, and the impact his crimes have had on his victims and their families.

Within one of these, Bellfield featured within a 'Born to Kill?' series (Levi Bellfield: The Bus Stop Stalker, 2014). The episode explored Bellfield's upbringing and early life, to determine whether there were any risk factors or triggers that may have led him to such prolific violence against women. The documentary shared early offending patterns, as well as relationships he had with other known violent criminals and sexual offenders. Aside from a handful of newspaper articles, this was the first real attempt to explore the motivations and triggers for Bellfield crimes.

In 2019, ITV ran a three-part drama titled 'Manhunt' which focussed on the crimes of Bellfield from the perspective of DCI Colin Sutton. The series explored, in chronological order, how the investigations unfolded, and the complexities involved in handing both operation Yeaddiss, with the case of Milly Dowler.

Similarly, in 2020, a documentary series 'Making a Monster' dedicated episode 3 of session 1 to the crimes of Levi Bellfield. Here, Bellfield's crimes were presented in summary, and the episodes that followed included that of Rose West, Robert Maudsley and Stephen Griffiths. This further reinforces the grandiose of attention that Bellfield's crimes have gained by the media and the public, and how his profile and crimes are now regarded as some of Britain's worst.

The reporting on Bellfield has followed in parallel within newspapers and online articles. There have been numerous articles detailing his behaviour and conduct whilst in prison, and also publicity surround his change of religion to Islam, and subsequent name change to Yusuf Rahmin in 2016. On 22nd September 2021, Birchall ran a piece within the Sun newspaper, which summarised his offences, updated on his whereabouts, and confirmed the change of name and religion which had been undertaken whilst at HMP Frankland, Durham (Birchall, 2021).

On 5th February 2022, The Sun published an online article detailing the contents of a 14-page confession which has been submitted by Bellfield, allegedly describing his involvement in the murder and attempted murder of Lin, Megan, and Josie Russel in 1996 (Hamilton, 2022). Commenting on the article, Sutton suggests the crimes will likely be re-investigated in light of the new evidence, but he likes to 'play games' and enjoys having the 'spotlight on himself' (Hamilton, 2022). This story was also run by ITV News on the eve of 6th February (ITV News, 2022), and has continued to ignite a flurry of 'who is he', 'what did he do' style articles divulging into the murder Levi Bellfield. If investigated and determined as truthful, these confessions mean the original suspect Richard Stone was wrongfully convicted, and previous requests for appeals and reviews were possibly denied prematurely, and without exploring other avenues (such as potential DNA evidence found on a shoelace). This investigation will no doubt develop over the coming years.

THEORETICAL REFLECTION

Criminal Narratives

Criminal narrative theory proposes the idea that the role an individual self-assigns, is a key driver for offending and subsequent reoffending, and the role undertaken can be identified through the experience of offending (Ioannou, 2006). The narrative role undertaken by an offender is also believed to be a way for individuals to 'make sense' of their world, and the part they play within it (Baumeister and Newman, 1994). In extension to this, narrative roles are considered to be part of a wider framework, which allows individuals to validate their emotional experience (McLeod, 1997). Canter (1994) argued that the role an individual self-assigns unfolds over the course of an individual's lifetime and gives 'purpose to action' during the build-up, commission and aftermath of an offence. When narrative roles become prescriptive of crime, is when the narrative story becomes ill-formed or confused, and just as narratives help shape the non-offending actions we take, they also shape the act of offending. It was therefore hypothesised by Canter (1994) that in any given criminal context there would be a dominant role the criminal chooses to take, and that role is related directly to a recognisable narrative.

Through his actions, the criminal tells us about how he has chosen to live his life. The challenge is to reveal his destructive life story, to uncover the plot in which crime appears to play such a significant part (Canter, 1994, p.299).

Initial attempts to determine narrative roles within a criminal sample, identified four archetypal themes, which ran parallel with Frye's (1957) Theory of Mythoi, and McAdams Life Story Model. Overall, the preliminary studies found that the roles played by criminals, could be categorised into four themes. Ioannou (2001; 2006) titled these themes The Professional (Adventure), The Victim (Irony), The Hero (Quest) and The Revenger (Tragedy). According to Ioannou (2001; 2006) the Professional theme reflected an Adventurer narrative, with offenders typically agreeing with statements such as, 'I always knew it would happen' and 'I was like a professional'. According to Ioannou (2001; 2006), this offender experienced calm, competency, and mastery during their offence. Similarly, The Hero reflected a Quest narrative, experiencing hubris whilst overcoming and taking on their challenges. This offender agreed with statements such as, 'It was nothing special' and 'I was looking for recognition'. In contrast to this, were Ioannou's (2001; 2006) Victim and Revenger themes. The Victim reflected the Irony narrative, and it is believed that this offender experienced disconnectedness and despair, agreeing with statements such as, 'I was a victim' and 'I was confused'. Finally, the Revenger theme reflected the narrative of Tragedy. This offender reported feelings of distress and blame, agreeing with statements such as, 'I was getting my own back' and 'I didn't care what would happen'. These four themes of criminal narratives, and their associated archetypal mythoi, were replicated in a later study by Youngs and Canter (2012).

These finding from these studies demonstrated support for the Criminal Narrative model, however, Ioannou, Canter, Youngs and Synnott (2015) indicate that these studies failed to differentiate across specific crime types and grouped the sample irrespective of index offence. In an attempt to overcome this, Canter Youngs and Synnott (2015) measured the prevalence of the four themes across varied crime types. Like the earlier studies, offenders were presented with The Narrative Role Questionnaire (NRQ-v1) (Youngs and Canter, 2012), and were asked to rate how much, or how little they agreed with statements relating to one of the four proposed narrative role themes. They discovered that for property offences, the predominant role was Hero (50%), for drug offences the most highly scored role was Professional (40%), for violence and murder the predominant role was Revenger (50%), and lastly, for sexual offenders, the most frequent role was Victim (45%). Ioannou, Canter, Youngs and Synnott (2015) suggest that these findings reflect early theories on crime motivation, such as Flemming's (1999) description of property crime being driven by excitement, Brain, Parker and Bottomley's (1998) description of drug offences as a means to sustain 'lifestyle', and Katz's (1988) exploration of violent offenders as individuals who are seeking 'righteousness and vengeance'.

However, the study by Ioannou, Canter, Youngs and Synnott (2015) explored only the prevalence of themes among the offending groups, and failed to recognise that within offending groups, there may be different themes present. DeBlasio, Ioannou and Synnott (2022), acted upon this limitation, and explored narrative roles within a sample of sexual offenders. Smallest space analysis (SSA) found support for three themes of narrative roles suggested within the literature, and these narrative role themes were titled: The Professional, The Adventurer and The Revenger-Victim. Whilst the three themes somewhat reflected the findings of earlier studies (Ioannou, 2001, 2006; Canter and Youngs, 2012; Ioannou, Canter, Youngs and Synnott, 2015), they also suggested that sexual offending was more likely concerned with seeking conquest of positive narrative roles than negative ones, which contrasts with the earlier findings suggested by Ioannou Canter, Youngs and Synnott (2015). In the progressive study, the fourth theme (Revenger) become merged with the third (Victim), creating one overarching theme Revenger-Victim, and this theme was found to reflect only 23% of the sample of sexual offenders (DeBlasio, Ioannou and Synnott, 2022). This suggested that despite Ioannou Canter, Youngs and Synnott (2015) finding higher prevalence of victim roles for sexual offending, there is still variation within the offending group.

Hypothesising the Narrative Role of Bellfield

It is clear through his actions, that Bellfield's narrative role during the evolution of his offending career was likely to be in line with the Adventurer or Professional theme. He 'stalked' his victims at bus stops, assaulted them with weapons such as hammers, and continue to re-offend in close succession, in order to satisfy his own needs. Bellfield was a confident, organised offender, often committing his offences in public spaces such as roads and parks. During the investigation of the offences, Bellfield remained confident in his ability to evade detection, and presented as a self-assured professional. These characteristics are not typical of a Victim or Revenger narrative role theme. Research suggests that these offenders often describe feeling confused during the crime, almost a 'victim' themselves, and suggest they didn't want to offend and what happened was 'nothing special'. These findings do not reflect what was exhibited by Bellfield.

The murders Bellfield was found guilty of, reflect what Santtila, Hakkanen, Canter and Elfgren (2003) describe as Instrumental homicide. Within their 'Classifying homicide offenders and predicting their characteristics from crime scene behaviour' paper, Santtila, Hakkanen, Canter and Elfgren's (2003) explore crime scene behaviours alongside personal characteristics, to generate a typology model of homicide offenders. The authors note, how instrumental homicide is typically categorised through crime scene behaviours such as a 'location known to the offender', 'gain from the victim' and the 'use of a weapon'. Bellfield was known to demonstrate all of these behaviours within his offences, stalking young girls at bus stops around the area close to his home, using blunt force trauma to disable his victims (in most cases, his weapon of choice was a hammer), and gaining sexual gratification from the murder of his female victims. In regards to personal characteristics, the Instrumental offender, according to Santtila, Hakkanen, Canter and Elfgren (2003), is known to use aggression to overcome problems, engage in a diverse array of offending (including burglary/robbery), is likely to come from a low Socio-Economic background, and has difficulty maintaining relationships (likely to be single or divorced). Again, this reflects the known personal circumstances of Levi Bellfield. He is described as being a violent individual who has a string of offences (including assaulting a police officer), also has a number of convictions relating to property (including that of burglary), has a troublesome relationship profile and comes from a relatively low socio-economic background. All of these factors, combined with the crime scene behaviour exhibited by Bellfield, demonstrate a likelihood of him categorising as an Instrumental offender.

This conclusion echoes what was originally considered in response to narrative role themes, that Bellfield was likely to experience Professional or Adventurer narrative during the commission of his offence. This analysis is reinforced by Senior Investigative Officer Colin Sutton, who was responsible for the investigation and later prosecution of Bellfield. Describing Bellfield, Sutton comments, '[Bellfield] has a massive ego to feed, he thinks he's God's gift to everyone'. Speaking to the media post sentencing, Sutton later commented, '*when we started dealing with him [Bellfield] he came across as very jokey, like he's your best mate. But he's a cunning individual, violent. He can switch from being nice to being nasty, instantly*'. These comments reflect the initial summary of Bellfield acting as a poised criminal.

Considering the evidence presented concerning his offending style, background information, personal characteristic, and crime scene behaviour, it is hypothesised that Bellfield adopted a Professional narrative role theme. The professional differs from the adventurer in the description of the offence. Professionals are known to describe their behaviour as a 'mission' which was 'fate' or 'something that would always happen'. Professionals seek 'recognition' for their 'job' which they believe was 'right' and 'didn't care' what would happen. Contrastingly, adventurers describe their offending as 'fun', 'interesting' and 'exciting', they do not seek the recognition of a professional, and counter the risk of detection with the need to gain emotionally from the crime. It is evident from the material presented, that Bellfield not only took pleasure in reoffending, but he done so in a calm, calculated and methodological manner. He saw his attacks on women as his mission and didn't really care what would happen in the long term. This is evidenced by his repeated exposure to violence, right up until his incarceration. This concluding Professional narrative role theme has remained consistent in his actions during the trial, sentencing, and behaviour in custody, and can be demonstrated through his attitude post-conviction.

CONCLUSION

On 27th January 2016, Surrey Police announced that Bellfield had admitted, for the first time, abducting, raping and murdering Milly Dowler. This confession came after being interviewed about whether he had acted with an accomplice. Bellfield later issued a denial that he made any such confession, but Surrey Police stood by their earlier statement. Similarly, in February 2022, it is alleged that Bellfield confessed in writing to the murder of Lin and Megan Russell, and the attempted murder of Josie Russell. These confessions undoubtedly trigger secondary trauma for his surviving victims and families, but perhaps that is the aim?

Speaking on the Russell confession letter, Colin Sutton suggests it is yet another attempt from Bellfield to stay in the spotlight, and this is fuelled by his narcissistic personality. However, as presented earlier, the suspected narrative role theme of a Professional, encourages the individual to 'seek recognition'. Should this analysis of Bellfield's criminal narrative be true, the recent confessions made by him are in line with the behaviour and motivations typically expected of someone who has experience professional narratives within their criminal career.

Moving forward, the police and media should reflect on the contributions that they both made which led to the evasion of detection and failing prosecutions against Bellfield. Surrey Police, among others, admittedly invested too much time around other suspects, and outlets such as the Daily Mail allowed Bellfield to escape conviction on crimes which were successfully brought against him. Whilst neither party is to blame for the actions of Bellfield, better decision making could have certainly lessened the trauma for surviving victims and families.

REFERENCES

Attorney General's Office and The Rt Hon Dominic Grieve QC. (2012). *Two newspapers fined for contempt of court over Levi Bellfield trial.* https://www.gov.uk/government/news/two-newspapers-fined-for-contempt-of-court-over-levi-bellfield-trial

Baumeister, R. F., & Newman, L. S. (1994). How stories make sense of personal experience: Motives that shape autobiographical narratives. *Personality and Social Psychology Bulletin, 20*(6), 679–690. doi:10.1177/0146167294206006

BBC News. (2008). *Bus Stop Killers Chain of Violence.* BBC News. http://news.bbc.co.uk/1/hi/uk/7230063.stm#mcdonnell

BBC News. (2011a). *News of the World hacked Milly Dowler phone*. https://www.bbc.co.uk/news/uk-14017661

BBC News. (2011b). *Milly Dowler trial: No evidence from Levi Bellfield.* BBC News. https://www.bbc.co.uk/news/uk-england-13792659

BBC News. (2011c). *Rachel Cowles angry at Bellfield case collapse*. BBC News. https://www.bbc.co.uk/news/av/uk-13909290

Levi Bellfield: The Bus Stop Stalker. (2014). *Born to Kill*. Season 6. Episode 6.

Birchall, G. (2021). EVIL LEVI Who is Levi Bellfield and where is he now? *The Sun*. https://www.thesun.co.uk/news/3892932/levi-bellfield-milly-dowler-now/

Bird, S. (2008). Profile: Levi Bellfield, psychopath who preyed on young women. *The Sunday Times*. http://www.timesonline.co.uk/tol/news/uk/crime/article3416155.ece

Canter, D. V. (1994). *Criminal shadows*. Harper Collins.

Davies, C. (2011). Milly Dowler 'lookalike' tells trial of encounter with stranger in red car. *The Guardian*. https://www.theguardian.com/uk/2011/may/13/milly-dowler-lookalike-trial-red

DeBlasio, S., Ioannou, M., & Synnott, J. (2022). Sexual Offending: The Intrepid Professional-Adventurer and The Dejected Revenger-Victim. *International Journal of Offender Therapy and Comparative Criminology*. https://doi.org/10.1177/0306624X221124836 doi:10.1177/0306624X221124836 PMID:36181297

Dowler, G. (2018). *My Sister Milly*. Penguin.

Edwards, R. (2008). Levi Bellfield: A violent control freak. *The Daily Telegraph*.

Flemming, Z. (1999). The thrill of it all: Youthful offenders and auto theft. In P. Cromwell (Ed.), *In their own words: Criminals on crime* (2nd ed., pp. 71–79). Roxbury.

Frye, N. (1957). *Anatomy of criticism*. Princeton University Press. doi:10.1515/9781400866908

Greenslade, R. (2011). Were the media wrong to report on serial murderer Bellfield? *The Guardian*. https://www.theguardian.com/media/greenslade/2011/jun/24/medialaw-judiciary

Hamilton, M. (2022). KILLER CONFESSES Evil Levi Bellfield admits to hammer murders of mum and daughter Lin and Megan Russell in chilling confession letter. *The Sun*. https://www.thesun.co.uk/news/17559472/levi-bellfield-confession-letter-russell/

Herald Scotland. (2008, February 26). He murdered two... how many more did Bellfield Target? *The Herald*. https://www.heraldscotland.com/default_content/12457142.murdered-two-many-bellfield-target/

Ioannou, M. (2001). *The Experience of Crime: Emotions and Roles Experienced while committing an offence* [Unpublished MSc Thesis]. The University of Liverpool.

Ioannou, M. (2006). *Hero or Villain: criminals emotional experience of crime* [Unpublished Doctoral Dissertation]. University of Liverpool.

Ioannou, M., Canter, D. V., Youngs, D. E., & Synnott, J. P. (2015). Offenders' Crime Narratives Across Different Types of Crimes. *Journal of Forensic Psychology Practice*, *15*(5), 383–400. doi:10.1080/15228932.2015.1065620

ITV News. (2022). *Milly Dowler killer Levi Bellfield 'confesses' to Russell murders*. https://www.itv.com/news/meridian/2022-02-06/millie-dowler-killer-bellfield-confesses-to-russell-murders

Katz, J. (1988). *Seductions of crime: Moral and sensual attractions in doing evil*. Basic Books.

Lavender, J. (2020, February 17). Terrifying childhood trigger that set Levi Bellfield on path to becoming killer. *Mirror*. https://www.mirror.co.uk/tv/tv-news/terrifying-childhood-trigger-set-levi-21498739

Mangan, L. (2019, January 6). Manhunt review – A sober, responsible drama about the murder of three young females by Levi Bellfield. *The Guardian*. Retrieved from https://www.theguardian.com/tv-and-radio/2019/jan/06/manhunt-review-a-sober-responsible-drama-about-the-of-three-young-females-by-levi-bellfield

McAdams, D. P. (1988). *Power, intimacy and the life story*. The Guildford Press.

McLeod, J. (1997). *Narrative and psychotherapy*. Sage. doi:10.4135/9781849209489

Rawlinson, K. (2016, February 12). Levi Bellfield denies confessing to Milly Dowler's murder. *The Guardian*. Retrieved from https://www.theguardian.com/uk-news/2016/feb/12/levi-bellfield-denies-confessing-to-milly-dowlers

Santtila, P., Häkkänen, H., Canter, D., & Elfgren, T. (2003). Classifying homicide offenders and predicting their characteristics from crime scene behavior. *Scandinavian Journal of Psychology*, *44*(2), 107–118. doi:10.1111/1467-9450.00328 PMID:12778978

Sutton, C. (2019). *Manhunt - how I brought serial killer Levi Bellfield to Justice*. John Blake Publishing.

The Guardian. (2011). Missing Milly Dowler's voicemail was hacked by News of the World. *The Guardian*. https://www.theguardian.com/uk/2011/jul/04/milly-dowler-voicemail-hacked-news-of-world

Youngs, D., & Canter, D. (2012). Offenders' crime narratives as revealed by the Narrative Roles Questionnaire (NRQ). *International Journal of Offender Therapy and Comparative Criminology*, 1–23. PMID:22247223

ENDNOTES

1 This is a phrase used by officers to promote feelings of justice for victims who are not able to bring charges/convictions against their perpetrators. It was used in the current case to offer victims a mutual feeling of justice once Bellfield was convicted of the murders.

2 'Single Suggestions' is a term used by police to refer to any public reports concerning possible suspects.

3 Sonia Salvetierra claimed to have been attacked over the head while out walking in Twickenham Green in late 2002. Following the attack, Sonia left her job as a Nanny and returned to Peru. She would not come to the attention of Police until her former employer reported the similarities of the ongoing cases with Sonia's attack. The Met Police contacted Sonia and asked if she would be able to recognise her attacker during an Identification Parade, she confirmed, but on the day of the ID Parade, Sonia was unable to make a positive identification.

Chapter 4
Fake It Until You Make It! The Crimes and Trial of Anna Sorokin (Delvey)

Angelo Kevin Brown
Arkansas State University, USA

EXECUTIVE SUMMARY

The chapter will provide an overview of the life, crimes, and trial of Anna Sorokin better known as Anna Delvey. Anna had invented a false persona and life so that people would think she was a rich German heiress instead of her real identity of a woman from a working-class Russian family. Anna used her false identity to defraud banks, hotels, and friends for about $275,000. Anna's life became internationally known with her story being published in major news and media articles including podcasts, 60 Minutes, HBO, a $300,000 book deal to her former friend Rachel Williams, and a $320,000 Netflix deal for Anna. Anna was arrested and convicted in 2019 and was sentenced to four to 12 years in New York State. After her release from prison, she was arrested again by U.S. Immigration and Customs Enforcement and held for overstaying her visa.

INTRODUCTION

Anna Sorokin born on January 28th, 1991, was a Russian woman from a working-class family. She created a false persona of a person who was extremely wealthy and changed her name to Anna Delvey. Anna with her new name and persona pretended to be a German heiress so she would be able to gain access to the social elite in New York City and elsewhere. Eventually, Anna and the false narrative she gave about

DOI: 10.4018/978-1-7998-9668-5.ch004

her life finally caught up with her, and she was arrested, convicted, and being held for overstaying her visa where she could be deported back to Germany. Anna was given various names including the Soho Scammer, Soho Grifter, and Fake Heiress. The media attention that was given to Anna during and after her trial made her internationally famous and her criminal scams became known as the "summer of scam" whose name was inspired by the "Summer of Sam" who was a serial killer in New York from during the 1970s (Bailey, 1999).

The criminal trial of Anna blew up on social media, which helped her story and name(s) be well-known through a line of T-shirts, various media outlets including books, podcasts, the *New York Times, The New Yorker, CNBC, The Guardian, HBO,* and an entire Netflix series. The criminal trial against Anna was brought upon after the arrest that was part of a sting operation planned by officer McCaffrey of the New York Police Department (NYPD) on October 3rd, 2017 in collaboration with the Los Angeles Police Department (LAPD). On April 25, 2019, Anna was found guilty of grand larceny, second-degree larceny, theft of services, and received four to 12 years imprisonment, a $24,000 fine, and $199,000 restitution (Gibson, 2022).

CON ARTISTS

This is not the first con artist to become nationally and internationally infamous. The media and especially pop culture has helped create an obsession with conmen and conwomen for decades, in fiction and nonfictional stories. These stories include *The Sting* (1973) a film about professional conmen, and more recently the award-winning *Catch Me If You Can* (2002) starring Leonardo DiCaprio, and *Oceans Eleven (2001)* with a star-studded cast including Brad Pitt, George Clooney, Julia Roberts, and Matt Damon which was a remake of a movie from the 1960s. These con artists often have lots of charisma and charm like Anna, and these movies based on the lives of con artists really helped highlight and even exaggerate these characteristics. Even Williams a former friend turned witness against Anna stated that Anna is "Clever, She can Be Funny… Amusing". As the American dream focuses on people becoming successful from nothing, these con artists do that in a unique way and use their personality and lies to get wealthy, and used the "fake it until you make it" slogan in criminal ways.

A con artist is a person who attempts to defraud an individual, business, or group of individuals by tricking them and gaining their trust (Dugatkin, 1992). The con artists use confidence tricks so they can exploit their victims by accessing their compassion, greed, confidence, vanity, naivete, and or credulity among other tactics. The 'con' is short for confidence in the name con, con man, con woman, con artist, etc. A con is also known by other names including a swindle, a scam, a grift, a hustle, among others names.

The purpose of these confidence tricks is to defraud a person by making the victim voluntarily exchange something without the victim knowing the true intent. The confidence trick first appears to be of mutual benefit to both parties but in actuality, it is not mutually beneficial but benefits the con artist at the expense of the victim(s). There are different types of cons including a short con and a long con, Anna was involved in the long or big con, which takes usually days, weeks, months or years to successfully complete, and is meant to take advantage of large sums of money or assets from the victim(s) (Konnikova, 2017).

There have been six main steps to a con according to Edward Smith (1923) from *Confessions of a Confidence Man*. The first step that Edward describes is the foundational work which includes preparing for the con such as studying the information needed, which for Anna included studying fashion and art and learning about people, trust funds, and business. The next step is the approach where the victim(s) are first approached by the perpetrator, this is when Anna had made contact with the victims and started to gain their trust by creating a false image of a wealthy German heiress. The third step is typically the build-up, where the victim is made to believe that they can benefit from the opportunity, this targets the victim's greed and impairs their judgment, Anna did this by making the victims believe their investment would bring them more money and status. The fourth step is then the pay-off/ convincer which the con artist gives the victim a small reward or payot to show that this is an effective opportunity, Anna would pay for various items including dinner, clothes, a personal trainer, and more to show her wealth and make the victims feel taken care of. The next step is the hurrah, which includes the creation of a crisis that coerces the victims to take immediate action, such as making the victims believe that they must take action immediately or the window of opportunity will be gone. The last step is the in and in which where a conspirator puts their resources into the scheme to show legitimacy and encourage the victim to follow, Anna attempted to do this by getting false documents and false wire transfers to show that others had invested in her and that she had the assets to cover the expenses in her trust fund.

The treatment of these white-collar criminals is much different in the media than other criminals (Holmes, 2017). The harm they do to people is a serious issue that often gets overlooked as they often ruin people financially but serve less time than people who steal much less value. The victims are not just hurt financially but they are also ashamed, betrayed, and embarrassed by someone that they trusted. The media often portrays con artists like Anna as Robin Hood figures (Shostack, 1990) as criminals like Anna stole from the rich. Another reason con artists are often given a positive perspective is that they are usually non-violent and do not look threatening.

The common representation of the victims of these con artists is oftentimes gullible, entitled, and naïve. Victims often are made to blame themselves for falling for the con (Titus & Gover 2001). This can seriously affect a victim's mental health and even make some victims suicidal. This negative mental health impact was described by Williams as she stated it was "destabilizing to have been so wrong about someone I trusted". Williams stated that she began writing about her perspective of Anna's crimes to learn from them and to be able to leave it all behind her.

Williams had been critical of her portrayal in the Netflix show as she had not been involved with the production of the series. The series portrayed her as "A natural-born follower whose blind worship of Anna almost destroys her job, her credit, and her life. But while her relationship with Anna is her greatest regret, the woman she becomes because of Anna maybe Anna's greatest creation." Anna and Williams continued to feud after the trial as Anna called Williams a hypocrite and a "Karen".

THE REAL LIFE OF ANNA SOROKIN

Anna was born in Domodedovo, Russia, a town about 23 miles south of Moscow. She was from a working middle-class family with her father Vadim Sorokin being a truck driver and her mother owning a small store. While Anna was 16 she and her family moved to Germany. Vadim had gotten an executive position at a transport company but after the business ended he opened his own company that was based on energy-efficient HVACs. During her time in Germany Anna Attended a local German Catholic school called Bischöfliche Liebfrauenschule Eschweiler (Episcopal School of Our Lady Eschweiler) in the town of Eschweiler. During her time at her new German school, Anna had struggled to make friends and had difficulties learning to speak German. While in Germany she had become highly interested in fashion and started following Vogue Magazine, fashion stars, and fashion blogs.

Following her graduation, Anna moved to the United Kingdom (UK) in 2011 and was admitted to Central Saint Martin's art school but dropped out in the first year and decided to get practical on-the-job experience. Anna then moved back to Germany and started to intern with a company in Berlin where she learned public relations. Anna then moved to France and in 2013 had started a new position with the fashion magazine *Purple* in Paris where she was an intern. During her time in Paris, she started to go by Anna Delvey for the first time.

Anna's life as a con woman started in 2013 as she created a false identity as a rich German heiress and changed her last name from Sorokin a Russian surname to Delvey in an attempt to hide her Russian background. After visiting New York City for Fashion Week Anna decided to transfer to the New York City office of *Purple* but soon after the move she had quit her position. Soon after leaving *Purple*

Anna had started to create a proposal for an art foundation called the 'Anna Delvey Foundation' and started to recruit wealthy donors for this exclusive member club. She made people believe that she had a $67 million trust fund that her father made for her. This helped give her legitimacy to gain acceptance into the high society of New York City, high-end hotels, and nightclubs with the rich and famous.

Anna had created an 80-page proposal that listed world-renowned artists like Urs Fischer, Cindy Sherman, Agnes Martin, Ed Ruscha, Anish Kapoor, and Helmut Newton to help legitimize her vision for her foundation. She had wanted to lease the Church Missions House a 45,000 sq ft building located in the middle of Manhattan, New York which was sold for around $50 million in July of 2014. Anna had even attempted to scam Billy McFarland a convicted felon who defrauded investors for over $27 million, who was known as the "ultimate conman" because he had orchestrated the Fyre Festival scandal that also became a story used for a popular Netflix documentary.

Shortly after moving to the United States of America, Anna began to connect with the social elite of New York City for her plans for the Anna Delvey Foundation. Anna had discussions with the son of the famous architect Santiago Calatrava, and investors like Roo Rogers. Anna was known to brag about her wealth and designer clothing but many of her acquittances became suspicious of her as she would ask them if she could sleep at their place, and at times she would even sleep in a car as she had nowhere to go. The parties that Anna organized included mostly people she did not know very well.

During her events and her stays in hotels, Anna was known to be especially rude to the servers and other people in the service industry. On various occasions, Anna had claimed that she had forgotten her credit cards or that they were not working which then she coerced her acquittances to pay the bill for dinner, drinks, and more. One of Anna's victims was the art collector Michael Haung. After meeting at a party Anna and Haung made plans to go to Venice for an art viewing. Huang had paid for Anna's flights and hotel stays believing that Anna would pay him back for the cost. As Huang tried to get reimbursed for paying for the flight and hotels Anna would claim that she had supposedly forgotten to pay.

In 2016 Anna had a public relations company contracted to plan her birthday party, but the credit card that was used for the dinner was declined. This made Haung who was attending the dinner suspicious of Anna as this was another instance that she could not pay. Later in 2016 Anna continued to stay in upscale hotels and had gotten a reputation for being rude to the hotel staff and also giving large $100 bills to other hotel staff to flaunt her assumed wealth.

During Anna's stay at the High Line Hotel, she met Williams who worked at Vanity Fair during a night out at a club. Williams soon became one of Anna's best friends in New York. Williams would travel and dine out with Anna regularly, which put Williams in debt. Williams became interested in Anna as she claimed that Anna "walked into my life in Gucci sandals and Céline glasses… and showed me a glamorous, frictionless world of hotel living and Le Coucou dinners and infrared saunas and Moroccan vacations. And then she made my $62,000 disappear." Williams had stated that she had never questioned who Anna was and trusted that she was a German heiress and a real friend.

During Anna's stays in hotels, she would create false documents to make people believe she was worth around 60 million Euros. Anna would claim that her main was stuck in a trust and she was having a difficult time accessing the money because it was in Swiss accounts. Anna had built connections with attorney Gibson Dunn, who had close ties with financial institutions and investment groups. Anna used Dunn to apply for a loan of $22 million to the City National Bank. City National Bank eventually declined Anna's loans because of her inability to provide proper documentation to her trust, as her falsified documents and stories were not enough. After she was declined from City National, she then attempted to go through Fortress for a loan, and they had started the process to consider Anna's application if she was able to pay $100,000 in legal expenses, which she failed to do so. Due to Anna's inability to pay for the Church Missions House, it was leased to another party.

In 2017 Anna was successful in getting City National to place a temporary overdraft for $100,000. Anna created false email addresses of business managers for her documents which created suspicions at City National. As Fortress investigated Anna's documents they started to see more discrepancies including that her passport claimed she was born in Russia, but she claimed to be German. Fortress had attempted to verify Anna's wealth by setting up a meeting with the Swiss banks, but Anna had soon withdrawn her application for the loan. After the withdrawal of the loan application, Anna had $55,000 left from the overdraft and started to spend the money on luxury items, and luxury activities.

Anna in April 2017 checked into a new luxury hotel in SoHo, Manhattan called 11 Howard. Anna was known for using cash and giving $100 bills for tips to the staff. Anna would often use the staff that she tipped to ask for favors in the hotel and even became friends with the employees. Anna would spend lavishly in the hotel, especially at the restaurant, where she would just bill the costs to her room. Anna had racked up around $30,000 before the hotel management had become worried that she did not have a credit card in the system. Anna had no way of paying the bill because she had used her money from the loan overdraft on her expensive lifestyle and would not even be able to pay for the bill when she took her friends out to dinner, where she would go out to dinner parties with people like Macaulay Culkin, Martin Shkreli, and even hired the celebrity personal trainer Kacy Duke.

Anna had gotten $70,000 from Citibank through fraudulent checks to pay for her hotel bill. Then in May Anna had forged a wire transfer and booked a business jet to Omaha to go to a meeting in hopes to meet Warren Buffet. Anna continued to use false documents and her false persona to meet wealthy business owners and celebrities. Anna had made CEO Robert Wiesenthal worried and even contacted the police as she failed to pay. The management of 11 Howard had also become suspicious of Anna as she still was unable to provide a credit card, and they blocked her from staying in the hotel and put her belongings in a locked storage area. Anna had then tried to get a $1 million ransom from the hotel managers through emails as she purchased the domain names of the managers. Anna eventually was able to move her belongings to another hotel, including the Bowery Hotel where she used a fake wire transfer.

Anna had promised her friend Williams, her personal trainer Duke, and a videographer a trip to Morocco where she claimed to cover the expenses of the trip. Anna had booked a 5-star luxury hotel, which was a $7,000 a night cost. She claimed the trip was to film a documentary that would be based on her foundation. Early in the trip, the hotel staff had not been able to charge the credit cards that Anna provided and requested a new form of payment. Anna had argued with the staff and even got an employee fired. Anna had no way to pay and convinced her friend Williams to use her card for the bill of $62,000 which was more than the annual salary Williams. Williams had used both her personal and work credit cards as she was promised by Anna that she would be paid back. Williams was also convinced to pay for other luxuries of the trip including the flights. After the trip, Anna avoided paying Williams, and she eventually paid Williams $5,000. This led Williams to have to borrow money just to pay her rent and living expenses. Williams had to go through American Express fraud services to get $52,000 removed from her charges. Williams continued to learn that she was not the only person that Anna had failed to pay back and learned that Anna was involved in various acts of fraud and deception. Anna had even defrauded a private jet company during her crime spree.

As Anna returned to New York City she moved to another luxury hotel and now stayed at the Beekman. Anna stayed in the hotel for weeks and failed to pay for the $11,518 bill until she was removed from the premises. Anna then moved to the W New York Union Square hotel and was removed after two days as she failed to pay her bill. On July 5th, 2017, Anna had nowhere to stay and became homeless and went to find her fitness trainer. Anna had found Duke out on a date and tried to convince her to allow Anna into her home, but Duke refused. Anna soon had the police called on her at the Le Parker Meridien hotel restaurant because of her inability to pay for dinner. In august of 2017, Anna had run out of money and was being invested for bank fraud and had deposited fraudulent checks at Signature Banks and was able to withdraw $8,200 before the checks had bounced and were returned.

Arrest

Anna was eventually arrested on October 3rd, 2017, during a sting operation. The sting was organized by the NYPD, Manhattan District Attorney, and the LAPD. Williams, Anna's former friend had been working with law enforcement to locate Anna at the Passages Malibu rehab center. Law enforcement had told Williams to set up a lunch meeting with Anna. As Anna was leaving the rehab center she was arrested. After the arrest, she was indicted through the Manhattan District Court for two counts of attempted grand larceny in the first degree, three counts of grand larceny in the second degree, one count of grand larceny in the third degree, and one count of theft of services.

Trial

On December 18th, 2018, Anna had been offered a plea deal by the New York City Criminal court. The plea deal for a three to nine-year sentence was rejected instead of a trial. The trial started on March 20th, 2019. Judge Diane Kiesel was appointed to the trial. During the trial, Anna requested a wardrobe stylist, and Anastasia Walker was hired as her personal stylist to provide luxury outfits for her trial appearances. Anna's outfits included Michael Kors, Saint Laurent, Vitoria Beckham, and other name-brand items. Anna had even refused to enter court because she did not want to wear her clothing. After all, it was not "pressed". Anna delayed the court appearance by over an hour because she refused to wear the clothes until she was forced by the judge to appear. Reporters stated that Judge Kiesel had become irritated with Anna and her attitude in court as she stated "This is a trial… She's a defendant. I'm sorry, her clothing is not up to her standards. Are you asking me to stop this trial because of her wardrobe?"

Anna's lawyer, Todd Spodek, had defended her through the trial creating a narrative that Anna had intended to repay all her debts through publicity via Instagram. Spodek claimed that she was she wanted to change clothes because the ones that she had from Rikers Island were dirty and she was needing to delay her trial appearance for "an aggregate of things, not just her clothes. She's feeling nauseous. She's been up since 4 am. She's not being treated well by other inmates and some officers …" Her lawyer had compared her tactics to that of Frank Sinatra and that it was part of the millennial culture, "Any millennial will tell you," Spodek said, "it is not uncommon to have delusions of grandeur."

Spodek did not attempt to deny that Anna had done what she was being accused of but focused on the intent of what she did. Spodek had attempted to argue in the trial that Anna was trying to "fake it until she could make it" and was "easily seduced by glamour and glitz" and that "There's a little bit of Anna in everyone… Everyone lies a little." Spodek had argued that Anna had not broken the law but just exploited the unequal capitalistic system, and that telling lies was not illegal. He even stated that "Anna had every intention of doing things the right way, but she couldn't open those doors without doing something a little bit grey to open the door." And that she had to lie or no one would listen to her if she was being honest. Anna had stated that she "never had a fraudulent intent".

During her detention at Rickers Island during the criminal trial, Anna had been given 13 disciplinary infractions for violating policies from issues like fighting and disobeying orders from staff which resulted in Anna being held in solitary confinement throughout Christmas. At the end of the trial on April 25th, 2019, the jury deliberated for two days and found Anna guilty of eight of the 10 charges. Anna was guilty of grand larceny in the second degree, attempted grand larceny, and theft of services but was not guilty of one attempt of grand larceny in the first degree (The loan application to City National), and larceny in the second degree (theft of $62,000 from Williams).

Anna was sentenced on May 9th, 2019, and was given a 4-to-12-year sentence, ordered to repay her victims $190,000 including $100,000 to City National, and $70,000 to Citibank. Anna also had to pay around $75,000 in legal fees for the trial. The restitution, fines, and fees were paid through her Netflix deal, after all, that Anna owed, she had a remaining $22,000 of her $320,000 deal. Anna had not had to pay for various other fees related to her trial and crimes including $160,000 legal fees to Perkins Cole for the attempted lease of Church Missions House, the $20,000 in fees to Lowenstein Sandler, or the $65,000 in fees to Gibson Dunn.

Anna did state that she was sorry for what she had done "I just want to say that I'm really ashamed and I'm sorry for what I did," and did acknowledge how she hurt the victims, "I completely understand that a lot of people suffered when I thought I was not doing anything wrong." This contrasted with what she had told the *New York Times* "I'd be lying to you and to everyone else and to myself if I said I was sorry for anything." The judge of the case had issued a statement about the problematic celebrity status given to Anna as she stated, "This sentence should be a message to the defendant and any of her fans out there".

Following the trial, Anna was placed in the Bedford Hills Correctional Faculty for Women for a short period and was eventually moved to the Albion Correctional Facility. On February 11th, 2021, Anna had been released and put on parole. Once released Anna had moved into the NoMad hotel and even hired a film crew to film her life on parole. Anna had started to film her life and stated that "I just got out of prison, like two days ago. So it's me like getting all this stuff from Sephora, me opening a bank account as soon as I get permission from my parole officer."

Anna had spent about six weeks on parole before she was arrested again. On March 25th, 2021, Anna was arrested by Immigration and Customs Enforcement

(ICE) for a violation of her visa and was put into a New Jersey jail. While in ICE custody Anna had been contesting her deportation. In January of 2022 while in custody Anna had gotten COVID-19 and was put into quarantine. The immigration judge had denied her release as the judge stated that she would continue to commit fraud. On March 1st, 2022, Anna joined a lawsuit by the American Civil Liberates Union against ICE, as she claims she was refused a COVID-19 booster shot.

THE MEDIA REPRESENTATION

The article *Maybe She Had So Much Money She Just Lost Track of It*, published in May of 2018 in the *New York* magazine by Jessica Pressler had been the start of the media frenzy about Anna's life and crimes. Pressler had also been known for other articles that became internationally known including an article that inspired the 2019 film Hustlers which starred Cardi B and Jennifer Lopez. *Hustlers* was another film about female criminals who stole money from wealthy men who attended a strip club, the men were drugged and conned by the women. Despite the crimes that were committed by the women in *Hustlers* the story was portrayed as 'Stripper Robin Hood' by various media outlets.

Pressler had been Anna's main journalist that brought the story to light and gave insight from Anna's perspective. Pressler was pregnant when she started visiting Anna in Rikers Island and would attend the trial hearings, she had even purchased designer accessories and clothes for Anna's trial outfits and was in contact with Anna's lawyer. Various media outlets portrayed the courtroom as a runway show for Anna, which helped increase her Instagram followers, and improve her image. The *New York Magazine* (Pressler, 2018) article allowed Anna to share her story before her conviction which is always a concern for the courts as it can lead to biased jurors (Meringolo, 2010). The article had become very popular and even claimed to "break the internet".

Soon after the *New York* article, Netflix paid Anna $320,000 to have exclusive rights to her story. The contract included that Anna has no participation in shows or documentaries while the next series goes through prediction as well as no posts on her social media accounts about her experience with the Netflix show without permission for there years after the premiere of the show, and no participation in talks shows. The contract also limits Anna's ability to write a book within the first year of the release of the show. The contract does not stop others from telling the Anna Delvey story but it does limit Anna from assisting with the production of any material about her life.

The nine-part series *Inventing Anna* became number one on Netflix when it was released on February 11th, 2022. The week of February 14-20th the series had a reported 3.3 billion minutes watched and were Nielsen's number one streaming ranking. The series was produced by Shonda Rhimes (producer of Grey's Anatomy and Scandal) and was inspired by Pressler's article (Presser was an executive producer for the Netflix series). Anna was played by Julia Garnder. The series starts with a disclaimer stating that "This whole story is completely true. Except for all the parts that are totally made up." The series makes it difficult to know how accurate the series is to the real story of Anna. The series had followed the journalist Vivian (based on Pressler) who was played by Anna Chlumsky, as she details Anna's life story.

The Netflix series takes tells Anna's story from the perspective of those who knew her, especially her friends. The show portrays Anna's ability to create a vision and convince others to believe in her vision, and her ability to convince high-level investors and businessmen, and women to follow along with her manipulation and lies. The series shows flashbacks to Anna's childhood where she was treated poorly for being working and class and Russian during her upbringing in Germany. The Netflix series was a dramatization that exaggerated and added fictional aspects of the story for entertainment value as various news articles had tried to distinguish what was real from the series.

Before the Netflix premiere, Anna's story was told in a variety of ways. Anna's story had been premiered on the CNBC series American Greed in February of 2020 a documentary series that focuses on white-collar crimes. The episode was called "Fake Heiress Cons High Society" and focused on how she made it through the New York City social scene as a fake German Heiress and her trial. The series concluded that she decided to go to trial and deny the plea offers to ensure that she would be on the front page of the news and become internationally known.

HBO Max explored Anna's story on an episode of *Generation Hustle* released in 2021 called *Anna Delvey Takes Manhattan*. The episode shows the transformation of Anna from an awkward young woman to a confident German heiress. The show shows how she convinces her friend Williams to pay for an expensive vacation with the false promise of paying her back which prompts the fall of Anna as the NYPD starts their investigation into her crimes.

ABC had interviewed Anna while she was detained by ICE and the interview was released on *20/20*. During Anna's interview shows her starting to seek fame again on social media right after her release. The episode also allows Anna to sit down and speak about her life for the first time on a television episode and Anna attempted to explain that she was not the person that the media portrays her as. Anna stated that "I'm not this dumb, greedy person".

Anna was also interviewed for an episode of *60 Minutes Australia* which aired on April 18th, 2021, called *Faking It*. The episode host calls her a "con", and a skilled charlatan. Anna in the episode claims she did not con anyone and claimed that she did not know what was going on and was just doing whatever she wanted to do. Despite the harm, she caused she is a "role model to some people" according to her lawyer.

The popular *BBC Radio 4* podcast released a documentary about Anna's story on December 16th of 2019. The documentary was a series with six episodes named the Fake Heiress. The series starts with Anna Sorokin as an intern with a fashion magazine and how she creates her fake identity as a wealthy heiress named Anna Delvey.

In the television series *Katy Keene* the character Pepper Smith was loosely based on Anna. Pepper was moving in and out of expensive hotels and was a socialite like Anna who got into trouble because she was not able to pay for the hotel bills and had been pretending to be reached. Pepper would not be honest with her friends and convinced an investor to fund an artistic idea of "Andy Warhol's Factory".

A stage play was released in July of 2021 called *Anna X* which was inspired by Anna and was played at Harold Pinter Theater. Anna has been in the process of producing a book about her experience incarcerated and a podcast. Anna has also signed a contract for a reality television show through Bunim/Murray Productions, who have produced *The Real World, Road Rules, and Bad Girls Club.*

Anna has a popular social media presence. She has connected with various celebrities including Julia Fox, who stated that they are collaborating on future projects together. Anna continues to try and profit off her identity including that she would reveal the identity of her former boyfriend for a $10,000 fee. As of March 21, 2022, Anna had over 977,000 Instagram followers, where she posted a former Tweet of hers that stated that she will "Only agreeing to go back to Europe when they give Black people reparations", on February 14th, 2021, during Black history month.

Anna's associates had also benefited from the publicity of the case, especially Williams who authored the book *My Friend Anna: the True Story of the Fake Heiress of New York City*, which was published through Gallery Publishing Group and paid Williams $300,000. The book detailed how Anna had defrauded and deceived Williams. According to Williams her experience with Anna had negatively impacted her mentally and financially because she had fallen into debt after she used her credit card for a trip that she assumed Anna was paying for.

Williams ended up receiving $35,000 from *HBO* for rights to her story for a television series. Williams had worked as an editor and producer at *Vanity Fair* as she became friends with Anna but was laid off in 2019. She had written in various outlets about her experiences with Anna including in a *Vanity Fair* article titled *As An Added Bonus, She Paid For Everything My Bright-Lights Misadventure With A Magician of Manhattan*, a Time Magazine article *Here's How I Helped Bring the Fake Heiress to Justice*, and an Air Mail's article *Re-Inventing Anna*, where she criticized the Netflix portrayal of her stating that it was a fictional story that rewarded Anna's crimes. Williams also gave her perspective on television as she was interviewed on an episode of the ABC network program, *20/20, The Sinfluencer of Soho*, which was released on October 1st, 2021.

Cost and Restitution

Despite Anna getting paid $320,000 for her story, most of the earnings went to pay for fees and restitution for her crimes. The New York Attorney General had sued Anna under the Son of Sam law that greatly limits people from profiting off their crime-related publicity. The lawsuit and "Son of Sam" law forced Anna to use most of the money for fees, fines, and restitution. The Son of Sam law was created because of the 1970s serial killer who was known as the "Son of Sam" David Berkowitz. There were serious concerns about Berkowitz profiting off selling the rights to his story to publishers so New York state passed legislation to prevent Berkowitz and other criminals from profiting off of their crimes, and other states also mimicked these laws. The publishers had attempted to fight against the Son of Sam law and argued it was against the first amendments freedom of speech clause. In one case in the 1980s Simon and Schuster had brought the law to the Supreme Court as they had been working on a book with a convicted criminal Henry Hill. The Supreme Court had found the law to be unconstitutional as it violated the right to free speech and the law was struck down. This allowed Hill to make around $480,000 from the novel *Wiseguy* which was the main inspiration for the *Goodfellas*. The revised Son of Sam Law was then reintroduced in 2001 and requires that the publishing company notifies the Office of Victims Services (OVS) when a convicted felon is paid in excess of $10,000 (Gold, 2014).

The OVS can freeze bank accounts and allow the victim(s) to file lawsuits against the convicted felon. This is what happened with Anna's case, as the banks who were victims of Anna had been notified and acted to recover money that they lost, including City National Bank which filed a lawsuit and got $100,000, as well as CitiBank which received $70,000. The third bank Signature Bank had not filed any legal actions under the Son of Sam law and Willims was not eligible for the lawsuit because Anna was found not guilty in the case against Williams. This was the first utilization of the Son of Sam law for a person profiting off a television show. Netflix had been engaged since the pre-trial stage of the criminal case, as employees were present during the trial along with the press. Netflix had initiated the payments and followed all the policies related to OVS and the Son of Sam laws. Netflix had continued to agree to all of the New York court orders related to the case and made payments to the accounts that were distributed to the victims.

Why the Fascination with Anna Delvey?

The media coverage of young female criminal defendants has been given extraordinary attention in the 21st century with the media wanting to know every detail of Anna's life. This fascination was like what was given to the murder suspect Amanda Knox who was also given international attention during her murder trial (Simkin, 2013) and after her conviction and was given a multimillion-dollar book deal and Netflix movie. Both women were in their 20s, middle class, and of European descent. When young white women are victims of crimes, they have been given disproportionately higher amounts of attention than women of color. For Anna being an offender, she was also given disproportionate attention which she was able to use to her benefit and profit from her crimes even after being convicted.

Streaming services like Netflix have capitalized on crime and con artists (Bluestone, 2021). Just before *Inventing Anna* was released another viral documentary was released called the *Tinder Swindler* which quickly became an international phenomenon. The movie was about a con artist who lied and manipulated women he met on Tinder. These shows help show viewers how easy it is to be tricked and conned by people you think you trust and that appear to be wealthy and successful.

Many news articles were critical of rewarding Anna for her criminal lifestyle, but the more the news published stories about her the more famous she was becoming. When she was released from prison, she started posting on social media just hours after she was released asking for $720 million in a Twitter post "Someone from Fortress Investment Group - I need $720m by the end of next week. DM me." Her Instagram bio states that she is a "Professional Defendant". Despite Anna being found guilty, she has continued to claim that her business plans for her foundation were legitimate.

CONCLUSION

The Anna Delvey story continues to show Western media's fascination with scammers, con artists, fame, and crime (Levi, 2006). Many young people go to great lengths for fame, and sometimes those include illegal activities. The rewarding outcome of fame for Anna allowed her to get the attention and notoriety she was seeking as well as a 6-figure payday from Netflix. It is important for media outlets to provide an accurate representation of crimes and events like Anna's story, but this can create an image that crime pays. When asked during an interview if crime pays Anna said "In a way, it did."

When crimes are able to make people tune in as it did with Anna and others who gained notoriety through their crimes and the media companies can help provide you with a great attorney to help the perpetrator, it can be a lucrative process for some. Fame can create a potential for a criminal to create a platform to create future financial opportunities and media attention as Anna is attempting to do. This is where a critical perspective can show the harm and pain that was caused by the crimes that Anna had perpetuated, and the loss of opportunities, friends, connections, freedom, time, and money this cost her and others.

REFERENCES

Bailey, B., Farber, D., & Lee, S. (1999). Summer of Sam. *The Journal of American History*, *86*(3), 1447. doi:10.2307/2568751

Bluestone, G. (2021). *Hype: How Scammers, Grifters, and Con Artists Are Taking Over the Internet—and Why We're Following*. Harlequin.

Dugatkin, L. A. (1992). The evolution of the "con artist". *Ethology and Sociobiology*, *13*(1), 3–18. doi:10.1016/0162-3095(92)90003-M

Gibson, K. (2022). Inventing Anna True Story: Everything to Know About Anna Delvey, Including Her Crimes and Where She Is Now. *People Magazine*.

Gold, S. D. (2014). *Son of Sam Case: Simon & Schuster Inc. v. Members of United States Crime Victims Board*. Cavendish Square Publishing, LLC.

Holmes, T. (2017). Professional Criminals and White-Collar Crime in Popular Culture. In Oxford Research Encyclopedia of Criminology and Criminal Justice. doi:10.1093/acrefore/9780190264079.013.215

Konnikova, M. (2017). *The Confidence Game: Why we fall for it... Every time*. Penguin.

Levi, M. (2006). The media construction of financial white-collar crimes. *British Journal of Criminology*, *46*(6), 1037–1057. doi:10.1093/bjc/azl079

Meringolo, J. C. (2010). The media, the jury, and the high-profile defendant: A defense perspective on the media circus. *New York Law School Law Review*, *55*, 981.

Pressler, J. (2018). *Maybe she had so much money she just lost track of It*. New York Magazine.

Shostack, G. L. (1990). Stand up for ethics. *The Journal of Business Strategy*, *11*(3), 48–50. doi:10.1108/eb039376

Simkin, S. (2013). 'Actually evil. Not high school evil': Amanda Knox, sex and celebrity crime. *Celebrity Studies*, *4*(1), 33–45. doi:10.1080/19392397.2012.750107

Smith, E. (1923). *Confessions of a Confidence Man: A Handbook for Suckers*. Scientific American Publishing.

Titus, R. M., & Gover, A. R. (2001). Personal fraud: The victims and the scams. *Crime Prevention Studies*, *12*, 133–152.

Chapter 5
The Murder of Sophie Toscan du Plantier and Its Implications for the Study of Media and Crime:
A Case Study in West Cork

Shane O'Mahony
University of Hertfordshire, UK

EXECUTIVE SUMMARY

Criminologists have often highlighted how the news media tends to disseminate simplified and stigmatised narratives to represent violence against women. Furthermore, these narratives often interweave with class-based fears, sensationalism, and mythology. However, recently, several authors have begun to examine the potential of new media sources (podcasts, documentary series, social media) to subvert these narratives. Drawing on a case study examining the murder of Sophie Toscan du Plantier in West Cork, Ireland (December 1996), the current chapter examines the ways in which three recent new media examinations of the case subvert and reinforce these narratives. The chapter demonstrates that while the new media sources foreground the victim's biography and background, give voice to her family, and situate the case within broader social and political contexts, they also reinforce class-based stereotypes relating to deserving and undeserving victims and problematically focus on the mythical elements of the case for entertainment purposes.

DOI: 10.4018/978-1-7998-9668-5.ch005

INTRODUCTION

On the 23rd of December 1996, just outside the small seaside village of Schull in West Cork, Ireland, French national Sophie Toscan du Plantier was violently murdered at her remote holiday home. This had been the first murder case in the local area in almost one hundred years and given that the victim was a married mother enjoying a holiday so close to the festive period, the case sent shockwaves throughout the community (Sheridan, 2014). The subsequent media coverage (Irish Examiner, 1998, 1999, 2000) of the case had all the hallmarks of a moral panic and attracted sustained media coverage both nationally and internationally.

In examining the media coverage, moral panic is obvious in declarations that this represented a watershed in the transformation of a multi-cultural rural idyll on the southwestern seaboard, to a modern community beset with fear of crime and risk of violence (Garland, 2000), murder, and other social problems. Another element of moral panic is visible in fanciful theories concocted to explain the murder. These ranged from discussions of French hitmen (Bailey, 1997), a Garda plot to cover up the murder by a member of the force (Sheridan, 2014), to folkloric stories involving castles and ghosts, to the most bizarre theory – that Sophie was killed by a horse (Sheridan, 2014).

The case took a particular sensationalist twist when the lead local journalist covering the case – Ian Bailey – was arrested and labeled the chief suspect by the media and the Gardai Siochana[1] (Netflix, episode two). In the years since, there has been intense focus on the character of the prime suspect, the victim's family's insistence that he is guilty, and his attempts to sue the Irish state and a variety of British and Irish tabloids for defamation of character (Sheridan, 2014). More recently, attention has turned to the chief suspect's conviction *in absentia* in a Parisian court, and subsequent attempts to have him extradited to France to serve his sentence (Brent, 2021). This recent legal struggle between the French and Irish justice systems has reinvigorated international attention to the case.

Having heard of the legal controversy, two London-based crime podcasters launched an in-depth multi-episode coverage of the case, which in turn sparked interest from Sky Atlantic and Netflix, both of whom released documentary series examining the case. While these series have in many ways been typical of the true-crime genre in their focus on the "who done it" element of the case (Rawlings, 1995), the supposed character flaws of the prime suspect, and their focus on the folkloric, sensationalist, and scandalous elements of the case, there is a more nuanced and comprehensive engagement in the case than is typical. This in-depth, International, and nuanced engagement provided the impetus for the current study and prompted two central research questions. These are:

1. To what extent is the recent podcast and documentary series coverage of the case like the gendered, classed, and sensationalised coverage of violent crime against women that the criminological canon (Heidensohn, 1985; Jewkes, 2011) has long highlighted?
2. To what extent does the podcast and documentary series format present an opportunity to offer a more nuanced and academically rigorous analysis of violent crime against women?

In addressing these research questions, the current chapter will be unconcerned with the question of guilt, or the specific details of the crime (except where they are relevant to the research questions), and various issues relating to Garda corruption, differences, and clashes between justice systems. Instead, the chapter will take this case study as an opportunity to compare traditional media (newspaper) and new media (podcast and documentary series) in terms of their gendered, classed, and sensationalised representations of violence against women.

The chapter will also be interested in the comparatively understudied topic of the capacity of podcasts and documentary series to provide more nuanced and academically rigorous analyses than has been the case with more traditional media outlets. As we will see, the current case study demonstrates that the podcast and documentary series platform does hold the potential to achieve this nuanced and academically rigorous analysis, but in the current case has *both* reinforced and subverted traditionally gendered, classed, and sensationalised representations of female victims of violent crime. The next section will critically examine the literature relevant to the current research. The following section will critically examine relevant academic literature, then we will deal with the results, before concluding with a discussion section.

BACKGROUND

Although Mendelsohn (1947) first coined the term Victimology to denote the scientific study of crime victims, it was not until the 1970s that the literature examining media representations of victims, and in particular, victims of violent crime began to develop significantly. Indeed, prior to this period, criminological based media analyses of crime victims tended to focus on the tendency of the media to contribute to an unwarranted increase in fear of crime and victimisation (Bonger, 1916; Selin, 1937; 1938), while debates surrounding the criminogenic effects of the media also dominated the literature (Gerbner et al, 1972). However, from this juncture onwards several themes began to emerge.

Firstly, researchers began to note that news and fiction coverage focused overwhelmingly on serious and violent crime and victimisation (Jewkes, 2011), as opposed to more statistically common but mundane types of crime. Secondly, the demographic profile of offenders and victims that attracted the most attention tended to be older and of higher status than those who were typically encountering crime and criminal justice systems (Jewkes, 2011). Thirdly, individual victims and their suffering increasingly provided the motive force of crime stories (Greer, 2019). Fourthly, attractive, and successful men who committed violent crimes (particularly serial murder) against women tended to be mythologised and gain folk status (with a particular interest in their biography), while their low status and marginalised victims tended to either be ignored completely or relegated to stigmatised signifier – prostitute, 'good-time girl', adulteress (Wattis, 2015).

These themes and their influence on media representations of crime were most comprehensively addressed in the literature that emerged around the concept of "news values" (Jewkes, 2011). This literature examines the values that determine whether a story becomes newsworthy or not. In other words, identifying what makes a story that will stimulate the audience's interest. The core elements of this are immediacy, dramatization, personalization, titillation, and novelty (Chibnall 1977: 22–45; Hall et al. 1978; Ericson et al. 1989). The value of novelty means that most news is about deviance (Ericson et al. 1989). The primacy of these news values explains the predominant emphasis on violent and sex offenses, and the concentration on higher-status offenders and victims, especially celebrities. It also accounts for the tendency to avoid stories about crime in general, or explanations of criminal trends and patterns.

More recently, researchers (Jewkes, 2011; Wattis, 2015) have noted that while the media tends to commonly cover stories of violence against women, it is very uncommon to place this violence in any structural context, preferring instead to represent these crimes as symptoms of offender pathology. Additionally, news reports rarely elevated the voices of survivors, advocates, and other experts, with a disproportionate emphasis on law enforcement, political and criminal justice perspectives (Heidensohn, 1986; Jewkes, 2011; Dyer, 2022). Moreover, the media has also been accused of simplifying complex issues using stereotypes. For example, while women commit a minority of crimes, women as perpetrators arouse intense media interest, especially when the crime is one of violence (Dyer, 2022). Jewkes (2011) argues that female offenders are constructed around a narrow range of stereotypes that relate to sexuality, physical attractiveness, maternity, and victimhood. Stereotypes also impact how women as victims of crime are portrayed; for example, female victims and victims of sexual homicide are more newsworthy than other homicide categories (Peelo et al 2004), a hierarchy corresponding to newsworthiness and informed by stereotypical notions of the ideal victim (Christie 1986).

While the Irish literature on this topic followed international trends (albeit a little later chronologically), in that its initial focus was on the role of the media in distorting the public view on crime and victimization (O'Connell, 1999; and O'Donnell, 2005), comparatively little has been written in the sociological, or criminological literature concerning media representations of violence against women and girls. However, given that these disciplines are institutionally young in Ireland, and given that they have developed from the 1980s – a period of radical socio-political and economic change (Ferriter, 2004), it is understandable that their interests lay elsewhere. For example, the period following 1996 witnessed a moral panic regarding organised crime in Ireland (O'Mahony, 2019). This moral panic followed the murder of Garda Gerry McCabe and Journalist Veronica Guerin by paramilitaries and organised crime groups, and the panic that followed led to the predictable rush for punitive legislation.

Furthermore, this period also witnessed scandals involving child sex abuse and institutional abuses of women and children in Catholic institutions (Ferriter, 2004), not to mention the Peace Process in Northern Ireland and the advent of the Celtic Tiger (Ferriter, 2004). However, while the issue of media representations of violence against women has been comparatively neglected in Criminology and Sociology, it has not been completely ignored. For example, Carr and Holt (2010) have explored the issue of femicide in newspaper reporting and found a binary of 'deserving' and 'undeserving' victims. Women deviating from the conventional role of wife and mother were viewed as less 'worthy.' This good/bad dichotomy (Inglis and MacKeogh 2012), evident in the news reporting of women as victims, is also present in the reporting of women as offenders, viewed as unnatural because of the stereotype of women as non-aggressive (O'Sullivan 2008). This is especially so with women in prison who are typically 'represented in a partial, hostile, indeed, mythical manner' (Quinlan 2011, p.244). Research into the treatment of female offenders in the Irish press has also found that women tend to be portrayed in a limited range of roles linked to gender stereotypes (Black 2009)

Crucially, however, while several themes have developed in the Irish and international literature in the last number of decades, there are notable gaps. Firstly, the bulk of this research at an international level has been concerned with traditional media such as newspapers and television. According to Pew research studies, between 30-40% of adults now claim that they primarily consume news and entertainment online rather than through traditional media sources (Pew, 2021). While this has historically been justified by recourse to access issues and elevated levels of readership among the populace, there is evidence that the Irish public, like their American and international counterparts, are now relying more heavily on the internet for news.

While the themes examined to highlight the media's tendency to simplify, stereotype, and sensationalise crime and violent crime, recent research suggests that the medium of the podcast may be able to overcome these tendencies. Researchers have found that podcasts have contributed to efforts to overcome issues relating to black representation in the US media (Serrano, 2022), and simplification and polarisation in political debate (Pew, 2014). The common finding seems to be that the podcast format enables a comprehensive engagement that goes beyond the surface, the presentation, or a diverse range of viewpoints, and distributes opportunities for coverage more evenly. However, authors' have pointed out that without traditional standards of fact-checking, and the potential for misinformed and bad faith actors to seize the platforms to push authoritarian agendas, the podcast also poses dangers (Cushion et al, 2021).

To attempt to address the question of whether podcasts can offer more comprehensive and informed analyses than newspapers, this chapter turns to the question of whether podcast and documentary series coverage of the current case study subverts or reproduces simplified and stereotyped coverage of violence against women, so common in traditional media formats. In doing so, it contributes to the international literature in comparing new media coverage of violent crime to that of more traditional media formats. It also contributes to the Irish literature by examining a neglected case study from an academic perspective and broadening the literature on media coverage beyond the traditional press. Before the results and analysis of the current study are presented, however, there are some methodological concerns to address.

METHODOLOGY

The data pertaining to this research comes from a variety of sources. Firstly, the Netflix documentary series, titled "*Sophie: A Murder in West Cork*" consists of three episodes ranging between 49 and 64 minutes in duration, and is available to anyone with a Netflix account. Secondly, the Sky Atlantic series is titled: "*Murder at the Cottage: The search for Justice for Sophie*" is available on Now TV, and consists of six episodes, each an hour long. Finally, the *West Cork Podcast* is by far the most comprehensive and length contribution and consists of fourteen episodes each lasting slightly more than half an hour. This podcast is available at: https://www.westcorkpodcast.com/. Furthermore, the Irish Newspaper Archives[2] was also examined to compare the coverage by more traditional media, to the coverage by new media. From the outset, the selection of these data sources presents methodological problems.

Firstly, the traditional media outlets were reacting to an evolving story, and therefore, it may seem unfair to compare the quality of their coverage, to well-funded documentary series, that not only have the benefit of being removed from the events, but also have the time, space, and financial resources to conduct more comprehensive analyses. However, it must also be recognised that there are no traditional media sources that could overcome this problem and allow for more direct and fair comparisons. Therefore, this limitation notwithstanding, it does seem that we can still draw comparisons while keeping this imbalance in mind.

Secondly, there are question marks concerning the impartiality of the two-documentary series. As regards the Netflix series, questions have been raised about the involvement of the du Plantier family in the editing and production process (Sheridan, 2021), with some claiming they were so heavily involved in every step of the production that its objectivity is effectively compromised. Relatedly, regarding the Sky Atlantic series, questions have been raised as to the nature of the relationship between the executive director Jim Sheridan, and the prime suspect Ian Bailey. Indeed, in the docuseries, Sheridan communicates the results of the French murder trial to Bailey in real-time. However, given that the aim of the current chapter is not to ascertain guilt, or to engage with any theories as to who committed the murder, this does not seem to pose a problem. Even series with biased agendas concerning guilt will reproduce or subvert class, gender, and sensationalised representations to some extent. Therefore, while it is important to keep this issue in mind when analysing the data, it does not pose any major limitations.

In terms of data analysis, each of the episodes of the three main sources was viewed multiple times, notes were taken and uploaded to NVivo Qualitative Data Analysis Software. These notes were then coded thematically under the nodes "gender," "class," and "sensationalism." This enabled thematic coding and analysis that was directly relevant to the research questions. As regards the newspapers, the archives were searched using various combinations of the terms "Sophie," "du Plantier;" "Sophie Toscan du Plantier," "Murder," and "West Cork." As these articles were typically quite short it did not prove too difficult to engage with them, despite the overall volume of hits being extremely high.

ANALYSIS

The sub-sections that follow will present the results of the thematic analysis of the podcasts, documentary series (docuseries), and traditional newspaper coverage, which were collated to address the research questions posed in the introduction. These sub-sections are: (1) A comprehensive and sympathetic exploration of Sophie's biography and background; (2) A comprehensive and sympathetic foregrounding of the victim's family; (3) An analysis of wider social and political contexts; (4) Class and gender biases and stereotypes; and (5) A fascination with the dramatic, sensational, and mythical.

As should become clear, the first three themes subvert many of the tendencies of traditional media formats and demonstrate the potential for long-form podcasts and documentary series to present comprehensive and academically rich representations of crime to the general public. However, the later two themes represent the risks that these formats may reproduce problematic tendencies and stereotypes long associated with traditional media formats, but in more damaging ways. These arguments will be elaborated on in the coming sub-sections.

Sophie's Biography and Background

A common theme that emerged from the new media sources was the comprehensive and sympathetic presentation of Sophie's biography and background. While traditional news coverage did include biographical information (Irish Examiner, 1997; 1998; 2000), this was often in snippet form, and most coverage tended to focus on the key suspect and details of the case rather than the details of the victim's biography.

For example, halfway through the first episode of the Netflix series, after the details of the murder have been introduced and the background has been established, journalist Laura Marlowe introduces the topic of Sophie's background and biography (Netflix, episode one):

My ex-husband and I were on holiday in Ireland over Christmas and New Year's 1996, and one morning he brought in the breakfast tray with the Irish times [...] 'French woman murdered in West Cork' [...]. I thought this is awful, I'd like to know more about this woman.

The episode immediately cuts to a discussion with the lead superintendent on the case explaining Sophie's background (Netflix, episode one):

She had been visiting here [West Cork] for a few years, bought this property. She is a person who kept very much to herself.

Next, Sophie's cousin Frederic Gazeau states (Netflix, episode one):

She was a documentary producer, she had her son Pierre-Louis and lived alone with him before Daniel came into her life. He was a filmmaker too and intellectual, so they were on the same level and just clicked right away.

Indeed, in a scene slightly later in episode one, Sophie's Aunt Marie-Madeleine Opalka, discusses the complexities of Sophie's life with her new partner Daniel (Netflix, episode one):

Every evening, they had people, they were with people, they had to go out. Sophie did not like that. I always said there was an Alice in Wonderland quality to Sophie. She liked to be alone, especially given her husband's life and high profile.

Sophie's son seems to concur with this assessment, as we see in the next scene (Netflix, episode one)

My mum did not like glamour, she always wanted to be private and authentic. She needed an escape, and Ireland was the perfect escape. She was not Sophie Toscan du Plantier over there, she was just Sophie.

Having heard from members of Sophie's family, we hear again from journalist Laura Marlow (Netflix, episode one):

When she was a child, she had lived with an Irish family for a time, so she had this idea that she wanted a house in Ireland. So, she went on a trip with her cousin and hesitated between two houses, one was in peaceful Irish landscape of green rolling hills and the other was, she called it 'violence.' They found that house

Her uncle then informs the viewer (Netflix, episode one):

If you really want to know Sophie, just go to her house in Ireland. The sun, the wind, the rain, all things that reflect Sophie. Tortured, calm, stormy, noise, wind, sea. You really get the span of Sophie's spirit there. She was also very bright, cheerful, sunny, and at the same time had a romantic side. Not in the sentimental sense, but a black romanticism. The dark side, attracted by the morbid, death, monsters. She had planned before she died to make a series about bodily fluids. That was her project, to make a film series about breast milk, blood, sperm, bile, our reactions to this sort of thing fascinated her. She had a very gothic side. This gave her a sort of contrast it gave her depth.

Developing this theme, the episode turns back to Laura Marlowe (Netflix, episode one):

She was a talented writer, and she wrote a great deal with great affection about West Cork. The most haunting passage I remember was that she recalled a dead lamb, she had seen on a path. It had been savaged by a fox […] It gives me shivers now, because that is exactly what happened to her.

While episode two focuses primarily on the chief suspect, Ian Bailey, episode three opens with Sophie's relative informing the audience that (Netflix, episode two):

Sophie is at the centre of this story. But its true that for almost 23 years, its often forgotten who my sister was.

In centering Sophie in the story, a West Cork writer makes the insightful observation that (Netflix, episode two):

So much Crime fiction involves the violent murder of women. Those lurid covers of old fashion detective stories. Sophie Toscan du Plantier really was very beautiful, but there was so much more to her. She was solitary, thoughtful, a romantic poet. I think for her West Cork was a place to reflect, to write, to read – she loved Irish poetry.

Indeed, while a substantial portion of the third and final episode does focus on the main character and the drama of the case more broadly, in the final third of the episode we are brought back to Sophie again (Netflix, episode three):

It is hard to remember everything in detail. There have been court cases for libel, court cases for other things, and it's been known as the Bailey case ever since, and I think the focus has to go back to Sophie.

While not providing the same level of biographical detail and background information as the Netflix documentary series, the Sky Crime series also contains rich information. Almost two minutes into the first episode, the director Jim Sheridan remarks (Sky Atlantic, episode one):

She was born, Sophie Buniol, she died Sophie Toscan du Plantier. She is buried here but her soul lives on in Ireland.

Two minutes later, the director asks the locals their opinion of Sophie. As one local publican comments (Sky Atlantic, episode one):

She used to come in the wintertime. She was a lovely girl. She was coming for a few years, and I got to know her each time she came a little more. She would come into the pub on her own and drink tea.

Just over halfway through the first episode, Sophie's diverse character and background are again discussed (Sky Atlantic, episode one):

Sophie was a documentary filmmaker and mother to Pierre-Louis. She worked for Uni France, the company that promoted French film to the outside world. It was here that she met her future husband, Daniel Tuscan du Plantier.

The *West Cork Podcast* also foregrounds Sophie's biography and background, devoting an entire episode to her, titled – Sophie Buniol (West Cork Podcast, Episode three). For example, four and a half minutes into the podcast the listener learns that:

Sophie Tuscan du Plantier was 39 years' old. She was a television producer, she made art house documentaries for French TV. Her father was a dentist, her mother was a Deputy major of a central district in Paris [...]. Sophie was just over 5 ft tall, with blue eyes [...].

The podcast goes on to discuss Sophie's marriage to Daniel, and her character more broadly (West Cork Podcast, episode 3):

It sounds like Daniel inhabited his own world. While Sophie embraced it, the diners, the public events, the movie premiers, that was only part of who Sophie was. [Sophie's brother speaking]. 'My sister was quite different. Yes, she liked glamour, but not all the time. She also liked to be alone, just to be in her mind. She liked to write, to read.

As demonstrated, all three sources represent the biography and character of Sophie Tuscon du Plantier in a complex and comprehensive manner. This representation presents Sophie as a filmmaker, a poet, and a writer. She was an adventurer who embraced solitary living, a socialite who thrived in Parisian high society, a gothic bohemian who marvelled in the esoteric and macabre, as well as an ordinary person who embraced the mundane. This portrayal subverts and transcends two key tendencies that academics have identified in traditional media representations of female victims of violent crime. As mentioned in the literature review, the first tendency is to de-emphasise female victims, and the second is to stigmatise them due to their violation of gender norms (Wattis, 2015 and Inglis and Mackeogh, 2012). Sophie is centered in these depictions, and a comprehensive and complex account of her character is provided. However, despite traditional media commentary focusing on how it was unexpected that a married French mother should be alone in West Cork so close to Christmas (Irish Examiner, 1997), new media contributors to each production are quick to emphasise that this reflects Sophie's adventurous spirit. Indeed, the contradictions, conformities, and complexities of Sophie's character are celebrated both when they conform to *and subvert* traditional gender norms.

Overall, the comprehensive and rich details of Sophie's biography and background demonstrate the potential of podcasts and documentary series to provide comprehensive coverage of crime stories, which are consistent with criminological research. The tendency is also apparent in the wider analysis of the political and social context within which the murder occurred. It is to this issue we now turn.

Social and political context in West Cork

Each of the three new media sources devotes substantial time to exploring the social and political context relevant to Sophie's murder. For example, the Netflix documentary explores the social dynamics of life in West Cork. In the very first episode, local woman, Florence Newman discusses the character of the community as follows (Netflix, episode one):

This area is very open-minded. In coastal communities there is always an ebb and flow of people coming in, so there is an acceptance of difference.

Indeed, there is a long tradition of inward migration to West Cork from Britain and countries in continental Europe, dating back to when Ireland joined the European Economic Community (EEC) in 1973 (Ferriter, 2004). As one news reporter put it (Netflix, episode one):

West Cork has provided a peaceful, beautiful, and anonymous escape for people of all nationalities. Every third or fourth house would be a foreigner of some description. We have French, Germans, Portuguese, English. It is certainly not your typical rural Irish community. In fact, West Cork is often considered an international rather than Irish region. Yet the locals are very traditional, but still welcoming of newcomers.

This sense of rural cosmopolitanism is also prominent in Toma McCullim's (Netflix, episode one) account:

There were all different sets of blow-ins[3]*. There were the artist community, the yachties, the writers, hippies, dope smokers, feminists, and radicals.*

Local writer Elizabeth Wessel best sums up the foreign-born community in West Cork as follows (Netflix, episode one):

These were people drawn to the more rugged, wild, West Cork lands. The lost children of Europe.

This theme of rural cosmopolitanism and alternative lifestyles in West Cork was explored in a 30-minute-long episode on the West Cork Podcast. The episode opens with the following statement (West Cork Podcast, episode one):

To understand why this murder occurred and what that has meant for West Cork, we have to go back to the 1970s where all of this began.

Next, we hear from people who moved to West Cork from other countries, which helps the reader gain a sense of the social context. First, we hear the story of Len Liptick. When Len was in his twenties, he was an accounting clerk in London. According to Len he hated London and wanted to getaway. For him West Cork was (West Cork Podcast, episode one):

It was a hideaway at the edge of Europe, a community that grew by word of mouth. It was a way to escape the modern world, in favour or a quitter more secluded and slow-paced lifestyle.

The narrator introduces us to more individuals who have comparable stories to Len, before summing up the appeal of West Cork to European individuals who rejected the modern world and sought alternative lifestyles (West Cork Podcast, episode one):

Like a lot of places out on the fringes, West Cork attracted lots of people for all sorts of reasons. You could reset or reinvent yourself. Maybe you were looking for something new, or maybe you were running away from something [...]. You could be whoever you wanted to be, reinvent yourself rather than be who you truly were. However, this all eventually led to trouble when one blow in was murdered, and another was accused of doing it. This horrid event unresolved created tension in the community, and rural idyll where people left their doors unlocked and looked after their neighbours, was transformed into a place where people locked their doors and were weary of strangers.

This notion that West Cork had once offered a rural refuge from the modern world, and was transformed by this murder, is most eloquently expressed by English immigrant Pete Bielecki (West Cork Podcast, episode one):

With the things that were going on in the UK and in Europe, high levels of crime and violence and political turmoil, you try to move to the edge to escape, and West Cork was about as far as you could go.

He continues (West Cork Podcast, episode one):

West Cork underwent a sort of rural regeneration in the 1990s then. The hippies pushed up the house prices, and soon they were joined by actors, and writers, and lawyers who bought second homes. It became a sort of playground where the pressures of modern life did not apply. For a time, it was perfect, but then there was murder here and everything changed. It took some place special and turned it into everywhere else.

Finally, in episode one of the Sky Crime documentary series (Sky Atlantic, episode one), Jim Sheridan also examines the social and political context:

This murder would shock the community. It would disrupt a once peaceful rural idyl of hippies, locals, writers, actors, and romantics of all nationalities. The prime suspects conviction in a Parisian court, and the refusal of the Irish justice system to charge or extradite would pit two legal systems against each other. It would raise questions of Garda corruption and incompetency, and indeed questions that go to the very heart of our society and democracy itself.

As researchers have noted, media representations of violent crime and murder, and this is particularly the case with the true crime genre, tend to ignore or de-emphasise the social and political context, in favor of a focus on the sensational and novel elements of the case (Jewkes, 2011). There is also a tendency in such cases to focus in on what is deviant or pathological about the suspect/offender, and a tendency to either ignore the victim or reduce them to one point on the deserving/undeserving binary.

However, as we have seen, the three new media sources examined seem to subvert and transcend this tendency. While there is certainly evidence that the themes just mentioned are also at play, the crime is not considered in isolation. As one contributor put it, while Sophie's death was a personal tragedy for her, her family, and her loved ones, it was also a social tragedy for West cork.

For local people, this represented the end of an age of innocence for an alternative community that had rejected modern life in favor of communal and self-sustained living. This murder seems to have ended a sense of safety and security in the local area. Therefore, as much as it was an individual tragedy, it could also be understood as being indicative of wider sociological phenomena. Moreover, as Jim Sheridan has pointed out, the case raised issues for Irish democracy, issues of jurisprudence in terms of the differences in standards of evidence in common law and French law, as well as issues around extradition (Sky Atlantic, episode three). The three new media sources analysed subvert the trend to obscure or ignore the social and political context relevant to violent crime.

Victims' Family

Contrary to media coverage of violence against women (Wattis, 2015) in general, the recent coverage of Sophie's murder by new media sources foregrounds the victim's family to a considerable extent. For example, the first episode of the Netflix documentary series spends a sizeable portion of time engaging with the emotional impact the case has had on Sophie's family. For example, Sophie's aunt Marie-Madeline Opalka states (Netflix, episode one):

We are a very close family, yes. That is true. I said it cannot be Sophie because she had just spoke to her husband the night before. But it was, and we were in shock.

Similarly, Sophie's mother and father also spoke of a profound sense of shock in the immediate aftermath of her death (Netflix, episode one):

We were listening to the TV news, and they did not give the name of the place where the murder happened initially, or the name of the victim, but Marguerite said, "oh no it is Sophie.' And from here our lives changed forever.

Most dramatically, Sophie's brother recounts in detail the phone call with Sophie's neighbour in West Cork that represented the first confirmation the family had received (Netflix, episode one):

I called Josephine, Sophie's neighbour. I tried 10-15 times, but she was always busy. Eventually, I managed to get hold of her and I still remember vividly Josephine screaming in my ear. I didn't remember anything she was saying between her accent, her screaming, and the emotion. So, I cut her off by saying 'Is it Sophie or is it not Sophie?' Then she said it is Sophie, and then our world was turned upside down.

This episode also contains extended discussions with Sophie's son Pierre-Louis. He recalls his experience of the events of December 1996 (Netflix, episode one):

I was 15 years old. We were preparing for preparing for Christmas and my dad came and told me in the middle of the night. He woke me up to tell me, and well the shock, its like an electric shock. I was very close to my mother because my parents divorced when I was one. So, for a long time, I lived with my mom during the week.

We were very close yes very close. It was a sudden transformation from childhood to adulthood. When she died, a little part of me died.

In episode three of the Netflix documentary series (Netflix, episode three), the family's quest for justice is examined in detail. However, as this has already been addressed in the section that dealt with Sophie's biography and character, a few examples will suffice to make the point. The family had two basic aims in this regard, one to foreground Sophie in remembrance of this case, and secondly to seek justice. As regards justice, there is a clear sense of frustration at what the family sees as the Irish state's failure to take their concerns seriously or to include them in the process of investigation (Netflix, episode three):

I did not meet the police, French or Irish. The Irish police told us that a resolution was just around the corner, but one never came. And they did not really leave any role for the victims' family.

Similarly, Sophie's aunt remarks that (Netflix, episode three):

Someone called saying tonight there will be some good news and the case will be closed, but the DPP refused to prosecute, and we heard nothing else from the police.

This foregrounding of Sophie's family can also be seen in episode three of the West Cork podcast. For example, Pierre-Lois describes his mother as follows (Netflix, episode three):

She was my mother. When she divorced, we lived in a small apartment in Paris. My mother was not an artist, but she liked an artistic lifestyle, which is why she did not last with my father as he is a very pragmatic guy. I am much more like my other, which is why we were so close.

Overall, the new media sources engaged with foreground the experiences of the victim's family much more so than in the newspaper coverage. In the newspaper coverage, Sophie's family, and the impact her death had on them is ignored, and they are only ever mentioned in passing. The current case study suggests that new media may have an advantage over traditional media formats in overcoming the historical silencing of victims and their families, a theme that criminologists have been highlighting for decades (Jewkes, 2011). However, while the discussion so far has focused on the potential benefits of new media, we will now turn to the ways in which the new media in the current study reproduces problematic tropes associated with media coverage of violence against women.

Class and Gender Biases and Assumptions

Criminologists have long noted that females who violate traditional gender norms are seen as at least partially responsible for their experience of crime and victimisation (Bickle, 1991). For example, a woman's choice of clothing and alcohol consumption are frequently highlighted in media representations of female victims of sexual assault. While the new media sources examined do not invoke gender norms to apportion blame, they do devote a substantial amount of time to the question of why a married mother was alone in a foreign country just before Christmas. For example, in the Netflix documentary series a news reporter wonders aloud (Netflix, episode one):

Just what a married French mother of three was doing alone in a remote part of West Cork so close to Christmas remains a mystery.

Similarly, the Sky Crime documentary series opens with the director Jim Sheridan claiming (Sky Atlantic episode one):

There are many aspects of this case that trouble me [...] Like what was a married mother doing alone so close to Christmas in a foreign country.

Furthermore, episode three of the West Cork podcast also contemplates this issue (West Cork Podcast, episode three):

The circumstances surrounding the murder of Madame du Plantier are quite mysterious, as to why she should decide to spend Christmas alone in West Cork when she had a child and a husband in France.

While each of the three new media sources mentions this fact, there is no attempt to discuss its relevance or significance to the case. Indeed, given that Sophie was a film producer and had an interest in art, it is hardly surprising that she would seek solitude to focus on her work. Indeed, this is the reason Sophie's family gave for her presence in West Cork, and in any case, she had booked a flight back to Paris on Christmas eve. However, the critical point here from a gender perspective is that it seems unlikely that this fact would have been mentioned or framed in this way had a married male film producer with kids been killed a few days before Christmas. Given the extensive engagement and analysis presented on other issues it is certainly a limitation that none of the various new media sources engaged with this issue, and certainly demonstrates that this media format can indeed reproduce (or at the very least fail to debunk) problematic gender-based assumptions.

More problematically, however, is the tendency of the three new media sources to extensively focus on the male chief suspect in the case. Indeed, while Sophie is foregrounded so too is Ian Bailey. For example, the West Cork Podcast dedicates episodes four, five, six, and a portion of seven and nine (West Cork Podcast, episodes four; five; six; seven; and nine) to the character of the chief suspect and an attempt to ascertain whether he is guilty. In episode five, the producers describe their interactions with Ian at length (West Cork Podcast, episode five):

Speaking with Ian became a very big part of our lives for a while. Sometimes Ian would phone us up with details like when he self-published a book of his poetry. This was a plan he'd been working on way back before the murder accusation put things like that on hold before he became a household name in Ireland.

Similarly, the entire second episode of the Netflix series is devoted to Ian Bailey and contains numerous interview extracts. For example, Ian's former colleague Vivienne Hargreaves (Sunday Times) recalls that (Netflix, episode two):

He set up a journalism agency in Cheltenham and did that extremely well. As I recall, he was excellent at getting information out of people, he was an excellent journalist.

Ian confirms (Netflix, episode two):

I was writing articles while I was still at school. I read a book by Bernstein and Woodward called "All the presidents' men," and I thought that is what I want to, that is what I'm going to be, I'm going to be an investigative journalist.

While both the West Cork and Netflix series devote time to Ian's background, his interpretation of events, and his life since, the Sky Crime documentary contains excerpts of the producer Jim Sheridan informing Ian (first time he is informed) of the guilty verdict served against him in Paris in absentia (Sky Atlantic, episode six):

Ian, the verdict is in. I am afraid it is not good news, its guilty. But I am sure you were expecting that anyway.

As feminist scholars (Wattis, 2015) have pointed out in the case of Peter Sutcliff and other famous male perpetrators of violence and murder against women, there is a tendency in media coverage of such cases to foreground the male perpetrator and even mythologise him (e.g., the Yorkshire ripper, Suffolk Strangler). While it is true that the victim, in this case, is foregrounded, the new media follow the old in reproducing the problematic tendency to foreground males in the case.

Finally, however, there is potentially something problematic in the foregrounding of Sophie in this case and the tendency to de-emphaise female victims more generally. Indeed, it cannot be ignored that Sophie was of high social standing. As mentioned in episode four of the West Cork podcast, and repeated in the other two documentary series (West Cork Podcast, episode four):

Sophie was a TV producer, she made art house documentaries for French TV. Her father was a dentist, and her mother was a deputy major of a city district in Paris. Her husband Daniel was a famous film producer.

It seems plausible that the foregrounding of Sophie's character and the emphasis placed on her biography was party a function of the resources her family poured into the *Justice for Sophie* campaign and their relentless campaign to include her voice in the story. While this is admirable, one cannot help wondering if the same would have occurred had Sophie been a poor woman from a low-status background. Indeed, this issue is not explored, and all the evidence indicates that such women do not receive such favourable coverage (Jewkes, 2011).

Fascination with Myth

Each of the three new media documentary series spent a significant amount of time discussing the mythical elements associated with the case. Most prominently, they focus on the claim that Sophie had seen the "White lady" at an old castle in West Cork the day before she died. Local folklore dictates that anyone who sees the White Lady will die within 24 hours of the sighting (Netflix, episode one). For example, in episode one of the Netflix documentary a contributor remembers (Netflix, episode one):

One of the national papers picked up a story of a lady that lives at Three Castle Head, Yvonne Ungerer. She told me that she had a visit from the victim the day before she died, and that Madame du Plantier said that she had a really strange experience.

A second contributor picks up the story (Netflix, episode one):

There is a ruined castle on Three Castle Head. There she saw something terrible, and it scared her. She felt a terrible fear. She arrived at the Ungerers house really scared saying 'oh my God, I saw a woman, it was like a white shape.

A third contributor to the episode adds (Netflix, episode one):

Three castle head is meant to be haunted by a melancholic female ghost called the white lady. I learned the story about this lady, this mythological, legendary character, who lives at a place by the lake, and when you see her, you are going to die in the hours that follow.

Similarly, in episode two of the West Cork Podcast, the presenters also speak extensively about the case of the White Lady (West Cork Podcast, episode two):

Apparently in the days leading up to the murder Sophie had visited Three Castle Head and seen the mythical White Lady. The White Lady is a mythical figure that haunts an old, ruined castle in West Cork. The legend goes that anyone who sees the Wite Lady will die in the hours after.

Finally, Jim Sheridan in his Sky Crime documentary also refers to Sophie's apparent sighting of the White Lady (Sky Atlantic, episode one):

West Cork is an ancient place, and its almost like the landscape is alive, like it remembers. Like all ancient places its full of folklore, like the case of the White Lady, a figure who apparently haunts a ruined castle at Three Castle Head. Sophie had visited the castle shortly before her murder, and a local family claim she had arrived at their door in a distressed state having seen a white figure on the lake. What are we to make of this?

As Criminologists have noted, a fascination with the divine, macabre, and with folklore is quite common in media representations of crime. For example, Crews et al (1996) demonstrates how media fascination with Satanists and ritualistic killings led to a moral panic in the later part of the 20th century in the United States. Furthermore, a fascination with the occult and its relation to violent crime and ritualistic crime has frequently gripped the media in the UK and Europe, leading to increases in public fear of such crime (Jewkes, 2011).

However, while it should be acknowledged that none of the New Media sources promote the myth, there is a sense in which they all take advantage of public fascination with the occult to increase viewer interest. While the myth is not promoted, it is not debunked either. For example, a quick examination of the facts demonstrates that Sophie had actually "seen" the White Lady multiple days before her death, which of course is inconsistent with the legend. Moreover, the media sources do not report that the day Sophie visited was extremely foggy (Sheridan, 2021) and that dense fog on a lake can obviously create visual impressions of white figures. So, while the three-documentary series are not guilty of promoting the occult, they certainly take advantage of the issue to spark viewer interest.

CONCLUSION AND DISCUSSION

The current chapter was guided by two research questions. These are:

1. To what extent is the recent podcast and docuseries coverage of the case like the gendered, classed, and sensationalised coverage of violent crime against women that the criminological canon has long highlighted?
2. To what extent does the podcast and docuseries format present and opportunity to offer a more nuanced and academically consistent analysis of violent crime against women.

In relation to the first question, the new media sources engaged with have reproduced two problematic tendencies, commonly identified by Criminologists in media coverage of violence and violence against women. These are: (1) class and gender biases and problematic assumptions, and (2) a fascination with the mythical. While the new media sources foreground Sophie's biography and character, they also unfairly focus on her violation of gender norms. Specifically, they focus on the fact that a married mother was alone in a foreign country so close to Christmas. Given that Sophie was a documentary maker and an artist, it is not unusual that she would seek solitude to contemplate her work. Indeed, it seems highly unlikely that a similar discourse would have emerged had Sophie been a married male with children. Therefore, while new media has the potential to disrupt problematic assumptions and stereotypes regarding gender, it can also reproduce them, as we see in this instance. Furthermore, the new media sources have repeated the fascination with male suspects/perpetrators that feminist scholars (Carr and Holt, 2010) have long argued is central to media representations of violence against women.

This tendency leads to male perpetrators gaining iconic status (Ted Bundy, Peter Sutcliff), while their female victims tend to be de-emphasised. While Sophie was certainly not de-emphasised, and Ian Bailey is only a suspect, the new media nonetheless reproduce this problematic tendency. Finally, one cannot help pointing out that much of the discourse around Sophie focuses on her high social status and professional standing. One cannot help but wonder whether a single mother from a poor background would have received the same level of attention or sympathy. Therefore, there is an argument that the new media sources reproduce problematic class biases in media coverage of violence against women. Indeed, while scholars (Black, 2009; Carr and Holt, 2010) have pointed out that women who violate gender norms are often treated harshly, and the notion of female victims and offenders are doubly deviant (Heidensohn, 1985) has long been identified in criminology, it may well be that having a high social status mitigates against this tendency.

Finally, the tendency to focus on the mythic/occult elements of Sophies case plays into problematic tendencies to sensationalise media representations of crime. As Criminologists have long pointed out (Garland, 2000), most crime is boring, mundane, and routine, and the tendency to focus on salacious, sensationalist, and quasi-mythic elements distorts the publics understanding of crime and violent crime. While the new media sources do not promote the 'White Lady' narrative, they do not critically engage with it or discuss its meaning. Instead, the story is used for dramatic effect, to attract the viewers attention by focusing overtly on unusual and mythical elements of the story.

Notwithstanding these limitations, the three new media sources have overcome problematic tendencies in media coverage of violence against women. Most importantly, while most female victims or crime are either ignored or reduced to gender-based stereotypes (Heidensohn, 1985; Black, 2009; Carr and Holt, 2010), Sophies biography and character are foregrounded in the sources this chapter has examined. Together, the sources represent Sophie as a complex and varied character. She is represented as adventurous yet fond of solitude, artistic, and intelligent. The focus is on Sophies familial relationships, her hobbies and interests, and her career. She is front and centre of the story in a way that transcends traditional gender-based tropes in media representations of crime against women.

While most media coverage of violent crime against women focuses on the individual and pathological aspects of the case (Jewkes, 2011), without reference to the broader context, the three sources examined engage comprehensively with the relevant social and political context. Indeed, the social dynamics of West Cork are represented as a rural cosmopolitanism (Woods, 2018). The three sources represent the region as the last refuge from modernity and modern consumer lifestyles. Importantly, if traditionally media has represented cases of violent crime as pathological and disconnected from context, Sophie's murder was indicative of broader social change in West Cork. The three sources tend to emphasise that locals viewed the case as a watershed, transforming West Cork from a rural idyl to a place typical of the modern world, with all its attendant social problems.

Finally, while the victim and the victim's family have long been underrepresented in media coverage and Criminological research (Klun, 2017), Sophie's family and their experiences have been foregrounded in the new media sources. In particular, the emotions following the discovery of her murder, and their quest for justice and attempt to foreground Sophie in the story are afforded considerable attention. This foregrounding not only affords the family space to tell their story, but it also further superimposes Sophie in the narrative of the murder.

Overall, the current case study demonstrates the potential for new media sources to overcome some of the problematic tendencies associated with traditional media representations of violence against women, and crime more generally. The long format of a documentary series or podcast provides the space to interview experts and witnesses with lived experience, and to unpack difficult and complex issues over a substantial period. Furthermore, the time available to produce also allows for a more careful examination of the available evidence and sources than would be available to a journalist working to a shorter deadline. However, there are aspects that should evoke caution.

Firstly, the sources engaged with have represented problematic gender based and other tendencies. Therefore, while new media offers the potential to overcome these issues, the format itself is no guarantee that this will be achieved. Secondly, new media will also probably be subjected to the same profit motive-based consideration that may entice producers to rely on seductive yet simplistic assumptions in their coverage of crime cases. This is obvious in cases where there is a mythic or occult element to the case. Indeed, it is highly likely that these elements are more popular and focusing on them more profitable than a careful engagement with facts that may be more mundane. In conclusion, the current case study represents an example of the potential and pitfalls of new media in the search for more accurate and illuminating media representations of violence against women, and of crime more broadly.

REFERENCES

Bailey, E. (1997). Du Plantier maintains silence on his wife's brutal murder. *Irish Examiner*. Available at: https://www.irishnewsarchive.com/free_search/?pub=IEX&search_olive=eoin%20bailey&yearFrom=1996&toYear=1997

Bickle, G., & Peterson, R. D. (1991). The impact of gender-based family roles on criminal sentencing. *Social Problems*, *38*(3), 372–394. doi:10.2307/800605

Black, L. (2009). *The representation of female offenders in Irish newspapers* [MA Thesis]. University College Dublin.

Bonger, W. (1916). *Criminality and economic conditions* (1st ed.). Creative Media Partners.

Brent, H. (2021). *Ian Bailey told French prosecutors to 'Pog mo Thoin' when they demanded he face trial in France*. Available at: https://www.irishpost.com/news/ian-bailey-told-french-prosecutors-to-pog-mo-thoin-when-they-demanded-he-face-trial-in-paris-215300

Bungey, S., & Forde, J. (2021). *West Cork Podcast: the unsolved murder of Sophie Toscan Du Plantier* [podcast series]. The West Cork Podcast. https://www.westcorkpodcast.com/about

Carr, N., & Holt, S. (2010). Outrageous Provocation? The Media Reporting of Domestic Violence in Ireland. In P. Share & M. Corcoran (Eds.), *Ireland of the Illusions: A Sociological Chronicle, 2007–2008* (1st ed.). IPA.

Chibnall, S. (1977). *Law-and-order News: An Analysis of Crime Reporting in the British Press* (1st ed.). Psychology Press.

Christie, N. (1986). The Ideal Victim. In E. A. Fattah (Ed.), *From Crime Policy to Victim Policy* (1st ed.). Palgrave Macmillian. doi:10.1007/978-1-349-08305-3_2

Crews, G., Montgomery, R., & Garris, W. (1996). Satanic, Occult, and Ritualistic violence in America. *Violence in America.*, *1*(1), 33–53.

Dower, J. (2021). *Sophie: A murder in West Cork* [documentary series]. Netflix.

DyerT. (2022). *Media conglomeration, Local News, and Capital Market consequences*. Available at: https://papers.ssrn.com/sol3/papers.cfm?abstract_id=4055618 doi:10.2139/ssrn.4055618

Ericson, R., Baranek, P., & Chan, J. (1989). Negotiating Control: A Study of News Sources. Open University Press.

Ferriter, D. (2004). *The transformation of Ireland: 1900-2000* (1st ed.). Profile Books.

Garland, D. (2000). The culture of high crime societies: Some preconditions of recent law and order policies. *British Journal of Criminology*, *40*(3), 347–375. doi:10.1093/bjc/40.3.347

Gerbner, G., & Gross, L. (1972). Living with television: The violence profile. *Journal of Communication*, *26*(2), 173–199. PMID:932235

Greer, C. (2019). *Crime and Media: A Reader* (1st ed.). Routledge. doi:10.4324/9780367809195

Hall, S., Critcher, C., Jefferson, T., Clarke, J., & Roberts, B. (1978). *Policing the Crisis: Mugging, the State and Law and Order* (1st ed.). Macmillan. doi:10.1007/978-1-349-15881-2

Heidensohn, F. (1985). *Women and Crime* (1st ed.). Macmillan Education UK.

Inglis, T., & McKeogh, C. (2012). The double bind: Women, honour and sexuality in contemporary Ireland. *Media Culture & Society*, *34*(1), 68–82. doi:10.1177/0163443711427200

Irish Examiner Reporter. (1998). *Gardai deny second murder trial claim.* Available at: https://www.irishnewsarchive.com/free_search/?pub=IEX&search_olive=Sophie%20Toscan%20Du%20Plantier&yearFrom=1998&toYear=1998

Irish Examiner Reporter. (1999). Family speak of anguish over killer of woman still being at large. *Irish Examiner.*

Irish Examiner Reporter. (2000). *A gruesome account of the Sophie Toscan Du Plantier murder.* Available at: https://www.irishnewsarchive.com/free_search/?pub=IEX&search_olive=Sophie%20Toscan%20Du%20Plantier&yearFrom=1996&toYear=2000

Jewkes, Y. (2011). *Media and Crime* (2nd ed.). Sage.

Mendelsohn, R. (1947). Victimology and contemporary society's trends. *Victimology, an International Journal, 1*(1), 8-28.

O'Connell, M. (1999). Is Irish Public Opinion towards Crime Distorted by Media Bias? *European Journal of Communication, 14*(1), 191–212. doi:10.1177/0267323199014002003

O'Donnell, I. (2005). Crime and justice in the Republic of Ireland. *European Journal of Criminology, 2*(1), 99–131.

O'Mahony, S. (2019). From shebeens to supervised injecting centres: The socio-historical construction and portrayal of addiction in modern Ireland. *Irish Journal of Sociology, 27*(2), 153–197. doi:10.1177/0791603519835437

O'Sullivan, C. (2008). The Nun, the Rape Charge, and the Miscarriage of Justice: The Case of Nora Wall. *The Northern Ireland Legal Quarterly, 59*(1), 305.

Peelo, M., Francis, B., Soothill, K., Pearson, J., & Ackerley, E. (2004). Newspaper reporting and the public construction of homicide. *British Journal of Criminology, 44*(2), 256–275. doi:10.1093/bjc/44.2.256

Quinlan, C. (2011). *Inside: Ireland's women's prisons, past and present* (1st ed.). Irish Academic Press.

Rawlings, P. (1995). True Crime. In *Papers from then British Criminology Conference.* Loughborough University.

Sellin, T. (1937). *Crime in the depression* (1st ed.). Ayer Co Publishers.

Sellin, T. (1938). *Culture, conflict and crime.* Social Science Research Council. doi:10.1086/217919

Serrano, N. (2022). *Five Ways Podcasts Are Redefining Black Representation.* (Online). Available at: https://www.adweek.com/partner-articles/5-ways-podcasts-are-redefining-black-representation/

Sheridan, J. (2021). *Murder at the cottage: The search for justice for Sophie Toscan Du Plantier* [documentary series]. Now TV, Sky Crime.

Sheridan, M. (2014). *The Murder of Sophie: how I hunted and haunted the West Cork killer* (1st ed.). Gadfly Press.

Wattis, L. (2015). Revisiting the Yorkshire ripper murders: Interrogating gender violence, sex work, and justice. *Feminist Criminology*, *12*(1), 3–21. doi:10.1177/1557085115602960

ENDNOTES

1 This is the name of the Irish police force.

2 https://www.irishnewsarchive.com/

3 Local term for somebody not born in the locality.

Chapter 6
Trayvon Martin:
A Black Boy Who Made an Impact

Michelle Eliasson
https://orcid.org/0000-0002-2915-2775
University of Florida, USA

EXECUTIVE SUMMARY

In 2012, while returning from a visit at a local convenience store, 17-year-old Trayvon Martin was fatally shot by George Zimmerman, a community watch group member, in Sanford, Florida. Zimmerman stated that he was being attacked by Martin and shot him in self-defense, and in 2013 Zimmerman was acquitted of the death of Martin. There was a significant public reaction to Martin's death and the subsequent acquittal of Zimmerman. This chapter will describe Martin's death, the news media and social media coverage of the case, and the implications Martin's death brought on the discussion of racial profiling, implicit bias, and police conduct and practices. The chapter highlights the various roles Martin's death and news media and social media coverage played in the mobilization for social movement and activism highlighting racial justice in the United States.

INTRODUCTION

On February 26th, 2012, at 7 pm Trayvon Martin, a Black 17-year-old boy, was fatally shot by George Zimmerman, a community watch group member, in Sanford, Florida. Martin was returning from the local convenience store to a gated community his father's fiancée lived in. Zimmerman passed through the gated community and spotted Martin and shot him after an alleged altercation. The death of Martin sent shockwaves through American society. Americans were faced with the disparate

DOI: 10.4018/978-1-7998-9668-5.ch006

treatment that non-Whites experience when encountering individuals in authority positions. Contrary to the televised brutal beating of Rodney King in 1992, which led to day-long riots in Los Angeles, Zimmerman's killing of Martin was not captured on camera. Despite this, Martin's death had a significant impact on the discussion of police officers' use of violence against non-Whites, especially Blacks.

Extensive research shows that non-Whites are more likely than Whites to get killed by officers and are more likely to experience police brutality (Cesario, Johnson, & Terrill, 2019; Donelson, 2017). For example, non-Whites who are shot by the police are less likely than Whites who are shot by the police to not have been attacking the police officer or other individuals while being shot, and Blacks are twice as likely than Whites to be unarmed when shot by the police (Nix et al., 2017). Thus, scholarship has during recent years, highlighted the racism perpetrated by the police against non-Whites. The death of Martin was one of the events that triggered extensive social reaction to the adverse treatment of non-Whites, especially Blacks, by authority such as the police.

In this chapter, I will discuss the influence the media coverage of Martin's death and subsequent criminal trial had on the formation of social movements that address racial justice and police use of violence against Blacks. The first of the four notions that will be discussed is social media coverage's role in highlighting racism perpetuated by the police and the criminal justice system against Blacks. Second, how social media coverage contributed to creating one of the most significant social movements against racism, the Black Lives Matter movement. Thirdly, discuss the implication of coverage of Martin's in relation to social reactions of other Blacks experiencing police brutality. Fourth, the formation of Blue Lives Matter as a response to the social media and social movements criticizing the police and the racism perpetrated by the police force.

THE KILLING OF TRAYVON MARTIN

The death of Trayvon Martin in 2012 was an event that highlighted how racial profiling and violence against non-Whites, especially Blacks, have contributed to extensive disparate treatment of Blacks in American society (Teasley et al., 2017). It was not only Martin's death that impacted the American society but also the trial and subsequent acquittal of Zimmerman which caused a wide rage response on social media, among activists and in the news. Below I will describe Martin, Zimmerman, the shooting, investigation, trial and the subsequent acquittal of Zimmerman.

Martin was a Black 17-year-old high school student who lived with his mom and older brother in Miami Gardens, Florida. Martin was 5 feet 11 inches and weighed 158 pounds and was a junior in high school. At the time of the shooting Martin had been visiting his dad's fiancée's apartment in Sanford, Florida for seven days. Martin had been suspended for the third time from his high school in Miami due to drug residues that were found in his backpack. Both Martin's father and mother agreed that taking him out of Miami for a few days during the suspension would benefit Martin and keep him away from his friends (Botelho, 2012). Martin was described by his mother as a boy who, although at times struggled with his academics and behavior, loved his friends, family, sports, and music (Fulton & Martin, 2017).

George Zimmerman a Hispanic and White male was at the time of the shooting 29 years old and resided in the same gated community where he encountered Martin on the 26th of February. That night Zimmerman was working the night shift as a neighborhood watchman and was driving around the apartment complexes (Torres et al., 2017).

Zimmerman was born in Virginia and grew up with 3 siblings. His mother was born in Peru and his dad was of German and American descent. After graduating high school Zimmerman moved to Orlando, Florida from Virginia and started working for an insurance company. In 2007 Zimmerman married his wife and in 2011 they moved to Sanford, Florida. During this time he was working on an associate degree in criminal justice and worked as an insurance underwriter and for a neighborhood watch group (Reuters, 2012). Zimmerman had previously been arrested in 2005 when an undercover officer attempted to arrest Zimmerman's friend and Zimmerman allegedly assaulted the undercover officer and was subsequently arrested. These charges were ultimately dropped and Zimmerman participated in an alcohol education program. Approximately a month after the charges were dropped, Zimmerman's then-fiancé filed a restraining order against Zimmerman and noted domestic violence as the reason she wanted a restraining order.

The Shooting

At 7 pm the evening of the 26th, 2012, Zimmerman passed through the gated community and spotted Martin as he was walking back from the convenience store. While Zimmerman was observing Martin from a distance, he called the Sanford Police's non-emergency number to report seeing a suspicious person in the community. The community had a history of several break-ins during the last few years.

Martin was talking to his girlfriend on the phone and told her that someone was following him. During the conversation with his girlfriend, Martin began to run towards his dad's fiancée's house, and as Zimmerman reported this to the dispatcher, Zimmerman was told by the dispatcher not to pursue Martin. However, Zimmerman disregarded the instructions from the dispatcher and began pursuing Martin on foot only to loose track of him after a few minutes. After ending the phone call with the Sanford Police, Zimmerman again encountered Martin and according to Zimmerman had an altercation initiated by Martin. During this alleged altercation, Zimmerman fatally shot Martin. During the shooting, a 911 call was made by a witness who alerted the police that a shooting had occurred (Graeff et al., 2014).

A few minutes after the call, the Sanford Police arrived at the scene. When the police arrived Zimmerman was standing next to Martin who was lying face down and unresponsive on the ground approximately 50 yards from his dad's finance's residence. At the scene Zimmerman admitted to shooting Martin, however argued that the shot was fired in self-defense. Martin was pronounced dead at the scene and paramedics treated Zimmerman for minor injuries and brought him to the Sanford police department, where he was released after being questioned for five hours.

The Investigation, Trial and Acquittal

On March 12th, 2012, Sanford Police Chief Bill Lee stated that there was no evidence which contested Zimmerman's claims that the shooting of Martin was in self-defense. Leaning on Florida's "Stand your ground" law the Police Chief stated that Zimmerman was not going to be charged or arrested (Graeff et al., 2014). The "Stand your ground" law notes that individuals are allowed to use deadly force when they believe it to be necessary in order to defend themselves against deadly force, great bodily harm, kidnapping, rape and in some cases robbery. However, the "Stand your ground" law cannot be invoked by someone who is the primary aggressor or by someone who is doing something otherwise illegal (Justifiable Use of Force, Florida Statute XLVI Chapter 776, 2021). Thus, when Zimmerman argued that shooting Martin was in self-defense and that Martin was the primary aggressor, Zimmerman, according to the "Stand your ground" law, was not criminally liable for Martin's death.

One day after the Police Chief's statements, homicide detective Christopher Serino, who also worked in the Sanford Police Department, recommended that Martin's death should be investigated further. On the 14th of March the case was turned over to the State Attorney's Office and the Justice Department and the FBI then announced that they were formally investigating Martin's death. A short while after these announcements the Sanford Police Chief temporarily stepped down from his position and was later officially fired. Zimmerman was charged with murder and arrested, however, was later released on a 150,000-dollar bond and plead not guilty to the charges (Graeff et al., 2014).

During the investigation Zimmerman's family doctor released a medical report, which stated that the day after the shooting of Martin, Zimmerman displayed a fractured nose, two black eyes, and two lacerations on his head. This was according to the defense evidence supporting the fact that there had been a violent altercation between Martin and Zimmerman, which caused Zimmerman injuries before he shot Martin.

A couple of weeks after Zimmerman was released on bond, the judge revoked Zimmerman's bond, claiming that Zimmermann's wife misrepresented their finances to the court which impacted the sum of the bond that was set. The new bond was set at 1 million dollars, and Zimmerman's wife was arrested and charged with perjury. Zimmerman posted 10% of the 1-million-dollar bond and was released. Once released Zimmerman and his attorneys filed a motion to request the judge to step down from the case due to the disparaging language Zimmerman claimed the judge used in his bail order. The judge refused to step down and Zimmerman appealed this refusal to an appeal court which granted a new judge for the case. In August, the prosecution accidentally released documents to the public containing photos of Martin's body and Zimmerman's school records (CNN, 2021).

In April 2014, Zimmerman waived his right to a "Stand your ground" pretrial immunity hearing. During this hearing, the judge would have assessed whether or not the "Stand your ground" law would have been applicable in the case and thus protected the actions of Zimmerman (CNN, 2021). Instead of using the "Stand your ground" law to justify Zimmerman's actions, his defense attorneys choose to argue self-defense as the explanation for Zimmerman's action during the night of the shooting. The difference between the "Stand your ground" law and self-defense is that with the "Stand your ground" law there would have been no requirement for Zimmerman to have retreated before he shot Martin. However, with the self-defense claim, Zimmerman would have to have retreated or backed away from danger before the shooting occurred (Catalfamo, 2006; Douglas Brown, 2015). Another difference between the two claims is that if a judge argued that stand your ground law was applicable, no trial would have been conducted. Whereas with claims of self-defense a trial would still occur (Ward, 2014).

In addition to changing defense strategy, the defense team filed motions to allow information about Martin's familiarity with guns, his marijuana use, and previous fights to be brought up in trial. However, this was denied by the judge (CNN, 2021). In July 2013, the trial against Zimmerman occurred, the jury which consisted of sex females deliberated for 16 hours and 20 minutes and found Zimmerman not guilty of both second-degree murder and the lesser charge of manslaughter (New York Times, 2013)

After the Trial

After Zimmerman was found not guilty, Zimmerman's wife pleaded guilty to perjury. Zimmerman filed a 100-million-dollar lawsuit against Martin's family and others, arguing that Martin's attorney aided the change of a reluctant witness and helped a new witness to prepare a false testimony (McLaughlin et al., 2019). Zimmerman's legal troubles continued after his acquittal of Martin's death. In 2013 he was arrested on misdemeanor accounts of domestic violence battery, assault, and criminal mischief. The prosecutors decided not to press charges because Zimmerman's girlfriend, who was the alleged victim, did not wish to pursue the charges. In 2015 Zimmerman was again arrested on suspicion of aggravated assault on another girlfriend. These charges were also not pursued because of the girlfriend's wishes of dropping the charges against Zimmerman (McLaughlin et al., 2019).

NEWS AND SOCIAL MEDIA COVERAGE OF THE MARTIN CASE

There was extensive news media coverage and social media attention put towards the killing of Martin and the subsequent trial and acquittal of Zimmerman (Graeff et al., 2014; Umoja Noble, 2014). The news and social media coverage of Martin's death highlighted the capacity these platforms have on shining light on institutional racism, racial justice and to influence aspects of the criminal justice process (Cohn Aizenman, 2012).

News Media

Throughout the course of the Martin case the news media had different ways of framing the events that occurred. For example, some news outlets framed the events using racism narratives which argued that Zimmerman was a racist vigilante that killed Martin, whilst other framings argued Martin was the primary aggressor and that Zimmerman only defended himself. These competing frames did not only influence society's expectation on the criminal justice system but also the outcome of Zimmerman's trial (Cohn Aizenman, 2012). By providing these competing frames news media outlets contributed to highlight certain aspects of the case as more influential than others, but also linked these aspects to religious or political beliefs. The news outlets did this by presenting the emotionally charged question of the motivation of why the killing of Martin occurred and responded to their own questions in a wide range of ways which often reflected political leniency. For example, Martin's death and Zimmerman's claims of self-defense became a funnel for news media to discuss the "Stand your ground" law in Florida and discussions about gun regulation. Furthermore, the subsequent acquittal of Zimmerman further sparked discussions in the news about systematically embedded racism within the criminal justice system. By, for example, arguing for or against gun regulations or racial justice the news media outlets used experts or political figures with specific political agendas to debate the facts of the case and linking them to larger societal questions. The level of conservativeness and the political affiliation of the news outlets impacted how often emotionally charged questions were asked, answered and contributed to the conflicted framing of Martin's death (Madison, 2015). This resulted in that the initial competing frames reflecting racism and self-defense were further expanded by news media by drawing upon other questions which rendered responses impacted by political and ideological perceptions.

Overall one could argue that the Martin case was covered and discussed by news media in a variety of ways, but with three aspects often influencing how and what was covered. Firstly, the events were discussed on what could be argued as a factual basis, reflecting what occurred during the evening of the 26th of February, secondly, motivations of why Martin died and the motivation for the actions of Zimmerman and Martin that caused the death. Thirdly, the facts and motivation why events occur lead to a broad discussion in the news in relation to gun rights, Florida's "Stand your ground" law and racism within the criminal justice system. Through these three major ways of presenting and discussing the Martin case in the news media, political and ideological leniency influenced the news coverage which adhered to pro-White, racist, conservative, liberal and critical viewpoints (Graeff et al., 2014; Hodges, 2015; Madison, 2015; Smith, 2021).

The news media framing of Martin's shooting is not a single phenomenon, but rather an example of how news media coverage adheres to specific framing of narratives (Hodges, 2015). Scholars argue that there are several frames that are used in news media when specifically reporting on officer violence and Black victimization. For example Smith (2021) argues that partisan news networks displayed ani-Black and pro-White framing when reporting officers murdering Black victims. The framing of Martin's death in the news media exemplified these frames and actualized how framing can impact not only society perception of one event such as the killing, but also how one event can highlight systematically embedded notions such as racism and the ideological and political viewpoints associated with various aspects of the killing.

Social Media

Aside from the news media, there were many other responses and reactions from society due to Martin's death and the subsequent trial and acquittal of Zimmermann. The reactions ranged from support for both Martin and Zimmerman on social media, mobilization of social movements and social activists and politicians speaking on the matters. For example, right after Martin's death, a petition created by Martin's parents on Change.org regarding the demand of an arrest of Zimmerman acquired over 1.3 million signatures. Furthermore the organization "Justice for Trayvon Martin Foundation" was created and hosted peace walks and remembrance events for Martin's death (CNN, 2021). Additionally, the president at the time, Barack Obama, publicly spoke out just a few months after Martin's death, saying that the incident required some nationwide "soul-searching" and "If I had a son, he'd look like Trayvon" (McLaughlin et al., 2019).

According to Lawson (2012), the reactions to the death of Martin related to different aspects of the case. For example, while some argued the case was an example of racism in the US and criminal justice system, others argue that the case was about neighborhood watch and illegal vigilante justice. Additionally, other individuals highlighted the need to further illuminate and critically discuss prosecutorial discretion and law enforcement accountability, and some emphasize the "Stand your ground" law. The mixed points of interest among the public reflected the wide range of narratives and angles that news outlets choose to display in their coverage of the case. According to Lawson, the wide range of reactions was a result of the many layers of the case highlighting race and law and the government's responses to both.

One of the most well-known social movements of modern times was created as a response to the many social issues that Martin's death highlighted. Martin's death became a catalyst for the "Black Lives Matter" movement and other movements associated with racial justice (Fabregat & Beck, 2019; Smith, 2015; Lane et al., 2020). The "Black Lives Matter" movement is often described as a leaderless anti-racism movement that incorporates intersectional perspectives of race, class, gender, sexuality, disability, and nationality in a sociopolitical network addressing the violence against Black Americans (Fabregat & Beck, 2019). The "Black Lives Matter" movement responded to the violence and oppression of Blacks by mobilizing ever-growing grassroots movements which emphasized the rights of Blacks and highlighting the racial structure within American society. When the acquittal of Zimmerman was announced to the public civil rights activist Aliza Garza responded with a message highlighting the disparities Blacks are exposed to in the US (Fabregat & Beck, 2019; Lane et al., 2020) and signed it off with "Black people, I love you. I love us. Our lives matter" and the hashtag #BlackLives Matter" (Day, 2019 p. 5). According to Lane et al. (2020) the hashtag became an affirmation for Black people in the US and a symbol for the fight against the oppression against Blacks.

Usage of News and Social Media

Beyond being used as a tool to report on the facts and current events of the death of Martin, the trial, and subsequent acquittal, the news and social media was used by Martin's family and Zimmerman and his family to communicate with the public about their experiences during and after the death of Martin. For example, Zimmerman's father spoke out in the Orlando Sentinel about the unfair portrait of Zimmermann as a racist and highlighted that he grew up in a Hispanic family. Zimmerman's father also appeared on television arguing that Martin beat Zimmerman and threatened to kill him which was why Zimmerman had to shoot Martin. This was later attested to by Zimmerman's brother who while appearing on CNN stated that Zimmerman's nose was broken by Martin before Martin was shot. Zimmerman himself appeared on a Fox News tv broadcast and stated that if presented with the same situation today "he would not have done anything differently." Furthermore, Zimmerman also sued CNN for allegedly editing the 911 call that was made on the night of Martin's death because the editing presented Zimmerman as a racist who was racially profiling Martin (CNN, 2021).

All these very public interactions with the media occurred before trial and highlighted an active interaction between legal parties and media before adjudication had taken place, which could be argued to further engage the general public in the facts of the case before a trial even had a chance to occur. The publicity and interaction with news media and social media are some of the notions which make Martin's death something that potentially contributed to an increased engagement of many individuals in American society. Not only did individuals have a chance to hear Zimmermann's and Martin's families make claims about the alleged events, but it also allowed the public through social media to publicly react to information that was presented to both parties, information which often only is presented in court.

IMPACT OF MARTIN'S DEATH

The death of Martin has had several implications and influences on society's perceptions of racial dynamics in society. Due to Martin's death and the subsequent acquittal of Zimmerman, mobilization of social movements specifically focused on the disparate treatment of Blacks in society and institutions such as the criminal justice system. The "Black Lives Matter" movement became a vessel to illuminate the many Black lives lost to police brutality or unjust treatment throughout various stages of the criminal justice system. As a result of the mobilization of social movements, society members became publicly involved in trying to dismantle the racist structures in society and by highlighting the voices of Black victims of racism (Day, 2015). Thus, the "Black Lives Matter" movement has become one of the largest social movements that utilized social media to facilitate a mobilization of activism and facilitating this activism on the streets which specifically promote racial justice (Rickford, 2016).

The United States has a long history of systematically discriminating against Blacks, and the criminal justice system has been an institution which specifically has facilitated the disparate treatment of Blacks. Some examples of this are mass incarceration, wrongful conviction, and police brutality, which Black men disproportionately are victim to compared to other genders and races. The death of Martin, the trial and the acquittal of Zimmerman became prime examples of these disparities since Martin, a young Black boy, was killed by a White individual with a position of authority (Lawson, 2012).

Martin's death and society's reaction to his death set the stage and created a platform for illuminating the disparate treatments of other young Black men, specifically by police officers. During the following years after Martins, several other young Black men were killed by officers due to excessive force. Some of these young men were Eric Garner, Michael Brown, Tamir Rice, and George Floyd. Although there was a wide range of implications and influence that Martin's death and the media coverage of the death and subsequent trial brought to the overall discussion of racial dynamics in American society, this section will focus on discussing the implications for policing and the racial dynamics in society. More specifically, implicit bias and racial profiling, police brutality, and the calls to abolish the police.

Implicit Bias and Racial Profiling

The Martin case brought up the issue of implicit bias and racial profiling of Blacks by individuals in authority positions. When Zimmerman called the dispatcher to report that he saw a "suspect" person in the neighborhood, many argued that much of Zimmerman's statement and presumption of why Martin was in the area was related to Martin being Black. At this moment, many argued that Zimmerman was practicing racial profiling and had implicit biases towards Martin because of his race (Lee, 2013; Thomas and Blackmon, 2015).

Racial profiling refers to police-initiated actions based on race, ethnicity, or nationality instead of individual behavior, leading to the belief that an individual is partaking in illegal activities (Risse & Zeckhauser, 2004), and implicit bias refers to negative beliefs and attitudes against racial minorities (Kang, 2005). Racial profiling and implicit bias are firmly integrated with negative stereotypes related to minorities, which can be promoted and generated in several ways. The historically negative depiction of Blacks in media has contributed to a negative image of Blacks in the US society and furthered normative stereotypes about both Black men and women (Chaney & Robertson, 2013). For example, Peffley and Hurwitz (2013) argue that due to the negative stereotypes of Black men generated by the media, most Whites believe that Black is more inclined to engage in criminal activity and shall receive more punitive treatment in the criminal justice system. One of the results of negative stereotypes that often are promoted about Blacks, they are often subjected to racial profiling and implicit bias by the police (Graziano et al., 2010).

Martin's death generated a massive discussion regarding racial profiling and implicit bias in the criminal justice system towards Blacks. This racial profiling and implicit bias have negative implications for Blacks who have committed crimes and Blacks who have been living their daily lives and have not committed any crime. For example, several scholars have highlighted the prevalence of racial profiling in traffic stops (Smith & Petrocelli, 2001) and the relationship between racial profiling and police officers' use of force when interacting with individuals in the streets (Legewie, 2016). Thus, for young Black men, racial profiling and implicit bias can change everyday situations into life-or-death situations (Ferguson & McClendon, 2013).

Martin's death highlighted that Blacks, especially young Black men, are often seen as an imminent threat because of their race and because of the negative stereotypes, young Blacks are often racially profiled and faced with life-or-death situations in their everyday life due to their race (Desai, 2019). A study by Thomas and Blackmon (2015) found that the Martin shooting invoked great worry among Black parents about the safety of their children. After Martin's death, many of the parents reported that they discussed the violent incident with their children and talked about what their children should do if faced with a similar situation. Thus, the racial profiling and implicit bias perpetuated by society and police contribute to social inequality and injustice for Blacks (Teasly et al., 2018), because it furthers the idea of how Blacks are not treated the same as other races and have to take specific precautions when conducting their everyday life (Thomas and Blackmon, 2015).

The media and news coverage have historically played a large part in creating an image of Black men and have continued to do so after Martin's death. Although the depiction of Martin's death varies across news outlets, several scholars highlight the influence that media coverage of cases of racial profiling and implicit bias has on society. Specifically, the media depicts the individuals who experienced racial profiling and implicit bias during encounters with the police (Graziano et al., 2010). The Martin case not only contributes to highlighting the implicit bias and racial profiling but also created further discussion in which modalities Blacks are depicted in media contribute to the negative stereotypes, which fuels the normative biases that facilitate implicit bias and racial profiling.

Police Brutality

Beyond engaging society in further discussion racial profiling and implicit bias in society the criminal justice system, Martin's death also brought to light what role authority has in the oppression against Blacks. Zimmerman was a member of the neighborhood watch and had before the shooting expressed interest in being a police officer. In his position of authority, Zimmerman utilized this power to interrupt Martin while walking back from the local store. Zimmerman's positions of authority and membership in the neighborhood watched, as well as his acquittal, further the discussion among the public on the use of force and brutality that authority positions utilize against Blacks, especially by police officers.

Extensive research further investigates the modalities of police brutality and police's use of force (Nix et al., 2017; Terrill & Reisig, 2003; Worden, 2015). For example, scholars have investigated the impact characteristics of the officers have on their use of force, noting that officers with higher education are less likely to use force (Garner et al., 2002; Lim et al. 2014, Paoline & Terrill, 2004, 2007; Terrill & Mastrofski, 2002). Other studies have focused on understating the situational factors which impact officers' use of force. For example, scholars argue that police are more likely to use force upon individuals who are from lower social classes, individuals who are under the influence of alcohol or drugs, mentally ill, or are non-compliant or disrespectful, when there is evidence that a crime has been committed or when the suspects are armed (Johnson, 2011; Engel et al., 2000; McCluskey & Terrill, 2005). In addition to these factors, scholars have begun to explore in-depth the racial dynamics of police brutality and the overuse of force during the last couple of years. Much of this scholarship highlights that non-Whites, especially Blacks experience police brutality at higher rates than other races (Brunson & Miller 2006; Nix et al., 2017; Russell-Brown, 1998).

Martin's death generated a widespread media response that called for further investigation and critical assessment of authorities' use of force against Blacks, specifically police officers' overuse of force. Martin's death and the responses after the death created a platform that highlighted the many lives lost to police brutality and the failures of the criminal justices system to address these issues and hold the officers who use excessive force to be accountable for their actions. There are many reasons why officers have not been held accountable for their overuse of force. For example, there is a lack of accurate data on the use of force (Fyfe, 2002), and the boundaries of when excessive force is used could be blurred by police officers' own recollection of the encounters when force is used (Dick, 2005). When Zimmerman shot Martin, his actions, to many, displayed an overuse of force and although not being a police officer, Zimmerman was in a position of authority as a part of the neighborhood watch group and resident of the neighborhood. Thus when using his position of authority and administering an overuse of force, and subsequently being acquitted for the shooting, the case became a prime example of how violence towards Black men is not taken seriously by society and the criminal justice system. After Martin's death, several other young Black men were victims of excessive use of force by police officers. Many of the officers in these altercations did not suffer legal repercussions, and scholars have argued that this is an example of how racism is systematically embedded within the criminal justice system and society, noting that Blacks' lives are not valued the same as lives in the eyes of the law.

Abolish or Defund the Police

As a part of the reaction to Martin's death, the "Black Lives Matter" movement was developed which challenged the practices of several institutions in society (Day, 2015). Most of these social movements highlight the systematic racism embedded in schools and the criminal justice system (Rickford, 2016). One of the implications of this focus has specifically related to law enforcement and their claims of practicing procedural justice. Racial profiling and police brutality are just some of the notions questioned within law enforcement practices and have led to a widespread call for questioning of the police. As a result of the reactions to the extensive violence towards Black bodies since Martin, social movements and activists have called for abolishing or defunding the police (Dowd, 2021; Seigel, 2017).

Scholars have recently begun to explore the calls for abolishing or defunding the police to understand if this could be the answer to improving racial justice (Lum et al., 2021). Although offering mixed results of the positives and negatives with abolishing or defunding the police, the core idea of improving police conduct, racial justice, and procedural justice has become a topic heavy discussed by many scholars and activists (Jacobs et al., 2021; Jefferson-Bullock & Exum, 2020; Weichselbaum & Lewis, 2020). Martin's death was not the ultimate catalyst for calls to defund or abolish the police. However, Martin's death and the reactions to his death created a platform in which racial injustice began to be discussed on social media and on the streets. Martin's death, the initial lack of effort to investigate, and the acquittal of Zimmerman highlight the systematic and cultural practices which further highlight the embeddedness of race (Dowd, 2021). More specifically, it highlighted that for Blacks, everyday activities could turn into an encounter with the police, which ultimately can lead to death, much often only because of racial dynamics between Blacks and police officers.

Blue Lives Matter

As society called for a more critical examination of criminal justice, racial justice, and police conduct through social activism and social movements such as the Black Lives Matter movement, another movement was formed to support the police. This movement is known as the "Blue Lives Matter" movement and was created as a countermovement to the "Black Lives Matter" movement (Mason, 2020; Solomon & Martin, 2019). After the shooting of another Black boy, Michael Brown, in 2014, the "Blue Lives Matter" movement was created to provide police officers support, raise money for legal fees, and support families of fallen officers. Specifically, the "Blue Lives Matter" movement aims to help officers and their families, which they believe are "targeted" by the "Black Lives Matter" Movement. Since the creation of

The "Blue Lives Matter" movement, the organization has maintained a presence on social media, both having national and local "Blue Lives Matter" groups on social media (Solomon & Martin, 2019).

While the "Black Lives Matter" and the "Blue Lives matter" movements share similar goals in that they aim to have generated after government-community relationships, the means of such they use and the perceptions of how to approach these goals differ (Solomon & Martin, 2019). One specific idea that the "Blue Lives Matter" movement has brought forward in the discussion of police officers rights is the notion of including police officers and other first responders as a protected victim category, specifically in an expansion of the hate crime statutes (Gray, 2017; Olson, 2017). Currently, four states in the US have adopted reforms to include officers in these hate crime statutes. This is the first successful effort in expanding a victim category to include representatives of the state. Although some argue that these reforms have been beneficial for police officers, some scholars argue that these reforms pin Blacks and police officers against each other and further ignites conflict between the two (Mason, 2020). Scholars argue that the creation of the "Blue Lives Matter" as a countermovement to the "Black Lives Matter" movement not only meant that their agenda of the movement was to support police officers and their families, but also that it brought adverse reactions towards the work created by "Black Lives Matter" movement (Solomon et al., 2021). Although the messages and ways of attaining the goals of better government-community relationships vary between the movements, scholars have found that strong support for one of the movements is not a predictor for weak support of the other movement (Thomas, 2021).

Although the "Blue Lives Matter" movement was created two years after Martin's death, there are clear connections between the social reactions after Martin's death and the creation of the "Blue Lives Matter" movement. Since many argue that the "Blue Lives Matter" movement was specifically created as a reaction to the "Black Lives Matter" movement, the support for police which the organization is promoted is, according to some scholars, tangled up with notions that counter racial justice such as ethnonationalism (Solomon et al., 2021). Martin's death highlighted racial justice and the idea that Black lives are not valued as highly as other lives due to the continuous disparate treatment in the criminal justice system and the mean lives lost to police brutality. When the "Blue Lives Matter" movement utilized a similar name as the "Black Lives Matter" movement and specifically highlighted their support for police officers but also in many contexts framed their organizations as counter-organization to the "Black Lives Matter" movement, the "Blue Lives Matter" movement also became a counter organization for racial justice.

SOLUTIONS AND RECOMMENDATIONS

Racism is a notion that has caused disparate treatment of racial minorities for several decades in the United States. Martin's death highlighted many of the issues present in today's society driven by racial injustices. The fact that Martin was a young Black boy who was shot on his way home after a quick visit to a local convenience store by a man in an authority position highlights how racial minorities, especially Black men, can be exposed to life and death situations while performing everyday tasks. The subsequent acquittal of Zimmerman further illuminated accountability issues for racial profiling, implicit bias, and other racist notions that have negative implications for racial minorities.

There is no quick fix or easy solution to the systematic racism that takes place in American society. However, Martin's death showed that large-scale engagement and reactions from society make a difference in racial justice visibility. Martin's death created a platform that has been used to highlight several cases of racial injustice all across America, most often racial injustice caused by actors in authority positions such as the police. Activists have called for the abolition or defunding of the police as one of the suggested actions to improve racial justice and disparate treatments against Blacks and racial minorities. Although the scholarly work provided mixed arguments for the call to defund or abolish the police, it is clear that the current practices within various societal institutions, such as the criminal justice system, needs to be further investigated by scholars, policymakers, and politicians to ensure that actions are taken, and efforts are being made to profile a society where no one should fear for their life after going the local convenience store to buy a drink and some candy.

FUTURE RESEARCH DIRECTIONS

Extensive research has been conducted in relation to the implications of Martins death (Brunson & Miller, 2006; Lee, 2013; Teasley et al., 2017; Thomas & Blackmon, 2015), how his death was depicted in media (Graeff et al., 2014; Hodges, 2015; Lawson, 2012; Madison, 2015) and society's reaction to the case (Lane et al., 2020; Torres et al., 2017; Umoja Noble, 2014). Despite discussing different aspects of Martin's death, this literature highlights many significant implications and impacts his death brought. Despite the existence of studies investigating the impacts and implications, many notions could be further investigated. For example, the current scholarship would benefit from more in-depth examinations of how negative racial stereotypes inform police conduct and police's use of force. More can be learned about the hidden and implicit biases towards racial manticores by further understanding the creation, adaptation, and internalization of negative racial stereotypes among police officers and other criminal justice professionals. Furthermore, by understanding more about negative racial stereotypes and how it informs biases, more knowledge can be gained on how to dismantle and prohibit the adoption of these stereotypes.

CONCLUSION

There has been a wide range of reactions and implications due to the death of Martin. News media and social media played a central role in how the case was portrayed and talked about among society members, activists, scholars, politicians, and other actors. Although death rarely brings any positives, Martin's death and the reactions afterward did create a platform where racial justice took center stage. Throughout decades of differential and disparate treatment in many different aspects of society, Martin's death highlighted the dangers and life and death situations Blacks face while conducting their day-to-day lives due to society's racial dynamics. Negative racial stereotypes often inform these racial dynamics, resulting in differential treatment manifested through racial profiling and implicit bias against Blacks.

When Martin's death became publicized, there were many different narratives and aspects of the case discussed in the news media. For example, notions such as racial inequality, "Stand your ground" laws, the right to carry guns, and police and criminal justice accountability were some of the notions often discussed. Furthermore, the reactions on social media after the death of Martin and the subsequent acquittal of Zimmerman lead to the mobilization of social movement and activism, which have generated one of the largest social movements in US history, the "Black Lives Matter" movement. Society's response to Martin's death had both short-term and long-term implications for how racial justice is talked about. For example, Martin's death publicly highlighted the racial profiling and implicit biases displayed by authority figures and highlighted notions such as police brutality and the criminal justice system's lack of accountability for overuse of forces and disparate treatments of Blacks.

The news media and social media aided the widespread share of knowledge and called for action related to racial justice by highlighting various problematic aspects in society, displayed in the Martin case. However, beyond creating a platform to discuss racial injustice, news media have historically contributed to generating the negative racial stereotype that feeds the systematic racism embedded in American society for decades. Thus, although contributing to illuminating the need for a debate on racial justice, news media specifically has and is still playing a significant role in how Blacks are depicted in society and continue to feed society with negative stereotypes, which ultimately contribute to disparate treatment of Blacks.

REFERENCES

Botelho, G. (2012, May 23). *What happened the night Trayvon Martin died.* CNN. https://www.cnn.com/2012/05/18/justice/florida-teen-shooting-details/index.html

Brunson, R. K., & Miller, J. (2006). Young black men and urban policing in the United States. *British Journal of Criminology*, *46*(4), 613–640. doi:10.1093/bjc/azi093

Catalfamo, C. (2006). Stand your ground: Florida's castle doctrine for the twenty-first century. *Rutgers JL & Pub. Pol'y*, *4*, 504.

Cesario, J., Johnson, D. J., & Terrill, W. (2019). Is there evidence of racial disparity in police use of deadly force? Analyses of officer-involved fatal shootings in 2015–2016. *Social Psychological & Personality Science*, *10*(5), 586–595. doi:10.1177/1948550618775108

Chaney, C., & Robertson, R. V. (2013). Racism and police brutality in America. *Journal of African American Studies*, *17*(4), 480–505. doi:10.100712111-013-9246-5

CNN. (2021, February 17). *Trayvon Martin Shooting Fast Facts*. CNN. https://www.cnn.com/2013/06/05/us/trayvon-martin-shooting-fast-facts/index.html

Cohn Aizenman, H. (2012). Pretrial publicity in post-trayvon martin world. *Criminal Justice*, *27*(3), 12–17.

Day, E. (2015, July 19). #Blacklivesmatter: The birth of a new Civil Rights Movement. *The Guardian*. https://www.theguardian.com/world/2015/jul/19/blacklivesmatter-birth-civil-rights-movement

Desai, S. R. (2019). Humanizing Trayvon Martin: Racial profiling, implicit biases, and teacher education. *Urban Education*, *54*(8), 1031–1057. doi:10.1177/0042085916646609

Dick, P. (2005). Dirty work designations: How police officers account for their use of coercive force. *Human Relations*, *58*(11), 1363–1390. doi:10.1177/0018726705060242

Donelson, R. (2017). Blacks, Cops, and the State of Nature. *Ohio St. J. Crim. L.*, *15*, 183.

Douglas Brown, K. (2015). *Stand your ground: Black bodies and the justice of God*. Orbis Books.

Dowd, N. E. (2021). Black Lives Matter: Trayvon Martin, the Abolition of Juvenile Justice and# BlackYouthMatter. *University of Florida Journal of Law and Public Policy*, *31*(43), 43–57.

Engel, R. S., Sobol, J., & Wordon, R. E. (2000). Further exploration of the demeanor hypothesis: The interaction effects of suspects' characteristics and demeanor on police behavior. *Justice Quarterly, 17*(2), 235–258. doi:10.1080/07418820000096311

Fabregat, E., & Beck, T. J. (2019). On the erasure of race in control culture discourse: A case study of Trayvon Martin's role in the Black Lives Matter Movement. *Social Identities, 25*(6), 759–774. doi:10.1080/13504630.2019.1572502

Ferguson, S. C., & McClendon, J. H. (2013). Indignity and death: Philosophical commentary on white terror, black death, and the Trayvon Martin tragedy. In G. Yancy & G. Jones (Eds.), *Pursuing Trayvon Martin: Historical contexts and contemporary manifestations of racial dynamics* (pp. 41–58). Lexington Books.

Fulton, S., & Martin, T. (2017). *Rest in power: the enduring life of Trayvon Martin*. Spiegel & Grau.

Fyfe, J. J. (2002). Too many missing cases: Holes in our knowledge about police use of force. *Justice Research and Policy, 4*(1-2), 87–102. doi:10.3818/JRP.4.1.2002.87

Garner, J. H., Maxwell, C. D., & Heraux, C. G. (2002). Characteristics associated with the prevalence and severity of force used by the police. *Justice Quarterly, 19*(4), 705–746. doi:10.1080/07418820200095401

Graeff, E., Stempeck, M., & Zuckerman, E. (2014). The battle for 'Trayvon Martin': Mapping a media controversy online and off-line. *First Monday, 19*(2). Advance online publication. doi:10.5210/fm.v19i2.4947

Gray, S. (2017). "Blue Lives Matter" laws: The extension of hate crime statutes to include law enforcement. *Kentucky Law Journal (Lexington, Ky.)*.

Graziano, L., Schuck, A., & Martin, C. (2010). Police misconduct, media coverage, and public perceptions of racial profiling: An experiment. *Justice Quarterly, 27*(1), 52–76. doi:10.1080/07418820902763046

Hodges, A. (2015). Ideologies of language and race in US media discourse about the Trayvon Martin shooting. *Language in Society, 44*(3), 401–423. doi:10.1017/S004740451500024X

Jacobs, L. A., Kim, M. E., Whitfield, D. L., Gartner, R. E., Panichelli, M., Kattari, S. K., Downey, M. M., McQueen, S. S., & Mountz, S. E. (2021). Defund the police: Moving towards an anti-carceral social work. *Journal of Progressive Human Services, 32*(1), 37–62. doi:10.1080/10428232.2020.1852865

Jefferson-Bullock, J., & Exum, J. J. (2020). That is Enough Punishment: Situating Defunding the Police Within Antiracist Sentencing Reform. *The Fordham Urban Law Journal*, *48*, 625.

Johnson, R. (2011). Suspect mental disorder and police use of force. *Criminal Justice and Behavior*, *38*(2), 127–145. doi:10.1177/0093854810388160

Justifiable Use of Force. Fla. Stat. Title XLVI, Chapter 776 (2021). http://www.leg.state.fl.us/statutes/index.cfm?App_mode=Display_Statute&URL=0700-0799/0776/0776ContentsIndex.html

Kang, J. (2005). Trojan horses of race. *Harvard Law Review*, *118*, 1490–2005.

Lane, K., Williams, Y., Hunt, A. N., & Paulk, A. (2020). The Framing of Race: Trayvon Martin and the Black Lives Matter Movement. *Journal of Black Studies*, *51*(8), 790–812. doi:10.1177/0021934720946802

Lawson, T. F. (2012). Fresh cut in an old wound a critical analysis of the Trayvon martin killing: The public outcry, the prosecutors' discretion, and the stand your ground law. *University of Florida Journal of Law and Public Policy*, *23*(3), 271–310.

Lee, C. (2013). Making race salient: Trayvon martin and implicit bias in not yet post-racial society. *North Carolina Law Review*, *91*(5), 1555–1612.

Legewie, J. (2016). Racial profiling and use of force in police stops: How local events trigger periods of increased discrimination. *American Journal of Sociology*, *122*(2), 379–424. doi:10.1086/687518

Lim, H., Fridell, L. A., & Lee, H. (2014). The impact of supervision and neighborhood context on police use of less-lethal force: A multi-level analysis. *Journal of Police Studies*, *14*, 155–182.

Lum, C., Koper, C. S., & Wu, X. (2021). Can We Really Defund the Police? A Nine-Agency Study of Police Response to Calls for Service. *Police Quarterly*.

Madison, E. (2015). Media Portrayals of the Trayvon Martin Tragedy. *Cultural Studies « Critical Methodologies*, *15*(4), 278–282.

Mason, G. (2020). Blue Lives Matter and Hate Crime Law. *Race and Justice*.

McCluskey, J. D., & Terrill, W. (2005). Departmental and civilian complaints as predictors of police coercion. *Policing*, *28*(3), 513–529. doi:10.1108/13639510510614582

McLaughlin, E. C., Lynch, J., & Simon, D. (2019, December 5). *George Zimmerman sues Trayvon Martin's parents and others for more than $100 million*. CNN. https://www.cnn.com/2019/12/04/us/george-zimmerman-lawsuit-trayvon-martin-mother/index.html

Nix, J., Campbell, B. A., Byers, E. H., & Alpert, G. P. (2017). A bird's eye view of civilians killed by police in 2015: Further evidence of implicit bias. *Criminology & Public Policy*, *16*(1), 309–340. doi:10.1111/1745-9133.12269

Olson, L. (2017). Blue lives have always mattered: The usurping of hate crime laws for an unintended and unnecessary purpose. *St Mary's Law Review on Race and Social Justice*, *20*, 13–55.

Paoline, E., & Terrill, W. (2004). Women police officers and the use of coercion. *Women & Criminal Justice*, *15*(3-4), 97–119. doi:10.1300/J012v15n03_05

Paoline, E. III, & Terrill, W. (2007). Police education, experience, and the use of force. *Criminal Justice and Behavior*, *34*(2), 179–196. doi:10.1177/0093854806290239

Peffley, M., & Hurwitz, J. (2013). Persuasion and resistance: race and the death penalty in America. In H. T. Greene & S. Gabbidon (Eds.), *Race and crime: a text/reader* (1st ed., pp. 355–366). Sage.

Rickford, R. (2016). Black lives matter: Toward a modern practice of mass struggle. *New Labor Forum*, *25*(1), 34–42. doi:10.1177/1095796015620171

Risse, M., & Zeckhauser, R. (2004). Racial profiling. *Philosophy & Public Affairs*, *32*(2), 131–170. doi:10.1111/j.1088-4963.2004.00009.x

Russell-Brown, K. (1998). *The color of crime: Racial hoaxes, white fear, Black protectionism, police harassment and other macroaggressions*. New University Press.

Seigel, M. (2017). The dilemma of 'racial profiling': An abolitionist police history. *Contemporary Justice Review*, *20*(4), 474–490. doi:10.1080/10282580.2017.1383773

Smith, A. (2021). *Breaking News: The Presence Of Framing In Partisan Cable News Network's Coverage Of Officers Murdering Black Victims* [Master Thesis]. University of Central Florida.

Smith, M. R., & Petrocelli, M. (2001). Racial profiling? A multivariate analysis of police traffic stop data. *Police Quarterly*, *4*(1), 4–27. doi:10.1177/109861101004001001

Smith, P. K. (2015). Black lives matter: A new movement takes shape. *International Socialist Review*, 96.

Solomon, J., Kaplan, D., & Hancock, L. E. (2021). Expressions of American White Ethnonationalism in Support for "Blue Lives Matter". *Geopolitics*, *26*(3), 946–966. doi:10.1080/14650045.2019.1642876

Solomon, J., & Martin, A. (2019). Competitive victimhood as a lens to reconciliation: An analysis of the black lives matter and blue lives matter movements. *Conflict Resolution Quarterly*, *37*(1), 7–31. doi:10.1002/crq.21262

Teasley, M., Schiele, J., Adams, C., & Okilwa, N. (2017). Trayvon Martin: Racial Profiling, Black Male Stigma, and Social Work Practice. *Social Work*, *63*, 1–9. PMID:29136232

Terrill, W., & Mastrofski, S. D. (2002). Situational and officer-based determinants of police coercion. *Justice Quarterly*, *19*(2), 215–249. doi:10.1080/07418820200095221

Terrill, W., & Reisig, M. D. (2003). Neighborhood context and police use of force. *Journal of Research in Crime and Delinquency*, *40*(3), 291–321. doi:10.1177/0022427803253800

Thomas, A. (2021). *Attitudes Toward the Black & Blue Lives Matter Movements.* https://mcstor.library.milligan.edu/bitstream/handle/11558/5827/Thomas_Alexandria_20210413.pdf?sequence=3&isAllowed=y

Thomas, A. J., & Blackmon, S. M. (2015). The Influence of the Trayvon Martin Shooting on Racial Socialization Practices of African American Parents. *The Journal of Black Psychology*, *41*(1), 75–89. doi:10.1177/0095798414563610

Torres, M., Cannito-Coville, M., & Rodriguez, D. (2017). Trayvon Revisited: Race, Fear, and Affect in the Death of Trayvon Martin. *Sociological Forum*, *32*(S1), 1112–1126. doi:10.1111ocf.12369

Umoja Noble, S. (2014). Teaching Trayvon. *The Black Scholar*, *44*(1), 12–29. doi:10.1080/00064246.2014.11641209

Ward, C. V. (2014). Stand your ground and self-defense. *American Journal of Criminal Law*, *42*, 89.

Weichselbaum, S., & Lewis, N. (2020). *Support for defunding the police department is growing. Here's why it's not a silver bullet.* The Marshall Project.

Worden, R. E. (2015). *The causes of police brutality: Theory and evidence on police use of force.* Routledge.

ADDITIONAL READING

Alvarez, L., & Buckley, C. (2013, July 13). Zimmerman Is Acquitted in Trayvon Martin Killing. *New York Times*. https://www.nytimes.com/2013/07/14/us/george-zimmerman-verdict-trayvon-martin.html?pagewanted=1&emc=eta1

Francescani, C. (2012). *George Zimmerman: Prelude to a shooting*. Reuters. https://www.reuters.com/article/us-usa-florida-shooting-zimmerman-idUSBRE83O18H20120425

Holmes, M. D., & Smith, B. W. (2008). *Race and police brutality: Roots of an urban dilemma*. SUNY Press.

Littlefield, M. B. (2008). The media as a system of racialization: Exploring images of African American women and the new racism. *The American Behavioral Scientist*, *51*(5), 675–685. doi:10.1177/0002764207307747

Omi, M., & Winant, H. (2014). *Racial formation in the United States*. Routledge. doi:10.4324/9780203076804

Rowe, M. (2012). *Policing, race and racism*. Routledge. doi:10.4324/9781843924685

Russell-Brown, K. (2009). *The color of crime*. New York University Press.

Russell-Brown, K., & Davis, A. J. (2017). Making Implicit Bias Explicit: Black Men and the Police. *Policing the Black Man: Arrest, Prosecution and Prison,* 136-61.

KEY TERMS AND DEFINITIONS

Abolish the Police: Refers to advocating for replacing police with other forms and systems of public safety.

Acquittal: Refers to when a person is determined by the court of not being guilty of the crime they were charged with.

Defund the Police: Refers to advocating for a divesting funds from law enforcement agencies and relocating these funds to other forms of public safety and community support.

Ethnonationalism: A version of nationalism where nationality and nation is defined in terms of ethnicity.

Implicit Bias: Refers to negative beliefs and attitudes against racial minorities.

Police Brutality: Refers to excessive or unwarranted use of force by law enforcement.

Racial Justice: Systematic fair treatment of all races and ethnicities which leads to equal opportunities and outcomes for all.

Racial Profiling: Refers to police-initiated actions based on race, ethnicity, or nationality instead of individual behavior, leading to the belief that an individual is partaking in illegal activities.

Systematic Racism: Refers to racism that is embedded within the laws and regulations of organizations, institutions, and society.

Chapter 7
Crime in Perugia:
The Murder of Meredith Kercher

Beatrice Ugolini
University "N. Cusano", Rome, Italy & British Society of Criminology, UK

EXECUTIVE SUMMARY

On the night between 1st and 2nd November 2007, a 21-year-old English student called Meredith Kercher was killed in Perugia, Italy. After a long and controversial court case, the American, Amanda Knox, and the Italian, Raffaele Sollecito, after initially being found guilty, were acquitted of the crime. The only convict remains the Ivorian Rudi Guede. The case aroused unexpected media attention and international outcries. Many questions on the whole affair remain unresolved, which has contributed to adding conspiracy-like theories to standard criminological analysis. This chapter intends to provide a reconstruction of the events, highlighting the reasons that explain the case's great media attention.

INTRODUCTION

On the night between 1st and 2nd November 2007, in a student apartment in Via della Pergola 7, Perugia a twenty-one-year-old Englishwoman called Meredith Kercher died after being stabbed in the throat. The American Amanda Knox, Meredith's roommate, the Italian Raffaele Sollecito, a computer engineering student, with whom Amanda was in a relationship, and the Ivorian Rudi Hermann Guede, Amanda's acquaintance, were accused of the crime. Both the victim and Amanda attended courses at "Università per Stranieri di Perugia", as part of an Erasmus project. Sollecito's lawyer was Giulia Bongiorno, now a member of parliament,

DOI: 10.4018/978-1-7998-9668-5.ch007

who is known for defending the famous Italian politician Giulio Andreotti from accusations of mafia.

After a long and very controversial court case, Sollecito and Knox were acquitted of the crime. The only convict, "in concerted action with unknown persons", remains Rudi Guede, from the Ivory Coast who refuses to confess. The motive, never fully understood, is thought to be sexual assault and robbery. The case aroused unexpected media attention and international outcries. The Italian judicial system was harshly criticised by the Anglo-American press which highlighted the numerous errors made during their investigation. Despite being acquitted, Amanda Knox, nicknamed "Foxy Knoxy", became the object of unhealthy curiosity for her casual sex life and disturbing beauty. The story becomes the subject of films and documentaries such as, for example, "Amanda Knox: Murder on Trial in Italy" (2011), "Meredith - The Face of an Angel" (2014), "Amanda Knox" (2016). Public opinion is divided over the girl's innocence, while the victim, Meredith, seems to have almost been forgotten.

Many questions on the whole affair remain unresolved, which has contributed to adding conspiracy-like theories to the standard criminological analysis. This chapter intends to provide a reconstruction of the events, highlighting the reasons that explain the case's great media attention.

RECONSTRUCTION OF THE CRIME

According to what was written in the judgement of the Court of First Instance, Meredith Kercher's body was found on the morning of 2nd November 2007, shortly after 1.00 pm, covered by a quilt. The young woman was half-naked, with her T-shirt rolled up over her breasts. On the body there were signs of strangulation, suffocation and numerous bruises. The cause of death, however, was a cut to the neck, which caused blood to build up in the airways, leading to asphyxiation. Other non-fatal wounds were also present on the arms, hands, abdomen and legs. One of the vaginal swabs indicated the presence of biological material, but it was not possible, from the gynecological examination, to clearly establish whether sex was consensual or not (Court of Assizes of Perugia, 4-5/12/2009, pp. 103-111).

When Meredith's lifeless body was found, officers of the Italian postal and telecommunications police of Perugia were also present, having arrived shortly before 13.00. The presence of the police was due to having found Amanda's mobile phone, a few hours earlier, and later a second mobile phone of another roommate. Both phones were found in the garden of Elisabetta Lana's house, in Via Sperandio. The house and garden are surrounded by trees and is in the Parco S. Angelo area, a short distance from Via della Pergola 7: by car it would only take a few minutes to get there and on foot 15-20 minutes, maybe even less. Amanda Knox and Raffaele

Sollecito tell the Italian postal police that they are waiting for the Carabinieri, who they had called due to upon returning to Via della Pergola that morning, they had found the door of the house open and a broken window (Court of Assizes, pp. 12-15). The death was initially dated, by the coroner, to be between the evening of 2nd and the night of 3rd November. Subsequently, however, the time of death was set between 9.00 pm of 1st November, when the victim greets a friend near her home, and 12.10 am of 2nd November, when Meredith's mobile phone receives a call a using a phone tower located in Via Sperandio.

A few days later, a fourth person appears to enter the scene. At dawn on 6th November, in fact, Patrick Lumumba, manager of the club "Le Chic", well known among university students in Perugia, where Amanda works as a part-time waitress, was arrested together with Sollecito and Knox. Lumumba's summons was directly caused by Knox who, after yet another interrogation, revealed him as Meredith's killer. However, the young American reported that she remembers only confused flashes, almost dreamlike images, perhaps due to the drugs her had taken; she also ambiguously declared that she did not know whether Raffaele was at the house or not. Lumumba was later completely exonerated, following both Amanda's retraction of her statement and the investigation carried out. What, however, would be the reason for Lumumba's involvement? Amanda would claim to have imagined his presence at the crime scene, following a text message she received on 1st November in which he wrote "see you later". The owner of the club would argue that the message was to warn Amanda that she didn't need to go to work at the club that night, as there was no one there. Knox justified herself by saying that she made those statements "under stress and in the unusual situation that had arisen" (Court of Assizes, pp. 55-56).

Nonetheless, a "fourth man", present at the crime scene, really exists and was identified following forensic analysis: he is the 21-year-old Rudi Herman Guede from the Ivory Coast, aided and then adopted by an entrepreneur from Perugia. When he found out that he had been identified as a suspect he tried to flee to Germany, as he already had a criminal record, but was stopped in Düsseldorf. Guede goes on to claim to have met Amanda and Meredith at the "Le Chic" club and to have had an appointment with Meredith, at her home, on the evening of 1st November. The young man claimed he had no sexual intercourse with the victim. That evening, while he was in the bathroom, Guede declares, he heard someone enter the house, and then heard some screams. Leaving the bathroom, the young man claims to have seen a man with a knife in his hand and glimpsed a woman, with the attacker. Following very hard questioning by the investigators, Guede recognized Sollecito and Knox as the two people he saw; and also claimed to have tried to save Meredith by stopping the bleeding with some towels. His friends, however did not confirm his vision of his movements of 1st November and Meredith's friends also casted doubt on his possible flirtation with the young woman and, above all, about the alleged appointment on the evening of 1st November. According to the testimonies of the victim's closest friends, in fact, Meredith had recently started a relationship, which she really cared about, with a young man named Giacomo Silenzi, who lived on the lower floor of the same house in Via della Pergola 7. All the victim's friend excluded the fact that Meredith had ever talked to them about Rudi Guede and declared that they did not know him (Court of Assizes, p. 24).

Footprints were found in the corridor, coming from Meredith's room and going towards the door of the house, left by a shoe stained with the victim's blood. Initially these footprints were considered compatible with Raffaele Sollecito's shoes. Subsequent investigations however lead to excluding this theory and show that they are, instead, shoes of the same type, brand and size as those that could have been in a shoe box found in Rudi Guede's home. According to the judgement of the Court of First Instance, it appears unlikely that Rudi decided to enter the house in Via della Pergola in a furtive and violent way, as the broken window pane would suggest; further evaluation supported this unlikelihood due to the fact that some of the inhabitants might be present in that house or, some of them could come and surprise Rudi Guede at any moment. Also, according to the judgement of the Court of First Instance, staging broken glass and furtive entrance is carried out by those who, having ready and free access to the house, try to move any suspicion away from themselves, instead directing it instead towards unknown criminals (Court of Assizes, pp. 30-48).

As for Raffaele Sollecito, at first, he declared that he did not spend the entire night of 1st November with Amanda. However, after this version of events was rejected by Jovana Popovic, his friend and alibi, he declared a second version to the Preliminary Investigations Magistrate, in which he admits to having spent the evening with Knox, but did not remember whether Amanda had gone out or not. Sollecito also justified his confusion with his frequent use of cannabis, which, he said, served to allay anxiety. The version according to which Amanda and Raffaele remained together, in Raffaele's house, until 10.00 am on 2nd November was again later contradicted. In fact, the witness Antonio Curatolo, a homeless man initially considered reliable stated he had seen Amanda Knox and Raffaele Sollecito in the area of Piazza Grimana, the square in front of the Università per Stranieri where there is a basketball court (Court of Assizes, p. 69). The sentence of the Supreme Court would later invalidate the reliability of the homeless person's statement, due to the decline of his cognitive faculties, caused by constant heroin abuse (Court of Cassation, 26/03/2013, p. 50).

According to the Public Prosecutor Giuliano Mignini, the motive for the crime would be a group sexual game, a sort of party in which the victim, who seemed to lead a more reserved and secluded life, was dragged in by force. The erotic game then went on to become extreme and violent, due to both the drugs taken by all the accused and the resistance of the victim. According to the hypothesis of the Public Prosecutor, Meredith found herself kneeling in front of the wardrobe, while Rudi attempted to rape her; Sollecito firmly held her arm to stop her moving, while Amanda was in front of her with a knife in her hand. The situation hastily worsened, also due to the vigorous opposition of the victim: and it was Amanda, according to this accusatory hypothesis, who delivered the fatal blow.

According to the judgement of the Court of First Instance, Rudi let himself get carried away by a situation perceived as full of sexual solicitations and, yielding to his own lust, tried to satisfy his impulses by going to Meredith's room, who was alone in her room. However, it is not known whether Rudi went to Meredith's room on his own initiative or, instead, at the request of Amanda and/or Raffaele. The reaction and refusal of the young woman were probably heard by Amanda and Raffaele who intervened for aiding and abetting Rudi thus becoming, with him, Meredith's aggressors (Court of Assizes, pp. 391-392).

Amanda, therefore, was also at the scene of the crime and she too participated in the violence against Meredith, bound to Raffaele and Rudi by the only goal pursued together: to subjugate Meredith, allowing Rudi to sexually abuse her, creating a situation of violence and eroticism. (Court of Assizes, p. 405). This reconstruction was confirmed on the whole by the Judge for the Preliminary Hearing Paolo Micheli, albeit with an important distinction. In fact, Micheli rejected the idea that the murder was premeditated, since both Amanda and Raffaele had already made plans for that evening and only at the last minute, for different reasons, did they learn that they would be free (Mastronardi & Castellini, 2009, pp. 10-14).

MEDIA HYPE

In the judgement of the Court of First Instance, the Court of Assizes of Perugia sentenced Amanda Knox to 26 years and Raffaele Sollecito to 25 years of imprisonment, for aggravated voluntary murder (including sexual violence), violation of the law on weapons, theft and the simulation of the felony. Amanda Knox alone was also convicted of slander. The reasons for this sentence were, in short, the following: firstly, the falsity of the alibi, since no one confirmed that the two were not in the house in Via della Pergola on the evening of 1st November. Secondly, simulating a break-in via the window: staged in order to mislead investigators about the way in which the perpetrator of the crime entered the house. Her involvement in the crime was demonstrated by the fact that a single attacker would not be able undress the young woman and perform the sexual acts nor, above all, cut the hooks of the bra: this action, which must be carried out by standing behind the young woman, requires the use of both hands. In fact, if the attacker had been alone the victim would have had the opportunity to free herself, also because Meredith had a strong physique and practiced karate. DNA analysis also revealed the presence of Sollecito's DNA on the hook of Meredith's bra.

The judgement of the Court of Appeal completely overturned the the judgement of the Court of First Instance. The alleged co-perpetrators of the crime were, in fact, acquitted and released from prison in 2011 by the Court of Assizes of Appeal of Perugia for not having committed the crime, in terms of the murder; for Amanda Knox, however the three-year sentence for slander against Patrick Lumumba was confirmed. In the course of that process, an independent forensic investigation, ordered by the Court of Appeal, concluded that much of the DNA evidence that indicated Amanda and Raffaele's guilt was unreliable.

The Court of Cassation, accepting the appeal of the Chief Prosecutor of Perugia, annulled the acquittal in appeal on 26th March 2013 and referred the documents to the Court of Assizes of Appeal of Florence which, in January 2014, again condemned Knox and Sollecito to 28 and 25 years of imprisonment. According to the judgement of the second Court of Appeal of Florence, the murderous will of the attackers, in fact, was evident, as they could not have spared the victim upon going too far: Meredith, therefore, had to be put in a position where she was unable to report the attack. It would be the the Court of Cassation that decisively put an end to the entire judicial proceedings: on 27th March 2015, the Fifth Criminal Section, with judge Gennaro Marasca presiding, annulled the judgement without renvoi for Raffaele Sollecito and Amanda Knox, acquitting them of the crime. This sensational sentence was motivated by the lack of reliable evidence and by the presence of numerous errors made during the investigation: Marasca cites the second paragraph of article 530 of the Italian Criminal Procedure Code according to which the judge may pronounce an acquittal when there is a lack of, insufficient or contradictory evidence that the accused has committed the crime. The judgement made by of the Court of Appeal, in fact, was based on an incomplete data platform, reaching illogical conclusions, contradicting other available evidence, and presented multiple profiles of shortcomings, contradictions and manifest illogicality. In other words, there was no evidence of Amanda and Raffaele's guilt: but a lack of combined proof that featured evidence "beyond reasonable doubt". For the judges of the Italian Supreme Court, therefore, the only confirmed participant in the murder was Rudi Guede.

The Public Prosecutor Giuliano Mignini declared the sentence of the Supreme Court unconventional, although no longer open to challenge in any case, since there is no revision in the event of acquittal, as it would be *unique* in the jurisprudence of the Supreme Court, in the subject of murder. In fact, the Court ruled on merits and not on legitimacy and, therefore, it was not possible to reinstate a judgment of acquittal based on merits. This final judgement, in fact, triggered a series of controversies that represent one of the factors that explain, in part, the media hype which accompanied the case even after the judicial process finished. The main target of criticism is the way the investigation was conducted. The absolute disagreement between the sentences finds, in fact, its origin in the problem of evidence contamination, confirmed by the statements of the two external experts, Conti and Vecchiotti. Paradoxically, the coroner, Dr. Lalli, could only inspect the body at 1 am on 3rd November 2007: being unable to carry out any checks himself because “he was asked to preserve the crime scene as much as possible in order to allow the ‘execution of scientific surveys’ (Court of Assizes, p. 103).

Again in regards to investigation methods, the European Court of Human Rights, with a sentence made on 24th January 2019, ascertains that Italy breached, from a procedural point of view, Art. 3 of the European Convention on Human Rights. The applicant, Amanda Knox, in fact, has denounced various violations relating to the way in which her questioning was conducted, on the night between 5th and 6th November 2007, in the police station of Perugia. During questioning, Knox made the slanderous statements against Lumumba which, according to her, had the sole purpose of interrupting the conduct contrary to her human rights. In summary, the American complains that, on the night in which she went to the police station simply to accompany her then boyfriend Raffaele Sollecito, she was questioned, again without the assistance of a lawyer, twice: once, starting at 1.45 am, by three police officers plus an official who acted as an interpreter; and a second time, starting at 5.45 am, in the presence of the public prosecutor. During questioning, defined as “spontaneous information”, she allegedly suffered not only physical abuse, as an officer gave her two blows to the head, but also abuse of a moral nature. Amanda, in fact, complains of having been threatened with thirty years of prison if she had not spoken out, of having been called a “stupid liar”, of being shouted and yelled at during the interrogation, alternating with moments in which a policeman embraced and caressed her. This situation of extreme psychological pressure, according to Knox, would have induced her to make defamatory statements due to the lack of full possession of one’s faculties, in violation of the right to respect for private life. Regardless of the judgement of the European Court of Human Rights, in the opinion of Gialuz (2019), professor of criminal procedural law at the University of Genoa, the documents cast a truly sinister shadow on the way in which the investigation was conducted in such a delicate case: repeated and prolonged interrogations during the night; completely irrational and heterodox attitudes of an police officer who had hugged the girl and caressed her while she was making the accusatory statements; lack of legal aid; the unorthodox choice of interpreter; short and incomplete reports, in the face of operations lasting up to a few hours (Gialuz, 2019).

The complicated procedural and judicial controversies, however, do not alone justify the extraordinary media attention surrounding this murder. As the British journalist Bill Emmott (2011) notes, «With a British victim and defendants from both America and Italy, media interest was always likely to be strong, but also what happens in these cases is that the national media start to feed off one another, reporting on each other's coverage, responding to each other's coverage, and fanning prejudices about each other's countries». The crime, involving people from four different countries, immediately becomes a case with political and international implications. After the judgement of the Court of First Instance, Washington State Senator Maria Cantwell contacted the State Department and the US Embassy in Rome. The senator criticised the judgement, pointing her finger at the Italian judicial system and accusing the verdict of being a reflection of the anti-Americanism that existed in the country. According to the senator, the trial highlighted a number of flaws in the Italian justice system, including aggressive behaviour to Amanda made by police officers, the fact that the jury was not held in solitary confinement and negligence shown by investigators when collecting evidence. Hillary Clinton, US Secretary of State at the time, declared herself free to continue following the affair and to listen to any complaints. The case was also commented on by ex-secretary of state Madeleine Albright who said she did not think that Perugia's sentence was dictated by anti-American sentiment. The US State Department, in turn, declared that it had no indications that the Italian trial may present irregularities. Both the press and several US legal experts called the verdict "scandalous". The Knox family themselves feed this media hype, giving interviews to the US media and appearing on talk shows (Capponi, 2009).

In Emmott's opinion, however, there is another reason why the crime in Perugia turned into a major media event: the case involved women, and moreover young and attractive women. According to the British journalist, «The idea, encouraged by the veline culture and Bunga-Bunga, that women are either mothers, whores or witches, surely lay behind the prosecutor's description of Ms Knox last week as a lustful, diabolical creature». For many foreign observers, therefore, the trial would have played to the Italian stereotype of a country that encourages sexist and male chauvinist behaviour: a stereotype, moreover, encouraged by the lawyers on both sides (Emmott, 2011).

The crime in Perugia immediately fascinated the public, both in terms of television ratings and newspaper sales. And, at least at the beginning, all the protagonists of the story, not only the female ones, attracted the attention of reporters who therefore started to dig into their young and exuberant lives. Thus, some personality traits of the victim and the accused were formed. Meredith, thanks to the sacrifices her parents had made, had attended an expensive private school; she was diligent, cheerful, smiling and well-liked. Rudi Guede, a 21-year-old from the Ivory Coast, was a decent basketball player with some marks on his criminal record; he had lived in Perugia for over 15 years, practically forgotten by his natural father and helped by a local entrepreneur who even went on to adopt him. He was addicted to cocaine and committed petty theft; he was a decidedly unreliable subject, a proverbial liar and reckless (Mastronardi & Castellini, 2009, pp.42-43). He was nicknamed "The Baron", because Rudi liked to pose, in front of the students, as a mysterious tigger man with equivocal contacts and shrewd intelligence (Garofano & Russell, 2011, pp.131-132). The house in Via della Pergola 7 seemed to Rudi a friendly house, in which he could find easy and immediate hospitality: it was inhabited by friends and girls with whom he could entertain and in whom he had an interest (Court of Assizes, pp. 27-28).

Amanda, nicknamed, since childhood, "Foxy Knoxy", was a "social chameleon": she moved without difficulty in new environments and in a cosmopolitan culture, whirling together knowledge and friendships. Amanda, however, also had a disturbing side: she had unstable, and theatrical mannerisms, she had an impulse to be the centre of attention and, if this did not happen, she assumed an extravagant and excessive conduct; in her work as a waitress, she was lazy and unreliable. Amanda was remembered, by a bizarre coincidence, for the story she wrote a year earlier in which she describes the murder of a raped student, who dies drinking her own blood (Mastronardi & Castellini, 2009, p. 110). As for young men, she was competitive with Meredith. Between Meredith and Amanda initially there was a pleasant coexistence and the two seem to become friends, but then the relationship cooled down. The two young women appear too different in temperament: Amanda was bold and uninhibited, Meredith was reserved; Amanda was chaotic, Meredith tidy; Amanda was perpetually penniless, Meredith more sensible. Raffaele was almost always represented as the classic Italian boy from a good family, lazy, spoiled and inconclusive; having lost his mother, his father was a doctor (Mastronardi & Castellini, 2009, pp. 42-43). He was a quiet, introverted, shy young man who had the habit of carrying a small knife in his pocket. The teachers at the boys boarding school, which he had attended in the past, were shocked by the hardcore, extreme pornographic films, which sometimes also included animals, that he was used to watch. (Corte di Assise, p. 50). His fondness for reading particularly violent stories was emphasised, for example, with the manga "Blood The Last Vampire" (Mastronardi & Castellini, 2009, pp. 103-110).

Since Amanda and Raffaele had met on 25th October 2007 at a classical music concert, where Amanda had gone with Meredith, their relationship and their frequentation was very assiduous and continuous (Corte di Assise, p. 51). Unsurprisingly, the most famous image of Amanda and Raffaele, repeated continuously on Italian televisions, was precisely the one in which they exchanged loving affections outside the house in Via della Pergola, while Meredith's body had just been discovered and the Police are carrying out their investigations. Similar behaviour was also seen at the Police station, as noted in the judgement of the Court of First Instance: "They were very close to each other, they caressed each other, they kissed. An attitude that is not in keeping with the environment and the situation; yet it was put in place, indicative, therefore, of the strong attraction existing between the two which also manifested itself in inappropriate contexts" (Court of Assizes, p. 390)

The hype of the story, however, had its main and undisputed protagonist as Amanda Knox: it was she who catalysed media interest, to the point of making the victim, equally young and beautiful, be forgotten, and to put the other defendants in the background. As argued by Luciano Garofano, criminologist and former commander of the Carabinieri Scientific Investigations Department, the figure of Amanda took on great prominence, favoured by the transgressive vitality and disturbing beauty of the young American (Garofano & Russell, 2011). In 2016, the crime in Perugia was reconstructed, with a project that lasted five years, by American directors Rod Blackhurst and Brian McGinn in the documentary "Amanda Knox", a work produced by Netflix and presented at the Toronto Film Festival. The intent of the documentary was to tell how and why ordinary people become media characters of worldwide interest. The main protagonist, here too, is Amanda who is aware of it, to the point of playing herself, with her character by declaring: "Either I'm guilty or I'm innocent. If I'm guilty I'm a psychopath dressed like a normal person, if I'm innocent I'm you".

The documentary also features Nick Pisa, a British journalist from the "Daily Mail", who followed the case from beginning to end and who managed to find Amanda's diary, written in prison. He candidly admits that journalists often report what they are told without verifying the truthfulness of the facts: otherwise, the risk would be to give the competition an advantage. A statement that sounds rather ironic, considering that today Amanda works as a freelance journalist and blogger.

THE CONSPIRACIST LINE

In the world of the web, conspiracy theories and their authors have a wide following and plangency (Coady, 2006), to the point of having attracted the attention of analysts and scholars for some time now. Conspiracy theories presuppose subjects of considerable power and influence who act in the shadows in pursuit of illicit goals. According to these stories, which convey many arguments of a magical-occultist matrix, a secret elite of powerful, supranational and "supra-Masonic", dominates the world by manipulating consciences and establishing a climate of fear and total enslavement. The elite may also act in ritual killings. From a conspiracy perspective, these killings have key characteristics: not only do they take the form of a sacrifice to some demonic entity, but also have multiple meanings, which intertwine until they become confused: for example, propitiate particularly relevant political and social events; send messages, by using precise ceremonial equipment, to those who will have to investigate the crime; discredit or destroy inconvenient people.

But what would the elements be that could lead us to think that the murder of Meredith Kercher was a ritual crime? In Italy, the main supporters of the existence of ritual killings, from a conspiracy perspective, are the lawyer Paolo Franceschetti and the journalist/writer Gabriella Carlizzi (2008), who have studied and investigated many Italian news stories, often in a controversial but, nonetheless, pioneering way.

According to Franceschetti, one of the most recurring elements in this particular type of murder is the lack of a murder weapon: the weapon that killed Meredith Kercher has never been identified with certainty. Traces of Meredith's and Amanda's DNA are detected on a kitchen knife seized from Raffaele's home, but this analysis was rejected in a series of subsequent reports that find only the American's DNA on the blade. The other typical elements of these crimes would be: a lack of a serious, strong motive; contradictory (or even false) witness statements; conflicting scientific evidence; esoteric symbology relating to the date, place and protagonists of the crime. In this case, the lack of motive is clearly defined as those "futile reasons" which constituted the aggravating circumstance of the murder for which Knox, Sollecito and Guede were convicted at the Court of First Instance. According to Franceschetti, "that a single murderer can kill for futile reasons is plausible; but that three people can kill for no reason becomes quite unlikely, unless it is proven that they were hardened killers for some time." All three defendants of Meredith's death have given multiple accounts of the events that happened that night, made even more confusing by the use of drugs, each of whom used regularly. Regarding the evidence collected, there has often been talk of a real "war of appraisals", in which the forensic results of the Police were strongly contested, as they had not followed the international inspection procedures and the collection and sampling protocols. Finally, regarding the symbology, Franceschetti notes that the date of the crime is the day of the dead; the theosophical sum of the date is 13, the number of deaths; the victim's second name is Susanna which indicates, in Hebrew, the lily; Amanda, on the other hand, refers to the basic concept of Rosicrucian philosophy and creed, namely love (Franceschetti, 2014).

According to Gabriella Carlizzi, the behaviour of the accused is frequent for subjects who are forced to cover up for someone, often terrified for their own safety. If we add to this the media attack, by some, against the investigators, then, behind a murder that appears as a real ritual, perhaps there is more to discover: for the writer, it is a question of knowing to look beyond a transgressive evening that ended badly. The murderer of Meredith, therefore, would be a "fifth man", still living free today (Carlizzi, 2008). On the motives of the crime, however, it should be emphasised that Carlizzi makes a very interesting and insightful observation: the Public Prosecutor on duty at the time of the murder was Giuliano Mignini.

Mignini, however, is not exactly any magistrate: he is the one who in 2002 reopened the investigation relating to the death, which took place in 1985 at Lake Trasimeno, of Francesco Narducci, a doctor from Perugia, in the belief that he was one of the main perpetrators of the crimes committed by the so-called "Monster of Florence" (Garofano & Russell, 2011, pp. 138-139). These crimes, which led to the murder of eight couples, killed in the outskirts of Florence, ranging from 1968 to 1985, represent one of the most famous and mysterious cases that occurred in Italy, and is still unresolved today. The legal proceedings concerning the Kercher assassination unfolded between 2009 and 2015: these are the years in which Mignini is not, therefore, only the Prosecutor of the crime in Perugia, but also the Narducci case, a side case, in the region of Umbria, investigating the Monster of Florence. In fact, Mignini ordered the reopening of the Narducci tomb and ordered that the exhumation of the body. According to the results of the reports, the doctor did not drown, but was killed: the man found in the lake, and identified seventeen years earlier, therefore could not be the same person, physically very different from Narducci. The staging the replacement of the corpse, according to Mignini, was done at a high level to mask the real death of Narducci, who did not commit suicide, but was, instead, killed, probably because he was then considered unreliable. This complicated Umbrian line of investigations into the "Monster" would end in 2014 with the archiving and acquittal, due to the limitation period, of all the suspects.

It should also be pointed out that, during the judicial process relating to the crime in Perugia, two singular and little-remembered facts occurred. On 18th February 2009, unknown persons enter the house in Via della Pergola, still under judicial seizure, breaking the seals and turning the rooms upside down. They then arranged, in different points of the apartment, four large knives and candles, all objects, however, that were already in the apartment. This was discovered during operations to return some objects to the two Italian roommates of the victim. One of the knives, probably taken from the kitchen cabinet, was found on the ground, on top of a blue envelope with the word "police" written on it, similar to those often distributed in advertising campaigns. The press began to hypothesize a Satanist type ritual or intimidatory measures against the police (Bertoldi, 2009). About a month later, Meredith Kercher's mattress, two pillows and a suitcase with some knives in it were stolen from the house in Via della Pergola. It should be emphasised that, in the second break-in, the victim's mattress was the one where, at the beginning of the investigation, the outline of a knife was found (Garofano & Russell, 2011, p.328).

Another fact, apparently unrelated to everything else, could be cited in support of the conspiracy theories: In 2020, John Kercher, journalist and father of the victim, also died in violent circumstances after an accident took place just a few feet away from his home, in the south London suburb of Croydon. The man was found on the ground, with multiple fractures to the body and head: in hospital, he regained consciousness, however, was unable to remember what happened. John Kercher died after a few days. The police opened an investigation: the episode is considered a "suspicious death" by unknown persons. A plausible hypothesis is that John Kercher was the victim of a robbery gone wrong or was hit by a car and who drove away without calling for help. Officially Scotland Yard currently considers his death as the result of "unexplained causes", as there are no reliable witnesses, nor CCTV images of the alleged robbery (Franceschini, 2020).

CONCLUSION

More than ten years on, the murder of Meredith Kercher still arouses great media attention. Despite the end of the judicial proceedings, public opinion, the so-called "social media", consider this crime as unsolved. The many questions that remained unanswered, the motive never fully clarified, the sentences completely overturned at every level of judgment, have, in fact, fuelled the conviction that, beyond the procedural findings, much still needs explaining.

Rudi Guede, the only one convicted of the crime in Perugia, has finished serving his sentence of sixteen years in prison now, and was freed in January 2022. While admitting his presence at the crime scene, he has always pleaded innocent, also claiming to have tried to rescue Meredith. But if Knox and Sollecito are definitively acquitted, with whom did Rudi Guede commit the murder? Who are those accomplices that the Supreme Court ruling explicitly admitted as existing without, however, being able to identify? This remains the crucial question.

And it is precisely this specific question that the so-called conspiracy theory builds its different and not negligible point of view: it offers, in other words, a key to understanding some aspects not to be underestimated. For example, is the presence of magistrate Mignini on duty on the day of Meredith's murder an extraordinary coincidence or something prepared in advance? The hypothesis presented by Carlizzi, according to which there is a connection between the story of the Monster of Florence and the crime in Perugia must, in our opinion, at least be taken into consideration. Mignini was dealing with a very delicate part of the investigation on the Monster, concerning not the material perpetrators of the murders, but their occult principals. Michele Giuttari, head of the "Serial Crimes Investigative Group" that investigated the Monster of Florence, and with whom Mignini worked with for a long time, recently declared that "the Perugia investigation led to considering the hypothesis of the existence of a sect, based on precise witnesses also from people linked to Masonry"(Caroppo, 2021). And it is this sect, powerful and dedicated to extreme and cruel occult practices, which would represent the true author of the crimes of the Monster of Florence, always carefully hidden behind the actual perpetrators.

The perpetrators of the crimes, which terrorised Italy between 1968 and 1985, are therefore to be found not only in Florence, but between Florence and Umbria. Umbria is not only a region geographically close to the Florentine countryside where the perpetrators of crimes moved undisturbed but is also an esoterically special place: It is, in fact, a famous land of saints (just think of San Francesco, Santa Chiara, Santa Rita, San Ubaldo, Santa Angela). From an occult point of view, a land rich in mysticism also always attracts the opposite forces: If there is Good, there must be Evil. For the followers of occultism, light only makes sense in relation to a shadow that it delimits and brightens, just as the shadow must exist to allow the light to stand out in the fulness of its radiance: therefore, evil represents an essential part, an indispensable force for forming the equilibrium on which the universe rests. According to occultists, this explains why destructive forces are particularly present in certain areas and places: for example, Turin is traditionally considered the city of Satanists to counterbalance the presence of the Shroud; Rome manifests its dark side, due to the powerful presence of St. Peter. Similarly, and for the same principles, typical of occult dynamics, also Umbria can easily attract dark and violent events that "compensate", in some way, for its intense religious spirituality. It is therefore no coincidence that particular sectarian groups develop in some areas, just as it is no coincidence that some characters involved in the events of the Monster of Florence are also found in Umbria.

According to this interpretative hypothesis, the real motive for Meredith's death lies in the intent to discredit and de-legitimize the magistrate who was dealing with the Francesco Narducci case, belonging to one of the most prominent families in Perugia: thus, reducing the risk of being traced back to any instigators of the Monster of Florence, having hitherto escaped justice. It is Mignini, in fact, who in the judgement of the Court of First Instance elaborates the accusations against Knox and Sollecito, which will later be definitively rejected in the subsequent degrees of the trial. The presence of some (weak) occult connotations in Meredith's death, such as the date being between All Saints Day and the Day of the Dead, the stab wounds, the cruelty, the weapon never found, the sexual violence, would represent a staging to divert investigations from what is, however, the very concrete and rational purpose of protecting the sect. The two break-ins at the house in Via della Pergola, with the discovery of candles and knives, could constitute a strategy to further sidetrack opinion towards a ritual explanation of the crime. As noted, however, ritual crimes, according to conspiracy theories, often pursue more than one intent: the ritual elements can actually serve specific occult objectives, but also represent a language, understandable only to a few, to send messages to those who will be, from various points of view, in charge of dealing with the case.

Therefore, according to an esoteric-conspiracist interpretation Meredith's death would have been indirectly prepared, or directly executed, by one or more people who never came into the investigation at all. The young and unwary Amanda, Rudi and Raffaele participated, obscured by drugs, in an exciting game, which solicited their attraction towards the union of sex and violence, with people, however, more adult and dangerous: they remain involved in the crime, but were used in a perverse strategy far greater than them. In this version, Rudi, black, foreign and untrustworthy, is the scapegoat who pays for everyone.

Regardless of any reconstructions or so-called conspiracy theories, if the legal truth is now established, other truths are still waiting to be explored.

REFERENCES

Bertoldi, C. (2009, Feb. 19). Violata la casa degli orrori: macabri riti nella stanza di Mez. Incursione notturna nella villetta del delitto della studentessa [House of Horrors violated: macabre rituals in Mez's room. Night raid on the student's crime cottage]. *Il Giornale*. https://www.ilgiornale.it

Capponi, A. (2009, Dec. 6). Amanda e Raffaele guardati a vista. Gli Usa contro la giustizia italiana [Amanda and Raffaele closely watched. USA against Italian justice]. *Corriere della Sera*. https://www.corriere.it

Carlizzi, G. (2008). *Meredith Kercher. Un delitto imperfetto* [Meredith Kercher. An imperfect crime]. Mond & Editori.

Caroppo, L. (2021, Aug. 23). Mostro, la pistola da Vinci a un avvocato. E Pacciani è stato sicuramente ucciso [Monster, the gun from Vinci to a lawyer. And Pacciani was definitely killed]. *La Nazione*. https://www.lanazione.it

Coady, D. (2006). *Conspiracy Theories. The Philosophical Debate*. Routledge.

Corte di Assise di Appello di Perugia [Court of Assizes of Appeal of Perugia]. 4/2011.

Corte di Assise di Perugia [Court of Assizes of Perugia]. 7/2009.

Corte di Cassazione [Court of Cassation]. 422/2013.

Emmott, B. (2011, Oct. 5). Ecco perché il delitto di Perugia è diventato un caso unico [That's why the crime of Perugia has become a unique case]. *La Stampa*. https://www.lastampa.it

Franceschetti, P. (2014). *Considerazioni sul delitto Meredith* [Considerations on the crime Meredith]. https://petalidiloto.com

Franceschini, E. (2020, Feb. 7). Morto il padre di Meredith Kercher, la studentessa uccisa a Perugia [Meredith Kercher's father died, the student killed in Perugia]. *La Repubblica.* https://www.repubblica.it

Garofano, N., & Russell, P. (2011). *Assassini per caso. Luci e ombre del delitto di Perugia* [Assassins by chance. Lights and shadows of the crime of Perugia]. Rizzoli.

Gialuz, M. (2019). La violazione dei diritti fondamentali nuoce alla ricerca della verità: La Corte di Strasburgo condanna l'Italia per il procedimento nei confronti di Amanda Knox [Violation of fundamental rights harms the quest for truth: the Strasbourg Court condemns Italy for the proceedings against Amanda Knox]. *Diritto Penale Contemporaneo*, *2*, 155–168.

Mastronardi, V. M., & Castellini, G. (2009). *Meredith. Luci e ombre a Perugia* [Meredith. Lights and shadows in Perugia]. Armando.

Chapter 8
Corpus Delicti?
Forensic Dimensions of the No-Body Murder

Anna Chaussée
https://orcid.org/0000-0001-6116-5683
University of Winchester, UK

EXECUTIVE SUMMARY

Corpus delicti, or body of evidence, is a fundamental to criminal prosecutions. This contribution takes a more literal perspective by exploring the 'no-body murder'. Body disposal is not a single event; it is a complex process that dynamically responds to social and environmental circumstances. This contribution explores the legislative response to no-body murders through the Prisoners Act 2020 and presents six dimensions explaining non-disclosure of location of victim remains. Four high-profile no-body cases are presented, demonstrating the complexities inherent in searching for the long-term missing, presumed dead. This chapter focuses on the offender deposition strategy, the operational response, and environmental dimensions that explain prisoner non-disclosure and the failures to detect clandestine depositions.

INTRODUCTION

In January 2021, the Prisoners (Disclosure of Information About Victims) Act 2020 was enacted in England and Wales. Part of the act codifies the duty of the parole board to make a public protection decision for those serving life sentences for murder or manslaughter cases where the prisoner fails to disclose the location of the victim's remains, colloquially referred to as 'Helen's Law'. There are many reasons

DOI: 10.4018/978-1-7998-9668-5.ch008

why a body may not be recovered beyond the psychological explanations offered in the literature. Yet these factors have not been reflected in debates surrounding the Prisoners Act 2020. The following aims to contribute a forensic perspective dealing with no-body murder convictions by offering an explanatory framework using prominent UK case studies featured within the news media over an extensive period. This chapter highlights environmental and investigative realities impacting body recovery. It presents the factors that may account for search complexities beyond psychological models and challenge the perceived erosion of a fundamental principle enshrined in the adage 'absence of evidence is not evidence of absence.'

Some may hold the erroneous assumption that a murder conviction cannot be returned if there is no-body. This notion misunderstands the *corpus delicti* principle, which refers to the evidence of a crime having been committed rather than the actual body involved in a crime. A no-body murder refers to the disappearance of an individual where no other explanation explains their disappearance other than having been killed. A case remains a no-body murder until the point the body is recovered. However, producing the body is not a legal requirement for homicide convictions in the UK.

There are several reasons why an offender might not reveal information relating to the location of the body they have subjected to clandestine deposition. Media representations of non-disclosure have focused on the control and power of the offender over those in authority and the loved ones of the missing (e.g. "Helen's Law: Killer Refused Parole for Failing to Disclose Where Body Hidden," *The Guardian* 2021) (see additional news reporting on the disappearance of Helen McCourt, and the Moors Murders). Research conducted into the devastating impact on families is recognized as ambiguous loss (Boss, 1999, 2006). Academic exploration into no-body murder has understood psychological components such as control and power as reasons for non-disclosure (Jansen-Osmann & Berendt, 2005; Janzen, 2006; Ryan et al., 2020). An offender may choose to disclose information at a time that is beneficial to them and when it might be used as leverage. Other explanations include the offender being in denial or they may not remember. There may be a risk of revealing aspects of the crime (additional aggravating factors such as a sexual motive), or the extent of their previously unknown offending is too great. The prisoner may also perceive non-disclosure as assisting an application for an independent case review by innocence projects or review commissions in the hope of an appeal or even a future acquittal. What has not been represented in the debate is that the offender might be of limited assistance because of external factors impacting the accurate identification of a location, perhaps because of the deposition environment or investigative barriers.

What follows holds its central premise that body disposal is not a single event; it is a complex process that dynamically responds to a set of circumstances. The chapter provides the necessary background into no-body murder convictions and legislation that impacts how no-body murders are dealt with post-conviction. Dimensions affecting the recovery of the bodies of those subject to clandestine deposition are explained, and case studies are presented to illustrate the environmental and investigative barriers involved. These environmental and investigative themes provide nuance to previously over generalized representations of non-disclosure.

BACKGROUND

'No-body murder' trials have a disconcerting history in England, provoking a wariness about the safety of resulting convictions. Several high-profile cases justify public reticence. An early example is that of the 'Campden Wonder', described by Sir Overbury (1676), recounting the disappearance of a gentleman known as William Harrison from his home in Chipping Campden, Gloucestershire, in the 1660s. When William Harrison failed to meet his servant at a pre-agreed rendezvous point, a search of the surrounding area was conducted. His son and servant discovered William Harrison's bloodstained hat and damaged comb on the highway (Overbury, 1676, p. 4). Suspicion fell upon the servant, John Perry, because William Harrison's wife had sent him out to meet his master, but he did not return that night to raise the alarm. John Perry was tortured and confessed to the murder and disposal of the body of his master. Under torture, John Perry implicated the involvement of his mother and brother.

Upon this Confession and Accusation, the Justice of Peace gave Order for the apprehending of Joan and Richard Perry, the Mother and Brother of John Perry, and for searching the Sink where Mr. Harrison's Body was said to be thrown; which was accordingly done, but nothing of him could be there found: The Fish-pools likewise (in Campden) were drawn and searched, but nothing could be there found neither: So that some were of opinion, the body might be hid in the Ruins of Campden-house, burnt in the late Wars, and not unfit for such a Concealment; where was likewise Search made, but all in vain. (Overbury, 1676, p. 12)

Despite the confession, the body of William Harrison was undiscovered. The primary account of what transpired indicated the reluctance of the judge to try the three for murder without the body.

Upon the last indictment, the then Judge of Assizes, Sir Christopher Turner, would not try them, because the body was not found; but they were then tried upon the other Indictment for Robbery, to which they pleaded Not Guilty. (Overbury, 1676, p. 16)

All three were found guilty of robbery. However, the assizes that followed a year later, presided over by Sir Hyde, permitted the indictment for murder. Consequently, John Perry, his mother, and brother were convicted of murder and hanged. In a strange twist, William Harrison reappeared two years later alive. He claimed to have been kidnapped and sold into slavery in Turkey. The situation delivered a stark warning about the consequences of trying a murder without direct evidence of a dead body.

Yet practicalities dictated the obvious problems if a 'no body no murder' rule was permitted, especially in maritime communities. *R v Hindmarsh* [1792] describes mutinous sailors relieving a captain from his duty by throwing him overboard. The defence argued that a judge in a previous case directed an acquittal because there was no certainty that a child had died when thrown into a harbour. In *R v Hindmarsh*, direct proof of death was not required to prove murder. Instead, circumstantial evidence, could infer that death occurred if there were no other possible outcomes. Circumstantial evidence is the evidence of facts from which other facts may be inferred indirectly, and when considered in totality, the combination of circumstantial evidence may offer a cumulative effect. Subsequently, Hindmarsh was found guilty of piracy and executed (Home Office, 1792).

On the trial of an indictment for murder, the death of the person charged to have been killed, may be collected from the circumstances, if incapable of being proved by other evidence (R v Hindmarsh, [1792] 168 ER. at 388)

The principle of inferring murder from circumstantial evidence is crucial to the no-body murder prosecution. Two notable cases in the UK broke with a long pause in no-body murder convictions. In *R v Thomas Davison* (1934), the defendant confessed to killing his son and burning the body. In *R v Onufrejczyk* [1955], the cadaver of the defendant's partner was allegedly fed to pigs. In the latter case, it demonstrated on appeal that circumstantial evidence can be sufficient to infer death where no other alternative rational hypothesis exists that could undermine the inference.

Most physical forensic evidence is circumstantial, requiring the most careful observation and interpretation. The evidential basis provides the framework of the case known as the *corpus delicti*, or 'body of evidence' (van Meter, 1961). To ensure only strong cases go before a court, the Crown Prosecution Service (CPS) tests cases according to its principles (CPS, 2018). The evidential test requires that the evidence put before the court is reliable and credible and, when considered together, will have a realistic prospect of conviction. The public interest test ensures the prosecution is proportionate; it considers the culpability of the accused, the harm caused, the seriousness of the offence, and its impact on the public as justification for proceeding with a charge.

The no-body murder is an extraordinary claim which requires extraordinary evidence, irrespective of the availability of evidence. In cases where a body has been recovered then its examination might produce information relating to the identity of the deceased, the manner which brought about death, the approximate time since death or deposition, traces indicative of a sequence of events, evidence of contact, and even the identity of those who may have had bodily contact. Any of these elements may be robustly challenged by opposing counsel. The absence of evidence supporting a claim advanced by the prosecution may fail to persuade the jury to meet the criminal standard of proof so that the jury is sure of the defendant's guilt (Maddison et al., 2020). Indeed, plenty of murder trials do not have all these pieces of evidence represented. Interpretative evidence from observations of human remains may be affected by deterioration, contamination, and unclear time frames of deposition (amongst many other limitations). The prosecution holds the burden of proof because there is a presumption of innocence and an imbalance in the distribution of resources. However, in the no-body murder, the prosecution necessarily relies on the absence of proof of life operating at the criminal standard so that the jury are certain that the missing person is dead. Proof of life rests on the assumption that an individual engages with social institutions such as medical, financial, educational, communications, support organisations, and a continuation of social interactions. Yet if an individual changes their identity, many of these indicators fail to produce proof of life.

Establishing the death of the missing person is a difficult hurdle, but legislation has been updated in response to public campaigns (e.g., 'Claudia's Law', 'Helen's Law', and 'Suzanne's Law' discussed below). There are significant pieces of primary legislation in England and Wales dealing with missing persons the Coroners and Justice Act 2009 (c.25), the Presumption of Death Act 2013, the Guardianship (Missing Persons) Act 2017, and the Prisoners (Disclosure of Information About Victims) Act 2020. The Coroners and Justice Act 2009 (c.25) sets out the duty to refer an investigation to the Chief Coroner where there is a reason to believe a death occurred and the body is absent or otherwise irrecoverable. The Presumption of Death Act 2013 was brought in to ameliorate issues in accessing death certificates for next of kin and is in line with legislation enacted in Scotland and Northern Ireland (Presumption of Death (Scotland) Act 1977, and Presumption of Death (Northern Ireland) Act 2009). The Guardianship Act 2017 sought to remedy some of the financial problems caused by the disappearance of a person financially connected to others. An amendment to legislation known as Claudia's Law, brought about by the father of missing Claudia Lawrence, allows recognised guardians to safeguard the missing person's assets (Ministry of Justice, 2019).

It is helpful to set the scale of missing persons and discover unidentified human remains before considering the number of no-body murders in the UK and the

Prisoners Act 2020. Unfortunately, there are no reliable figures for assessing the scale of missing persons in the UK because of under-reporting and the lack of standardized reporting across police forces (National Crime Agency, 2021). Bettels et al. (2022) assess the number of people reported missing in the UK between 2015 and 2020 to be around 161,000 (±16,000) each year. However, most individuals return after a couple of days. Out of missing incidents in England and Wales, the gender of missing persons is 43% female, 56% male, and 0.1-0.2% transgender. Very similar figures are reported for Northern Ireland and Scotland, with more males missing than females (National Crime Agency, 2021). Missing person incidents are categorized according to high, medium, or low risk (College of Policing, 2021). Exploration of gender according to risk categories indicates that females and transgender people have proportionally more missing person incidents than males in high and medium risk categories during the last three years (National Crime Agency, 2021). Whereas most missing persons return of their own accord and are unharmed, between 1% and 3% of missing persons remain unaccounted for after 12 months, and some do not return. As of March 2020, the UK Missing Person Unit has 974 cases of unidentified remains across the UK. This figure includes 769 cadavers and 149 partial remains. Moreover, there are 1068 unresolved unidentified human remains' cases dating from the 1950s. Many of these remains will not be able to reveal the manner of death, and suitable identification efforts may have been exhausted or reference DNA is unavailable.

The Prisoners Act 2020 legislated the issues Parole Boards have historically considered. Parole may be refused to a prisoner who fails to provide the identities of victims subjected to indecent images or in cases of unlawful killings (murder and manslaughter) where information about the post-mortem disposal of the body has not been disclosed. It is referred to as 'Helen's Law' following the 1988 disappearance of Helen McCourt and the subsequent media campaign by her mother to stop the release of her daughter's convicted killer from prison unless he discloses the whereabouts of the body (Ng, 2020). At the time of writing, Scotland is reforming the Parole Board (Scotland) to reflect 'Suzanne's Law'. The proposed law is named after the murder and clandestine deposition of Suzanne Pilley (*HMA v David Gilroy* 2010), which similarly campaigns for the no release of prisoners in cases where they fail to disclose the location of the body. David Gilroy was convicted of Suzanne Pilley's murder and thought to have disposed of her body somewhere in the Argyll region of Scotland, which is characterised by its rugged mountainous terrain, thick forests, and lochs.

The Prisoners Act applies to parole on initial release (as opposed to re-release following recall). It places a statutory duty on the Parole Board to explicitly reference the disclosure of information about the victim in decision letters and oral hearings. Those convicted of no-body murders may be released on parole even if they fail to disclose the location of the victim's body as long as they are deemed to be no risk to the public. However, the Parole Board must consider the extent the prisoner has assisted the investigation. Since its enactment and at the time of writing, two prisoners' parole has been refused because of their non-disclosure of information relating to victim disposal. The Parole Board reflects upon the reasons for non-disclosure in making their determinations. While Parole Boards may consider a range of evidence, decisions on the non-disclosure of information about body disposal need to consider factors beyond the psychological explanations presented in the academic literature. Parole Boards are invited to view the dimensions given below and engage with appropriate experts to understand better the search and recovery of corporeal concealment and destruction of human remains.

During a House of Lords debate on the Prisoners Bill, Baroness Barker suggested there may be as many as 100 UK cases of non-body murders where prisoners fail to disclose the whereabouts of their victims (House of Lords Hansard, 2020). While there are no official national figures to provide the scale of no-body homicide convictions, it is unclear the timeframe Baroness Barker was using. However, such cases tend to be widely reported in the press. In the last 75 years, over 60 no-body homicide convictions have taken place in the UK. The no-body murder conviction is not a common occurrence, especially when considering an average of 306 murder convictions in England and Wales per annum (based on a median number of murder convictions 2011 – 2021) (Office for National Statistics 2022). Despite no-body murders representing a tiny fraction of homicide convictions overall, the issue's relevance is underpinned by the media attention these cases attract, the long-term commitment required for public resources, the costs involved in preparing and trying complex cases, and the costs of maintaining prison places.

A wealth of literature across forensic, psychology and criminology disciplines exist to understand aspects of how offenders make decisions, how traces of those behaviors might be detected, and how their detection might be avoided (Beauregard & Bouchard, 2010; Beauregard & Martineau, 2014; Chopin et al., 2020). Attempts to conceptualize detection avoidance have led to greater theoretical understandings through rational choice theory and the formulation of typologies explaining offender strategies of concealment and investigation manipulation (Bitton & Dayan, 2019; Ferguson, 2021; Ferguson & McKinley, 2020; Ferguson & Petherick, 2016). Anticipating offenders' detection avoidance strategies is a critical driver in all areas of forensic science research, enabling trace evidence to be recovered and even render valid results many years after the crime occurred.

Some concealed human remains are discovered because of dogs scratching at undergrowth or a particularly observant jogger (Killam, 2004). Other deposition sites are identified following sensitive lines of inquiries (Doyle & Barnes, 2020). Intelligence may be constructed from the analysis of soil samples, perhaps taken from a tool or vehicle available to the suspect, which might prompt a search of a broad area (Ruffell & McKinley, 2014; Young et al., 2021). Witness statements, automatic number plate recognition (ANPR), cell site analysis, and CCTV may be cross-referenced to form corroborative evidence and narrow the area of interest (Innes et al., 2021). The process of discovering clandestine depositions can depend on identifying a suspect. The preservation of potential trace evidence corresponding to an environment assists in narrowing down landscapes. Forensic professionals such as forensic archaeologists might then be employed to locate surface disturbances caused by clandestine depositions such as burial or identifying areas of intense burning.

An entire subdiscipline of archaeology, known as forensic archaeology, is dedicated to understanding clandestine depositions in search, location, and excavation (Hunter & Cox, 2005). The forensic archaeologist is best placed demonstrating if a body was deliberately concealed or obscured because of a natural process (e.g. leaf litter, snow, silt accumulation) (Pokines et al., 2018). Both phenomena indicate that corporeal depositions are dynamic environments (Hunter et al., 2013). In respect to the present context of body disposal, forensic archaeologists utilize a system of recording that captures differences in burial activities represented through perceived differences in the soil or layers of material (To, 2017). Archaeological perspectives carefully reconstruct formation processes involved in concealing a body or its destruction. Since concealment and destruction are not single events but complex processes representing sequences of actions, they rely on a recording system that captures differences in activities (Evis, 2016). For instance, the context numbering system may differentiate between the activities involved in the burial of a body. Separate 'context' numbers are given to the surface (e.g. the ground or a floor), the disturbance made through the act of digging through the ground surface (known as the cut), the filling of the cut feature (the fill) and the positioning of the body within the fill (deposit/body). These contexts are documented as separate archaeological events within a complex but connected process. The nuance becomes valuable when evaluating the circumstantial evidence related to alleged attempts at corporeal concealment. For instance, a feature has been dug with the suspected intention to act as a receptacle for human remains, but it was backfilled and not used for that purpose. The factfinder, the jury, is welcome to make an inference but the forensic archaeologist must avoid over-extending interpretations by ascribing intention to empty features. The distinction between such activities and unbiased presentation is of paramount importance to cases dealing with claims of this nature.

Forensic archaeologists are just one of several professionals who could be involved in the search for suspected body disposal, usually where clandestine burial is a concern (Dubsky & Christensen, 2018; Horsman, 2016; Pringle & Jervis, 2010). Forensic archaeology has followed a research trajectory of refining methods to locate clandestine depositions. However, little attention has been paid to some of the problems that emerge operationally concerning no-body murders and their relationship to broader issues in criminal justice (Chaussée, 2019). A partial explanation is the apparent publication bias of body recoveries rather than focusing on cases where bodies remain outstanding. There are legitimate operational sensitivities and concerns over *sub judice,* which means negative searches are not routinely reported on within academia, restricting the understanding of investigative errors to those operationally involved. Systematic case review remains a confidential process, and opportunities for disseminating lessons learned are extremely limited within academic and public arenas. While most work focuses on pre-trial investigation, a growing potential now exists following the enactment of the Prisoners Act in supporting post-conviction case review about the environmental aspects that may or may not interfere with locating clandestine depositions. The conceptualization of dimensions of non-disclosure goes beyond the psychological factors considered in current Parole Board decision-making (Parole Board, 2021).

DIMENSIONS OF NON-DISCLOSURE

The dimensions offered in Table 1 are a consequence of a larger research project dealing with the conceptualisation of corporeal concealment which systematically reviewed recorded homicide featuring concealment in England and Wales over a 20-year period. 61 no-body murder convictions (UK) over the last 75 years were examined. Accompanying news coverage of long-term searches in the UK from 2010-2020 has also informed the construction of these dimensions. The systematic review of academic literature (dealing with detection avoidance, body concealment in related disciplines such as psychology, criminology, forensic archaeology, forensic taphonomy), and professional search literature have also developed the framework below. The dimensions are not mutually exclusive since these factors are interconnected, and categories are not exhaustive. The presentation of dimensions aims to distinguish between reasons that non-disclosure remains a choice and where disclosure may be outside the prisoner's control.

'The Campden Wonder' case demonstrated the sheer horror of the wrongful no-body murder conviction resulting in three executions. Yet it is not the only case which has rendered unsafe no-body convictions. *R v Shirley Banfield and Lynette Banfield* [2013] is a more recent example in the UK of an acquittal of two women convicted of murder and concealment, and the appeal court stated in its judgment (paragraph 51):

Table 1. Dimensions of non-disclosure

Dimension	Examples
Factual innocence	The prisoner is factually innocent – the prisoner is not responsible for the murder or disposal of the body The alleged victim disappeared of their own volition and is unharmed.
Power and self-preservation	Manipulation, mischief-making, Maintaining power, propagating fear and confusion To protect another individual involved To avoid additional criminal charges Following legal advice Avoid repercussions (e.g. increased risk of harm)
Impairment	Memory impairment Limited knowledge Learning difficulties Communication difficulties Impairment at the time of deposition
Strategies of obliteration	The offender destroyed the body The body was cremated through a legitimate process Location facilitates partial or complete destruction
Environment	Part of a complex sequence of depositional events The remains are scattered across several locations Additional taphonomic agents moved, concealed or destroyed remains Environmental changes distort spatial reconstruction (cultural and natural changes) Remains unlikely to be recovered due to the deposition strategy adopted No reference points available to facilitate reconstruction or navigation
Investigative barriers	Media coverage The search required would exceed the resources available Duration since deposition Investigative errors or misrepresentation of the limitations of investigative techniques Remains recovered unlikely to render an identification Target is undetectable The search would be too dangerous/inhospitable Distrust in process

This was an alleged joint enterprise murder with no body, no suggested mechanism of death, no identified day when the murder was said to have occurred, no time and no place and no suggestion of what happened to the body.

Therefore, the first dimension acknowledges that those who are factually innocent cannot assist the investigation and are likely to fail to explain their non-disclosure to the satisfaction of the Parole Board. The Criminal Justice System is poorly prepared for dealing with factual innocence post-conviction and even more so when convictions are based upon the absence of evidence. Qualifying for an appeal or an official case review is set at a high threshold, and without fresh substantive evidence, the appeal is likely to be rejected or fail. Human rights campaigners are concerned that factually innocent people have the impossible task of satisfying the Parole Board.

The Parole Board recognises psychological factors such as power and self-preservation. Manipulation, mischief-making, maintaining power, and propagating fear and confusion can be achieved through the refusal to disclose information about victims. There is very little control a prisoner has in their lives within prisons, and control-seeking behaviours are well established within prison populations. Further examples for this dimension include protecting another person from implication, perhaps because there might be a connection through access to resources such as land ownership used for disposal, borrowing a vehicle, or other associations. The individual convicted of murder may have relied upon others to dispose of the body and may not wish to divulge that information. Moreover, a prisoner may be motivated by avoiding additional criminal charges. The revealing of a body's location might provide evidence of further crimes, other victims, or further aggravating factors (e.g. a significant degree of planning or premeditation, a sexual motive, or physical suffering before death). Claims that are accurate, exaggerated, or false presented in the media enter wider prison knowledge, increasing the risk of harm to the prisoner from the wider prison community. While prisons have processes in place to segregate vulnerable prisoners (e.g. sex offenders), it may influence the motivation to cooperate if new details enter the public domain as an act of self-preservation.

Concerns raised in the House of Lords during the debates of the proposed legislation centred on mental capacity and forms of long-term cognitive impairment including memory recall (House of Lords Hansard, 2020). Memory impairment may also be an issue where drugs and alcohol are involved. Alcohol use appears to be a theme in body disposal, hindering memory recall. However, the extent of alcohol use post-homicide behaviour is unknown but is likely to impact the ability of a prisoner to provide the detailed knowledge needed to assist in locating clandestine deposition(s).

Media coverage of cases has assisted in gathering information and raises the profile of cases which attracts political support (e.g., the unsolved disappearance of Madeleine McCann in 2007 continues to attract global attention). However, some cases receive so much attention that they can distort fact from fiction and flood inquiries with poor quality intelligence. Therefore, details not in the public domain are integral to this process for verification when a potentially credible claim is supplied. Other investigative barriers may include the health and safety risks to searchers (including cooperative prisoners), the level of specialist work required, and competing caseloads; each has a resourcing implication. The financial resourcing of resolved cases may mean only discrete searches of specific targets are considered instead of wide-area search and elimination exercises associated with unsolved cases. Even targeted searches can be unfruitful when dealing with credible intelligence and the correct application of techniques. Some searches need to be revisited because of search methods and recording changes. For instance, a search for a suspected female victim of Fred West focused on a café where she worked and where he was a regular customer, and he may have carried out some renovation work there. The café was searched in the 1990s but nothing of significance was found. In 2021 a TV production company contacted police, informing them of previously unknown voids in the cellar of the café. A victim recovery dog was deployed and indicated in the toilet area at a void below. A targeted forensic archaeological excavation was performed, but no human remains were found.

Police searches will use victim recovery dogs to indicate where a body may be buried or the presence of decomposition or blood. They are usually trained on dead pigs and synthetic 'death scents'. Their training is reinforced operationally through exposure to decomposed human remains, and they have proven successes in the field. However, they are also known to provide false positive and negative indications. Indications can influence the level of search intervention or be used to eliminate areas. The presence or absence of a signal by a dog is a guide only. It is not suitably reliable to be presented as scientific evidence to a jury for the presence or absence of human remains. The over-exaggeration of the reliability of methods may lead to premature elimination or over-interpretation, which is not limited to victim recovery dogs but includes forensic archaeologists ascribing empty holes as 'graves' and forensic anthropologists confirming the presence of human remains unsupported by the evidence. Investigative errors and over-extended interpretations breed distrust in the process and could undermine future cooperation with the accused.

The process of hiding something in an indoor or outdoor context may be premeditated or adaptive to the realities of the environment, available resources, and other external pressures. The prisoner cannot be expected to fully understand environmental conditions promoting decomposition or factors that may facilitate further concealment, even if the motivation was complete detection avoidance or delay. Environmental conditions distort recognition of clandestine depositions, lacking or disrupting reference points to aid navigation. Even remains that are likely to be well-preserved because the geological conditions may not be recovered if they were deposited in highly dynamic environments. Hunter, Simpson, and Sturdy Colls (2013, pp. 104–116) provide an excellent overview of natural and cultural changes to environments that may inhibit discovery of clandestine depositions. If the offender destroyed the body, the likelihood of recovery is minimal, and even if bone fragments are suspected to be found, it may be challenging to establish identification. It is unclear what standard of proof the Parole Board are working towards and how it can be consistent. The deposition of remains might be subject to additional or unanticipated natural and cultural taphonomic agents that may move, damage, or conceal remains or simply not recognise their significance. The environment is beyond the prisoner's control.

The onus is on the prisoner to explain the reason for the non-disclosure of the location. Yet it may not be apparent to the prisoner why the remains have not been found if a search has already been conducted. Prisoners are unlikely to have access to the resources for expert advice that might assist in explaining failure. Four cases of no-body murder convictions have been selected for presentation and discussion to illustrate further some of the dimensions presented above. Each case has a male perpetrator and a female victim. While the proportion of females as victims is not representative of homicide in general, it is representative of no-body murder conviction cases in the UK. No-body murder cases receive significant reporting in the news media (but discussions on disproportionate reportage of missing white women see Jeanis & Powers, 2017; Liebler, 2010; Liebler et al., 2020; Slakoff & Fadella, 2019; Stillman, 2007). Notable cases involving male victims include the post-conviction recovery of Adam Alexander (*HMA v Thomas Pryde* 2010) in Scotland and the no-body murder of Michael O'Leary in Cwmffrwd, Wales (2020) (see *R v Andrew Jones* 2020). The cases below have been selected because of the accessibility of case documents and their explanatory potential.

Case 1 deals with the disappearance of a child in 2012, where a mix of obliteration strategies was present, leading to the recovery of suspected partial remains. Case 2 presents body disposal at a pig farm with the body undiscovered. Case 3 presents the eventual post-conviction body recovery, but the prisoner had difficulties identifying the exact location. Case 4 presents the disappearance of a woman whose absence was not noticed for 19 years, but the circumstantial evidence suggested no reasonable alternative hypothesis exists other than her murder. Each case attracted significant media attention in the UK because of the relative rarity of no-body murder trials. The selected cases are no-body murders resulting in a UK criminal court conviction. They illustrate specific dimensions that may be applied to no-body murder cases. The substance of the cases has been reconstructed from triangulating original trial information, appeal judgments (where relevant) and reporting in the news media. While there may be examples of the power and self-preservation strategies or cognitive impairment, these aspects are not focused on here. The cases demonstrate the interconnectedness of the dimensions presented above. So, after their presentation, the cases are discussed according to the themes of obliteration, environmental changes, and investigative barriers influencing the ability to recover corporeal remains.

Case 1: Disappearance of April Jones, Machynlleth, Wales (2012) (*R v Bridger* 2013)

On the evening of 1 October 2012, five-year-old April Jones was abducted while playing in her housing estate in Machynlleth, mid-Wales. Her disappearance prompted one of the most extensive police searches in the UK with the involvement of 45 police forces. The investigation into her disappearance was called Operation Tempest. Initial scenarios considered were that she might be alive but had difficulty in the surrounding steep rural terrain, with its hidden mine shafts and fast-flowing watercourses. She could not be located despite using search helicopters, thermal imaging, ground search teams, victim recovery dogs, police divers, and kayakers. Once police received information that children had seen April Jones climbing into a 'grey van', suspicion fell on a local man in his late forties who was known to April.

Mark Bridger lived in Ceinws, a hamlet around 4.6 miles from the Bryn-y-Gog estate where April Jones was last seen. He was described as someone with extensive local knowledge of Machynlleth's rural areas. On 5 October 2012, Mark Bridger was charged with the abduction and murder of April Jones after a search of his cottage revealed indecent images of children, blood spots on a sofa, blood staining in the area in front of the wood burner and under the carpet of the corresponding area. The blood was later confirmed to belong to April Jones through DNA analysis. Blood was found in the grouting of bathroom tiles, indicative of clean-up. More staining was discovered in the hallway and on the washing machine. A tiny fragment of apparent bone (3 mm x 2 mm) was recovered from the waste pipe of the bath. The wood-burning stove in the living room continued to be hot and, inside, between 16 and 17 fragments of apparent bone and a burnt knife were recovered. An interpretation of the evidence presented at trial was that Mark Bridger had dismembered the body of April Jones in front of the stove and fragments were transferred into the wood burner and bath during the clean-up.

In April 2013, Mark Bridger stood trial at Mold Crown Court accused of abduction, murder and perverting the course of justice. Mark Bridger's defence included an admission that he had caused the death of April Jones by accidentally crushing her with his Land Rover. However, he could not recall what he had done to the body because he panicked and consumed alcohol.

During the trial, four forensic anthropologists agreed that the fragments represented burnt bone. One suggested that the interpretation could not go further than suggesting bone and not the skeletal element, species, or age due to its size. Another forensic anthropologist confirmed that the fragment was human. Two others agreed and identified five of the pieces as consistent with burnt fragments from a human child's cranium. The absence of elements from facial bones and teeth was suggestive that the whole skull had not been placed within the stove. Another forensic anthropologist disagreed that these inferences could be drawn from the fragments alone, which constituted confirmation bias. The remains in the stove would not render a DNA profile because of the extensive burning, and the piece recovered from the bath pipe was too small to undertake DNA analysis without destroying it.

Police do not believe the whole body was burnt in the stove but that April's body was dismembered and concealed in multiple places across the landscape. The tributaries in the *River Dyfi* catchment area were particularly fast-flowing and high. A witness confirmed they saw Mark Bridger on 2 October, the day after April Jones' disappearance, walking along the tributary close to his home holding a partially filled black bin bag. He was filmed by a police helicopter walking along the swollen tributary with the smoking chimney of his cottage visible in the background. Mark Bridger's grey Land Rover appeared to have travelled 400 miles in the two weeks between having his vehicle serviced and when police seized it.

Mark Bridger was found guilty, and upon sentencing him to life imprisonment, Mr Justice Griffith Williams commented,

How you disposed of her body must remain a mystery. It will serve no purpose for me to speculate as to what happened but all the indications are that you burnt at least a part of her in the wood burner... Your offences were aggravated by their premeditation and by the destruction of at least a part of her body and the concealment of the rest.

To date, the remains of April Jones have not been recovered.

Case 2: Disappearance of Tina Baker, Egham, Surrey (2002) (*R v Baker* 2006)

Tina and Martin Baker married in 1996, and within three years, their marriage became difficult with periods of separation. They lived in a bungalow in Egham, and they bought a 14-acre smallholding on Chobham, Surrey, where they raised rare poultry, cows and pigs. Tina Baker routinely visited the farm to feed the animals. Tina Baker, then 41 years old, disappeared one month after announcing she was leaving her husband. Around the time of her disappearance, she informed her husband that she wanted a divorce and planned to live with an old school friend with whom she was having an extramarital affair.

Tina Baker was last seen on 8 July 2002 after meeting a friend in Sunbury-on-Thames before feeding her animals at the farm just a few miles away. She is thought to have arrived at the smallholding at 1 pm. She was due to meet her new partner in Heathrow later that day but failed to turn up. Martin Baker reported his estranged wife's disappearance to the police two weeks later. Missing person posters were distributed, and her family and friends made appeals for information. Since the last known sighting of Tina Baker on 8 July, there was an absence of any further sightings of her or her Vauxhall Astra estate vehicle. Tina Baker's dog was discovered abandoned. There was no sign of life of Tina Baker including no activity on her bank account and her mobile phone could not be located.

By October 2002, police announced they were no longer pursuing a missing person enquiry and had commenced a murder investigation. They turned their attention to Martin Baker, a man in his fifties, previously married, and a former SAS reservist. Police thought Martin Baker might have been devastated at the prospect of losing the smallholding. Immediately following her leaving, Martin Baker had anxiously attempted to contact his estranged wife. All attempts to contact her abruptly ceased after she disappeared.

Martin Baker had once threatened his first wife before they divorced that he could make her disappear permanently by dismembering her body and feeding the remains to pigs. The prevailing theory was that Tina Baker's body was fed to pigs at their smallholding on Pennypott Lane. In November 2002, aerial photography surveyed the Chobham smallholding for recent ground surface disturbance. The land was searched using victim recovery dogs and licensed search officers, but her body was not located. The animal feed and excrement was searched. It was thought that Tina Baker's body had been fed to pigs and the animals sent for slaughter some time days after. There were no traces of the body, the car, or a suspected weapon.

Martin Baker claimed he had been sent home from work on the 8 July after breaking a piece of equipment and did not see Tina Baker that day. Cell site analysis demonstrated his mobile phone had been in the area that morning. He denied being at the smallholding, but a witness came forward claiming she had seen Martin Baker behaving in an agitated state and that he had made her presence feel unwelcome. Later that day, he contacted an associate at a breaker's yard, which offered same-day car disposal.

Martin Baker's behaviour also suggested he knew that his estranged wife would not return. Eight months after Tina Baker's disappearance Martin Baker allowed an associate to use her identity (using her unmarried name Tina Doyle) on a DVLA License with a stolen car. In November 2004, while investigating the suspected murder of Tina Baker, police arrested Martin Baker for cannabis cultivation at the marital home. The bungalow had been used as a hydroponics factory with 258 cannabis plants worth £16,000. He went on trial at the Central Criminal Court, was found guilty and handed a four-year custodial sentence. While already serving a sentence for growing cannabis, on 11 October 2005, Martin Baker was charged with the murder of Tina Baker. He was convicted of her murder and sentenced to a minimum of 14 years imprisonment. In 2008 Baker was unsuccessful in his appeal (*R v Baker* [2008]).

In response to new information, a renewed search took place in 2020 at a smallholding previously owned by Martin Baker on Priest Lane, some three miles from the Chobham farm. The British army and specialist search officers were involved, and, to date, Tina Baker's remains are undiscovered.

Case 3: Disappearance of Kate Prout Gloucestershire (2007/2011) (*R v Prout* 2010)

The remains of Kate Prout were recovered while Adrian Prout, her husband, was serving a life sentence for her murder. It was known that Kate Prout was in an acrimonious divorce with Adrian Prout. She had increased her settlement demand from him, which would require the selling of their 276-acre property at Redhill Farm, Redmarley, in Gloucestershire. Adrian Prout owned a pipe-laying business, and he used the land at the farm to run commercial pheasant shoots for clients. On the 5 November 2007, the last confirmed contact was between Kate Prout, aged 55, and her bank. All signs of medical, utility, social and financial activities ceased. Kate Prout's handbag, clothes, shoes, bank cards, mobile phone and passport had not been taken, and her car was left.

On 10 November 2007, five days after his estranged wife disappeared, Adrian Prout reported her missing to the police. On 27 November 2007, police arrested Adrian Prout on suspicion of murder without any direct evidence of Kate Prout having come to any harm. The police had been aware of an accusation of domestic violence the previous year, but there was not enough evidence to prosecute. Adrian Prout was released the following day. Extensive searches were conducted at Redhill Farm and land surrounding the marital property between November and mid-December 2007. Gloucestershire police embarked on their largest-ever search involving victim recovery dogs, ground-penetrating radar, police divers, licensed search officers, thermal imaging, aerial photography of the property and its surrounding area, including a reservoir and mass storage facilities for grain and bark. Pig excrement was sifted in the possibility that her body had been fed to pigs, but the search concluded without locating a body or suspected weapon.

In January 2008, the police announced they suspected Kate Prout had been murdered. In March 2009, Adrian Prout was arrested and charged with his wife's murder after the police had found Kate Prout's diary in her car, which detailed the physical abuse she received within the relationship. It appeared that from 2006 the marriage was volatile, with arguments and alleged episodes of violence from Adrian Prout directed at his wife. In 2006 Kate Prout recorded a violent outburst by her husband, and the following year Kate Prout claimed her husband had attempted to kill her, prompting her to leave home temporarily. Kate and Adrian Prout reconciled the relationship two months later. The relationship appeared to be particularly volatile between February and November of that year. Kate Prout grew suspicious that her husband was conducting an extramarital affair with their house sitter. Adrian Prout's defence suggested the diary was an orchestrated attempt to give the impression she had come to harm by framing him for murder. Their view was that Kate Prout had left of her own accord and was alive and unharmed.

On 12 January 2010, Adrian Prout stood trial at Bristol Crown Court, and on 5 February, he was found guilty of her murder. He was sentenced to 18 years imprisonment. Three years was added to a 15-year sentence to reflect the aggravating factor that he concealed the body and failed to disclose the location. The police stopped actively searching for Kate Prout's remains shortly thereafter.

In November 2011, Adrian Prout failed a voluntary lie detector test arranged by his supporters, who believed he was innocent. Adrian Prout later confessed to his new fiancée and then to the police that he strangled Kate Prout and revealed where he believed he had concealed her remains in Cobhill woods in a pheasant pen. On 18 November 2011, Adrian Prout was escorted to the farm, where he spent 25 minutes there showing police where his wife's remains had been buried. He identified an area of 5 m x 15 m correlating with the boundaries of a pheasant pen under a feeder. Adrian Prout struggled to pinpoint the exact location because it emerged that the feeder had been moved in the intervening four-year period. Ground penetrating radar, victim recovery dogs and forensic archaeologists assisted in searching the area to establish the exact location.

After a four-day search focusing on the area identified by Adrian Prout, a buried feature 1.5 m long and a depth of 1.5 m was excavated. The trench had been dug originally by machine. Human remains wrapped in a curtain, and white plastic sheeting were discovered. The following day, the identification was confirmed through odontological analysis (dental records) as belonging to Kate Prout. An inquest into Kate Prout's death was held in May 2012 at Gloucestershire Coroner's Court. Evidence of fractures consistent with compression of the neck was presented at the inquest, although the exact manner of death could not be ascertained. The verdict of unlawful killing was given.

Case 4: Disappearance of Margaret Fleming (1999/2019) (*HMA v Cairney and Jones* 2019)

In April 2019, Edward Cairney and Avril Jones were found guilty of murdering Margaret Fleming in a televised no-body murder trial at Glasgow High Court. The prosecution argued that Margaret Fleming was killed between 18 December 1999 and 5 January 2000 at nineteen years old.

Margaret Fleming had learning difficulties which required lifelong support. She was entitled to claim incapacity benefits because she was unable to work. After her father died in 1995, Margaret Fleming lived with Edward Cairney and Avril Jones at Seacroft, a home they shared on the outskirts of Inverkip, a remote village on the west Scottish coastline. Edward Cairney and Avril Jones became recognised carers for Margaret Fleming and Avril Jones managed her financial affairs.

At the end of October 2016, it became apparent to social workers that they had no direct contact with Margaret Fleming since July 1996. Regular payments of Margaret Fleming's benefits had continued to be paid to Avril Jones. In the application for universal credit on Margaret Fleming's behalf, Avril Jones claimed that Margaret Fleming needed constant care and that she was self-harming. She also described problematic behaviours that had not previously been attributed to Margaret Fleming. Social workers were not given access to Margaret Fleming when they attempted to visit her at Seacroft. Social workers reported their concerns to local police, who conducted a welfare check at the property. Police were unable to ascertain Margaret Fleming's well-being, having been told by her carers that Margaret Fleming was scared and fled the property as the police arrived. On 28 October 2016, Margaret Fleming was reported missing by her carers.

The police searched the Wemyss Bay area but failed to find any sightings or establish Margaret Fleming's movements through CCTV. The police conducted a wide-ranging proof of life investigation extending to the USA, where some of Margaret Fleming's distant relatives lived. Police established that Margaret Fleming did not have a current passport and had not renewed it. She had not accessed her GP, social services, or aid organisations, and no mobile phone records existed. Neighbours and local community members were unaware that Margaret Fleming lived at Seacroft. Police established the last independent sighting of Margaret Fleming was on 17 December 1999 at a family event.

Edward Cairney and Avril Jones produced letters that had allegedly been written by Margaret Fleming purporting to be alive and well. One letter dated 9 January 2000 had been sent from Carlisle, and two others sent from a hotel in London on 13 January 2000. It later transpired from an invoice found at Seacroft that Edward Cairney and Avril Jones had stayed at the hotel when the letter was sent. Margaret Fleming's former teacher did not recognise the literacy abilities demonstrated in the writing of these letters as correlating with Margaret Fleming's capabilities.

Seacroft was one of four houses situated on a section of the A78 in an area described as rural and isolated. Seacroft was a dilapidated bungalow with rooms full of debris and windows missing. A fingertip search of the property was carried out without finding anything of significance. Luminol was used for the detection of blood, but nothing was found. There was no evidence of Margaret Fleming living there around the time of the search. Edward Cairney and Avril Jones provided some items claiming to be belongings of Margaret Fleming. These items were subjected to DNA testing, but none of Margaret Fleming's DNA was detected on the belongings, contradicting the claim that Margaret Fleming had handled the objects regularly.

The garden of Seacroft backed onto the boulder-strewn banks of the Firth of Clyde (Inverkip Bay). A range of location methods was deployed, focusing on the Seacroft property and garden. Police also concentrated on the surrounding area using a helicopter and police search divers. In December 2016, the entire back garden was excavated with mechanical top-soil stripping to detect subsurface disturbance. The spoil was retained and sieved. The ground was probed, and victim recovery dogs were used for systematic search. A victim recovery dog indicated at two areas interpreted as sites of decomposition. Areas of burning were identified, and 298 fragments of bone, many of which were burnt, were recovered from the garden. A forensic anthropologist was unable to confirm any of the remains as human. Some fragments were recognizably animal in origin, including deer and fish.

In a remarkable televised BBC interview recorded on 4 October 2017, Edward Cairney claimed Margaret Fleming was alive and often travelled to Europe operating under aliases. He claimed she was a gang recruiter and drug trafficker. The interview became a key piece of evidence in the subsequent prosecution case. Later that month, on 27 October 2017, Edward Cairney and Avril Jones were charged with abduction, murder, and fraud. The prosecution accused the carers of abusing Margaret Fleming between November 1997 and January 2000. In 2019 the trial found the defendants guilty of murder and attempting to defeat the ends of justice motivated by financial gain. Avril Jones was also convicted of defrauding the Department of Work and Pensions of £182,000. Both were sentenced to a minimum of 14 years. Both protest their innocence. The body of Margaret Fleming has not been recovered to date.

DISCUSSION

The value of the disclosed information is governed by its veracity, accuracy, specificity, reliability, completeness, timeliness, and applicability to the present day. The dimensions presented above explain why long-term searches might fail independently of the prisoner's cooperation. The Prisoners Act 2020 expects prisoners to understand their own offending and, albeit implicitly, to possess an insight into the taphonomic processes between disposal and recovery. Three of the dimensions, namely the interconnected themes of investigative barriers, the environment, and obliteration strategies, form the foundation of this discussion in light of the cases above.

In the six months preceding April Jones' disappearance (Case 1), the catchment area for the *River Dyfi* received extensive rainfall as tributaries transported vast quantities of water off the Cambrian mountains. The accumulative effect made the landscape exceptionally wet, with watercourses bursting their banks. According to river archives, the *Dyfi* was flowing at a 'notably high' level (UK Centre for Ecology and Hydrology, 2022). The water levels presented a risk to the life of the searchers, causing the search to be paused until water levels receded. Searches are temporarily abandoned when presented with an unacceptable level of danger by the surrounding environment; for example, prolonged wet weather exacerbates the risks associated with steep ground or subterranean structures like caves or mines. The willingness to overcome these barriers is striking, especially in the stages when the missing person might be alive and more so when there is a child at the center of the investigation. However, willingness to take risks may be reduced when a missing person is presumed deceased, and a conviction is secured.

The search surrounding Machynlleth required search specialists to navigate steep terrain with hidden caves and waterfalls. Towards the north and northeast of Ceinws, where Mark Bridger lived, is a landscape scattered with disused slate quarries and water sinks nestled within the Cambrian mountains. Mark Bridger was suspected of taking advantage of the environmental conditions to facilitate disintegration and rapid transportation of the remains by depositing them in watercourses. While on remand, Mark Bridger allegedly confessed to a prison chaplain, stating he had dismembered April Jones' body and disposed of her remains in the fast-flowing tributary *Afon Dulas* behind his cottage, which runs into the *Dyfi*. These conditions would quickly promote fast disarticulation of remains with a meagre chance of recovery. In cases where disposal in flowing watercourses has been employed, and human remains were not found in the initial search, then subsequent recovery is highly remote. However, investigators may need to consider any unidentified human remains discovered downstream in succeeding years.

Investigations associated with complex concealment are expensive because they require expertise for different search specialisms, each requiring the deployment of technical and forensic resources and significant police overtime. As described in Case 1, the search for April Jones was the most extensive search recorded in the UK, covering over 60 km^2 and quickly exceeded the resources of Dyfed-Powys Police. A FOI request made by the author to Dyfed-Powys Police (10/05/2021) revealed the total costs recorded for Operation Tempest as £8,923,994, and the Home Office contribution under Special Grant was £7,877,054. The deployment of resources generally follows the level of risk of the missing person. The police had to demonstrate to the public that everything was being done to try and find the five-year-old alive despite simultaneously investigating abduction and murder as a line of enquiry. After six months, the intense search was halted just before the accused stood trial for her murder and was convicted.

Homicide cases that have resulted in a conviction without the body being recovered are 'resolved' instead of 'unsolved' cases that have not secured a conviction. Unsolved cases are more of an operational priority than resolved cases. Therefore, post-conviction searches are unlikely to be an operational priority. The levels of resources and central financial assistance seen in Operation Tempest are not available post-conviction. Moreover, police cuts are expected to impact missing person investigations, and so there are also likely additional impacts on cold cases and searches associated with resolved cases (Greenhalgh & Shalev Greene, 2021).

Landscape searches have made use of 'winthropping' which is a navigation technique used by armed services in Northern Ireland before becoming declassified. Winthropping relates to the tendency to navigate towards landmarks and is mostly applied in wider landscapes but its definition seems to be extended to wayfaring in more targeted location exercises. This part of search theory is relatively undeveloped, with few offerings in the literature beyond what is already known in the armed services and by search professionals (Keatley et al., 2022). Offenders utilising wayfaring techniques have been anecdotally observed in drugs, intelligence, arms caches, and searches involved in no-body murders. Archives have revealed details for the recovery of Soviet-era intelligence and communication caches which may be located by following precise wayfaring. Instructions contained in the Mitrokhin archives describe the number of steps required to correctly locate and recover Soviet caches hidden in landscapes, many of which were marked by innocuous stones (Andrew & Mitrokhin, 2000).

Wayfaring using discrete waypoints is thought to feature in cases where there is an expectation perhaps to recover the item at some point or to monitor the area for signs of activity. There is little need for additional markers for offenders with extensive knowledge of the site, such as land owned by the offender. However, relational details between features may still be used for precise relocation and obstacles may be placed over the deposition. An easily overlooked aspect is that the components used as part of wayfaring may offer little permanence or meaning to another navigator. For this reason, witnesses and prisoners may be required to conduct site visits to show police the deposition location. Escorted prisoner visits have been associated with high profile cases such as the Moors Murderers Ian Brady and Myra Hindley, as well as Ian Simms and Adrian Prout. The perception in the news media is that the prisoners are having a 'day out' rather than offering genuine assistance because sometimes the prisoner fails to identify the location.

Re-searching areas where searches have been carried out decades earlier poses problems because of the inconsistent recording of search interventions. Anomalies indicative of ground disturbance can be destroyed in early searches, and an abundance of anomalies may have been created as part of the search but poorly recorded. It limits the value of techniques used to detect ground disturbance including geophysics and aerial photography where anomalies have been superfluously created and left unrecorded. Where necessary, the prisoner may be escorted on a site visit to assist narrowing down the area or attempt to show the exact location. It is not uncommon for suspects to assist the investigation by retracing their steps only to find those physical, relational details relied upon can change over a short amount of time, leading to disorientation or failure to locate. Myra Hindley attempted to assist police in 1987 in finding the bodies of Pauline Reade and Keith Bennett on Saddleworth Moor. However, when the site visit was conducted, there was snow on the ground, obscuring landscape features. Moreover, police also took Myra Hindley by an unfamiliar route rather than allowing her to retrace her steps (Hunter et al., 2013). Police successfully recovered the remains of Pauline Reade but were unsuccessful in locating the body of Keith Bennett, whose remains are still outstanding (at the time of writing). Site visits should be attempted in good visibility and with seasonality closely matching the approximate time of year the deposition occurred to create familiar conditions. Even if willing, not all offenders may be physically capable of undertaking a site visit, so alternative visualisation methods need to be considered.

Some of those who have concealed an object or a body might be able to position it in relation to other natural or cultural features within the immediate surroundings to a high level of precision and confidence. For example, take this account provided by the detective investigating the Christopher Halliwell murder and subsequent recovery of Rebecca Godden, who was killed by Halliwell in 2003, in Wiltshire, UK.

Taking his bearings from a dip in the wall, he began pacing into the middle of the field, putting one foot in front of the other. After taking a precise number of steps, he stopped and indicated that the body was beneath his feet. (Fulcher, 2017, p. 177)

Halliwell initially failed to navigate from the correct dip in the stone wall because, since the deposition, the wall had other areas of collapse where stones were missing. The forensic archaeologists involved did not find anything at that exact spot. However, the deposition was later found after reapplying the same method of wayfaring from an alternative section of the wall and observing the surface for soil texture and colour changes. Similarly, with Case 3 (Prout), physical features can change dramatically over relatively little time. The renewed search was only four years after his conviction. Halliwell used near latent and somewhat unstable features to navigate the deposition site's location. The pheasant pen and the feeder in Case 3 had provided Prout with a clear set of relational details used to relocate the clandestine deposition beneath. Prout struggled to locate his victim's remains because the feeder had moved in the intervening years.

Prout's reliance on the positioning of the feeder in a pheasant pen and Halliwell's reference point from a stone wall (*R v Halliwell* 2016) highlight the fragility of some of the strategies of navigation used through the incorporation of physical, relational details. Cases like this demand deeper understanding of how offenders navigate landscapes using micro-markers. If those details can be reconstructed with a cooperative prisoner, then disruption to those relational details may be anticipated. If a site has been searched, 360° imaging may be helpful to pick up potential microfeatures that could be used as navigational reference points. Three-dimensional modelling may draw out these textures more effectively and communicate spatial relationships better than two-dimensional maps. Contemporaneous aerial photographs and map regression are critical tools for tracing how deposition sites may have changed in the ensuing years. Reliable methods to facilitate prisoner cooperation in the search for clandestine depositions must be devised alongside psychologists and search professionals. An essential aspect of any process needs to consider site evolution and taphonomy to have real-world application.

In some cases of no-body murder, the target is small and difficult to detect using victim recovery dogs and geophysics. If much time has passed between the disposal and the search, the target might be undetectable using available technology. Buried infant remains can quickly degrade depending on the burial environment. Sometimes, only wrappings or containers might be recoverable, if at all (Davenport & Harrison, 2011). In cases where the remains are deliberately dismembered and scattered, investigative and environmental barriers will be significant factors in not being able to recover remains even with the offender's cooperation.

The search of the back garden of Seacroft in Case 4 (Fleming) produced nearly 300 fragments of bone and reports of victim recovery dog indications interpreted as 'the smell of decomposition'. The evidence of positive indications was presented at trial as inculpatory evidence of Margaret Fleming's death despite no blood found or human bone confirmed. None of the fragments could be confirmed as human because pieces were too small to identify the diagnostic characteristics associated with human bone (Corrieri & Márquez-Grant, 2019; Ubelaker & Wu, 2020). The presence of bone material is not surprising for an archaeologist excavating anywhere in the British Isles but especially in a domestic setting, given the propensity for people to bury dead pets in back gardens and dispose of kitchen waste (Davenport & Harrison, 2011). The relationship between bone and other evidence types is significant to articulate. Map regression, satellite photographs from previous years, and accounts of locals may aid understanding the legitimate and archaeological presence of bone, such as sheep grazing. More recent satellite images might also corroborate ground observations of possible bonfire sites and may be located at the site using geophysics such as magnetometry. The bonfire perceived archaeologically in Case 4 was also visible in earlier satellite images, but it was also explained by Edward Cairney that he had a bonfire to burn old furniture renovation projects.

Even when human bone material is suspected, its condition may be too fragmented and damaged to render a DNA profile (Case 1 Jones and Case 4 Fleming). Apparent human bone fragments recovered from Mark Bridger's stove would unlikely yield a DNA profile because the comparatively low temperatures required >90°C (194°F) to denature DNA. With only small samples to work on and the technique's destructive nature, the family may not wish to sacrifice the only tangible remains for identification purposes. Therefore, the spatial relationship between suspected human bone fragments and nearby intensive blood staining belonging to April Jones lends corroborative weight. Such relational details become easily disrupted as time progresses as evidenced in Case 4 (Fleming).

Attempts of corporeal obliteration are very serious and not uncommon within the context of homicide cases in the UK. Where fire is the agent of destruction, temperatures maintained around 1000þC are needed to reduce the body to dry cremated bone. The bone then requires additional processing to reduce further its volume, such as crushing. Corporeal obliteration through burning is relatively difficult to achieve because to do so requires the maintenance of high temperatures for long enough while generating a distinctive smell and plenty of smoke. Burning as an obliteration strategy tends to be more successful in rural locations where bonfires are a common practice to eliminate waste. There may be a plentiful supply of fuel and access to containers to maintain temperatures without attracting concern (see *R v Andrew Jones* 2020). Surviving bone fragments may offer tool marks on bone surfaces indicative of dismemberment (Mata Tutor et al., 2021; Thomson & Black, 2017). The clearing of all bone fragments and transportation is extremely difficult if a container is not used in the burning process.

An alternative strategy of obliteration presented in Cases 2 (Baker) and 3 (Prout) is the 'fed to pigs' scenario. Within media representations, the 'fed to pig' hypothesis plays on the visceral fears of the body being consumed by animals. The trope gleefully presented within fictional depictions (e.g. *Snatch* 2000) is that it can be achieved without a trace – an assumption not borne out in the literature and requires challenge. It will be a concerning situation if the pig as a taphonomic agent theory has been used as a convenient way to explain away the absence of evidence without considering the steps involved. The mention of which may be prejudicial in the absence of evidence of pigs being a taphonomic agent. Yet the scenario has been presented in two of the no-body murder cases presented above and other failed prosecutions or abandoned searches (see Harrison, Dawson, & Mackinnon, 2016). The reality is more likely that feeding a body to suids (pigs) would entail extensive pre-processing through the dismemberment of the body. Each stage of processing would leave detectable evidence in the form of bone fragments, teeth, hair, and blood unless extensive steps were carried out to avoid detection at the point of dismemberment, transportation, and the location for feeding. Carrying this out requires a high level of forensic awareness and organisation. The process of detection avoidance generates the need to acquire knowledge (e.g. knowledge of butchery or internet search), equipment for pre-processing risking witnesses, or a paper trail of financial activity.

Suids are omnivores and are common in Europe, with the domestic pig (*Sus scrofa domesticus*) associated with agricultural settings and the wild boar (*Sus scrofa*) common in the woodlands across mainland Europe. In the absence of pre-processing of remains, the literature may assist in understanding how suids scavenge carrion. Indra *et al.* (2022) reviewed literature associated with suid scavenging and its implications on human remains in forensic settings. They produced taxa of bone damage indicative of suid modification of human bone compared with other species. Suid species are associated with soft and hard tissue consumption with no evidence of transporting or caching of remains in the way that rodents or dogs typically carry out when scavenging. Unconsumed bones exhibit the teeth marks of pigs; such markings include pitting, punctures and scoring of the bone surface with observable long and flat grooves (Domínguez-Solera & Domínguez-Rodrigo, 2009). Remains subject to suid scavenging are highly fragmented, and crenulated edges, spiral fractures and splintering of bone may be observed. Pig scavenging is also associated with prying off the caps of long bones (known as epiphyses) (Berryman, 2002). Epiphyses are not easily recognised by non-specialists but generally have a high level of preservation. Ethnoarchaeological evidence suggests pigs are more selective than tropes suggest, leaving bone remains according to size and diminished nutritional values (Greenfield, 1988). The idea of complete obliteration is challenged by the observations of Greenfield (1988) and Domínguez-Solera & Domínguez-Rodrigo (2009). Their independent observations corroborate that suids consume small skeletal elements, mid-size elements exhibit widespread damage, especially to nutritionally higher portions such as cancellous bone, and become highly fragmented. However, larger skeletal elements remain relatively undamaged (Domínguez-Solera & Domínguez-Rodrigo, 2009; Greenfield, 1988).

Those fragments of bone and teeth that pass through the digestive tract are likely to survive and could be recovered from excreta through sieving. Extensive systematic sieving with < 5 mm mesh sieves would be required to capture relevant fragments and due to their size, would require anthropological specialists. Although an unpleasant job, sieving could yield results if the site's search occurred within a reasonable timeframe to the date of assumed death. It would cost an extortionate amount of overtime and relevant expertise to complete such a detailed search. The slaughtering of pigs (as was suspected in Harrison, Dawson and Mackinnon (2016, pp. 203–204) and Case 2 (Baker) would only remove the remains in active digestion and not those that had not been consumed or the fragments present in excreta. Suppose the aim is to obliterate the body; in that case, the taphonomic agent, the pig, is outside the offender's control. The above suggests that additional measures with expert knowledge of how to recognise fragmented bone and teeth would be required to thwart detection.

The potential of suids as a taphonomic agent, usually based on offender access, has led to police and prosecution offering the 'fed to pigs' explanation to juries. Arguments have been presented without additional evidence to support suids as managing obliteration of the body without leaving any evidence behind. Suspicions raised by Harrison, Dawson and Mackinnon (2016) and work conducted by Greenfield (1988), Berryman (2002), Domínguez-Solera & Domínguez-Rodrigo (2009), and Indra *et al.* (2022) do not recognise suids as obliterators. The presence of teeth marks and damage patterns on detritus demonstrate bone's observable nature and recoverability following pig scavenging. Yet as Case 3 (Prout) shows even when an offender has access to a notorious disposal method, it does not necessarily mean it met the offender's requirements. Perhaps investigators should have paid a little more attention to the suspect's skills as a pipe-layer and his role hosting pheasant shoots and less confidence on pigs as the taphonomic agents.

If a conviction is based upon the presentation of an obliteration theory without the presentation of supporting evidence, it raises a potential problem for the Parole Board. In the UK, juries do not provide reasons for their verdicts, and so the Parole Board must assume the jury accepted the prosecution's version of how the remains were obliterated. The destruction of the body or its concealment is an aggravating factor which carries a sentencing penalty which is generally between three and six years added to the starting point (Criminal Justice Act, 2003 see Schedule 21, Criminal Justice Act 2003 - (s.269(5)(a)). The sentence has already been adjusted for the concealment or destruction, so the Parole Board needs to consider avoiding double-counting. The statutory task of evaluating the extent of knowledge of where and how the victim's remains were disposed of and if the prisoner has further information (Prisoner Act 2020 c19 s.1(d,c)) needs to be balanced with expert opinion on the prevailing theory in light of current forensic understandings.

FUTURE RESEARCH DIRECTIONS

The above has provided an initial theoretical framework to understand some of the variables in corporeal concealment and its relationship with non-disclosure. Forensic psychologists and forensic archaeologists (and other search professionals) might now use these insights to develop interview methods specifically for prisoner cooperation in long-term body searches by taking environmental and investigative dimensions into account.

It is hoped that the above provides a starting point to enable further deeper conceptualisation of clandestine deposition incorporating the perspectives and observations of investigative personnel. Forensic archaeology and anthropology have much to offer in developing the conceptualisation of concealment, and corporeal destruction given their first-hand observations. However, greater understanding is required of how concealment and destruction of human remains are understood in the sentencing exercise and how Parole Boards ultimately understand these cases. Stronger links between the relationship between public understanding of corporeal concealment/destruction upon sentencing are needed so that efforts to record, recover, and understand concealment within a range of environments can be tailored to the needs of the court and the broader criminal justice system. Secure access to more detailed data on search contexts and body recovery of resolved cases involving the concealment or corporeal destruction would benefit this area of research.

This work has revealed that assumptions persist surrounding offender behavior because of integrating several areas of academic study and professional literature. It is time for assumptions dictating offender behavior to be revisited, such as choosing a disposal strategy governed by a rational choice and principles of least resistance (also known as least effort). Decision-making in the immediate aftermath of homicide continues to be poorly understood. It cannot be reliably simulated without first understanding post homicide behaviors from analyzing homicide data and contextualized case studies. Other assumptions relating to postmortem taphonomy, such as pigs destroying human remains without a trace, can be empirically simulated but they only have real value if they have the opportunity to inform the court or subsequent proceedings.

CONCLUSION

Media representations assume the only barrier to disclosure is self-preservation of sadistic control. Yet, reasons for non-disclosure may extend beyond those initial recognitions of self-preservation or some cognitive impairment. Psychological explanations are highly significant in the disclosure process, but this is not the only lens to consider factors impacting perceived non-disclosure. Non-disclosure may also be understood by analyzing the disposal strategy undertaken, the environment in which it was undertaken, and the investigative context of previous searches. The presentation of the theoretical model reveals a more interconnected picture of behavioral factors and the environment in which corporeal concealment or destruction occurred. One of the intentions behind the Prisoner Act 2020 is to enshrine in law Parole Board practices in ascertaining the body's whereabouts or an explanation why the remains might be irrecoverable. Yet not all environments offer the same potential for recovery regardless of the prisoner's cooperation. The full deployment of search and location methods cannot guarantee to find a concealed body and even less so when operating on tighter budgets.

Environmental conditions and disposal strategies can hasten decomposition or obliteration. A mix of disposal strategies, as seen in *R v Bridger* accompanied with detection avoidance cleaning, produces a straightforward narrative, the veracity of which is supported by corroborative relational details and overwhelming inculpatory circumstantial evidence. However, such information does not enable a complete reconstruction of deposition events, and even if a full account were to be provided, the remains themselves are unlikely to be recovered.

Environments are dynamic and change over time, disrupting the prisoner's ability to pinpoint a clandestine deposition. Sometimes seemingly minor changes to the environment occurring over a short period can disrupt the ability of offenders to retrace their steps. The cases presented show a range of strategies and decisions are made in depositions. The recovery of Kate Prout shows that access to methods of corporeal obliteration does not mean the offender employed it as a strategy. The correlation between the availability of a disposal strategy and the absence of a body is not sufficient evidence that the strategy was employed.

While the law allows for murder to be inferred from circumstantial evidence, search professionals need to maintain their independence by providing a complete account of the limitations of their evidence and the factors that impact the likelihood of detecting concealments. The absences of data need to be acknowledged, and false-negative and false-positive results need to be explained. Independent expertise is required to assess the reliability and suitability of search methods used. Moreover, current understandings of taphonomic expectations must be reflected so that assumptions are robustly challenged, and interpretations are not extended beyond their limits. Not only should this occur in the trial at first instance, but it may provide much-needed context for the Parole Board. This contribution has attempted to broaden understandings of the complexities involved in corporeal concealment. It highlights dimensions which reside outside the control of the investigative team and the offender(s) and, in part, explain why some prisoners might be released without their victim's body ever being recovered.

REFERENCES

Andrew, C., & Mitrokhin, V. (2000). *The Mitrokhin Archive: The KGB in Europe and the West*. Penguin. doi:10.1080/03071840008446488

Beauregard, E., & Bouchard, M. (2010). Cleaning up your act: Forensic awareness as a detection avoidance strategy. *Journal of Criminal Justice, 38*(6), 1160–1166. doi:10.1016/j.jcrimjus.2010.09.004

Beauregard, E., & Martineau, M. (2014). No body, no crime? The role of forensic awareness in avoiding police detection in cases of sexual homicide. *Journal of Criminal Justice*, *42*(2), 213–220. doi:10.1016/j.jcrimjus.2013.06.007

Berryman, H. (2002). Disarticulation pattern and tooth mark artifacts associated with pig scavenging of human remains: A case study. In M. H. Sorg & W. D. Haglund (Eds.), *Advances in Forensic Taphonomy: Method, Theory, and Archaeological Perspectives* (pp. 487–495). CRC Press.

Bettels, K., Grimstead, D., Allsop, C., Chaussée, A., Bolton-King, R., Sturdy Colls, C., Chapman, B., Keatley, D., Tilley, E., Turner, J., Spence, S., & Marquardt, A. (2022). (in press). Finding the missing and unknown: Novel educational approaches to warming up cold cases. *Science & Justice*. Advance online publication. doi:10.1016/j.scijus.2022.03.007

Bitton, Y., & Dayan, H. (2019). "The Perfect Murder": An exploratory study of staged murder scenes and concealed femicide. *British Journal of Criminology*, *59*(5), 1054–1075. doi:10.1093/bjc/azz015

Boss, P. (1999). *Ambiguous Loss: Learning to Live with Unresolved Grief.* Harvard University Press.

Boss, P. (2006). *Loss Trauma and Resilience: Therapeutic Work with Ambiguous Loss*. Norton.

Chaussée, A. (2019). The language of forensic archaeology: Discourses in field and in court. In K. Moran & C. Gold (Eds.), Forensic Archaeology: Multidisciplinary Perspectives (pp. 75–89). Springer Nature.

Chopin, J., Beauregard, E., & Bitzer, S. (2020). Factors influencing the use of forensic awareness strategies in sexual homicide. *Journal of Criminal Justice*, *71*(April), 101709. doi:10.1016/j.jcrimjus.2020.101709

College of Policing. (2021). *Missing Persons*. https://www.app.college.police.uk/app-content/major-investigation-and-public-protection/missing-persons/#risk-assessment-and-response

Coroners and Justice Act, (2009).

Corrieri, B., & Márquez-Grant, N. (2019). Using nutrient foramina to differentiate human from non-human long bone fragments in bioarchaeology and forensic anthropology. *Homo*, *70*(4), 255–268. doi:10.1127/homo/2019/1113 PMID:31701996

CPS. (2018). *The Code for Crown Prosecutors* (8th ed.). Crown.

ActC. J. (2003). (2003). https://www.legislation.gov.uk/ukpga/2003/44/contents

Davenport, A., & Harrison, K. (2011). Swinging the blue lamp: The forensic archaeology of contemporary child and animal burial in the UK. *Mortality*, *16*(2), 176–190. doi:10.1080/13576275.2011.560706

Domínguez-Solera, S., & Domínguez-Rodrigo, M. (2009). A taphonomic study of bone modification and of tooth-mark patterns on long limb bone portions by suids. *International Journal of Osteoarchaeology*, *19*(3), 345–363. doi:10.1002/oa.987

Doyle, R., & Barnes, G. C. (2020). Targeting missing persons most likely to come to harm among 92,681 cases reported to Devon and Cornwall Police. *Cambridge Journal of Evidence-Based Policing*, *4*(3–4), 160–177. doi:10.100741887-020-00051-2

Dubsky, A., & Christensen, A. (2018). Can intentionally compacting a clandestine grave make it more difficult to detect with a soil probe? *Journal of Forensic Identification*, *68*(1), 147–156.

Evis, L. (2016). *Forensic archaeology: the application of comparative excavation methods and recording systems*. Archaeopress Publishing Ltd. doi:10.2307/j.ctvxw3nq9

Ferguson, C. (2021). *Detection Avoidance in Homicides Debates, Explanations and Responses*. Routledge. doi:10.4324/9780367266851

Ferguson, C., & McKinley, A. (2020). Detection avoidance and mis/unclassified, unsolved homicides in Australia. *Journal of Criminal Psychology*, *10*(2), 113–122. doi:10.1108/JCP-09-2019-0030

Ferguson, C., & Petherick, W. (2016). Getting away with murder: An examination of detected homicides staged as suicides. *Homicide Studies*, *20*(1), 3–24. doi:10.1177/1088767914553099

Fulcher, S. (2017). *Catching a Serial Killer*. Ebury Press.

Greenfield, H. (1988). Special studies: Bone consumption by pigs in a contemporary Serbian village: implications for the interpretation of prehistoric faunal assemblages. *Journal of Field Archaeology*, *15*(4), 473–479. doi:10.1179/jfa.1988.15.4.473

Greenhalgh, M., & Shalev Greene, K. (2021). *Impact of Police Cuts on Missing Person Investigations*. https://pure.port.ac.uk/ws/portalfiles/portal/28691081/Final_version.pdf

Guardianship (Missing Persons) Act (2017).

Harrison, K., Dawson, L., & Mackinnon, G. (2016). Interdisciplinary approaches to the search and location of buried bodies. In H. Kars & L. van den Eijkel (Eds.), Soil in Criminal and Environmental Forensics (pp. 201–212). Springer.

HM Advocate v David Gilroy, (2012) Edinburgh High Court of Justiciary (unreported).

HM Advocate v David Gilroy [2013] HCJAC 18.

HM Advocate v Edward Cairney and Avril Jones, (2019) Glasgow High Court of Justiciary, (unreported).

HM Advocate v Thomas Pryde, (2010) Glasgow High Court of Justiciary (unreported).

Home Office. (1792). *Criminal Registers of Prisoners in Middlesex and the City*. London Lives 1600-1800. https://www.londonlives.org/browse.jsp?div=NAHOCR70005CR700050193

Horsman, G. (2016). Unmanned aerial vehicles: A preliminary analysis of forensic challenges. *Digital Investigation, 16*, 1–11. Advance online publication. doi:10.1016/j.diin.2015.11.002

House of Lords Hansard. (2020). *Prisoners (Disclosure of Information About Victims) Bill*. https://hansard.parliament.uk/Lords/2020-07-01/debates/5FEFEC9B-F6D7-4648-9CF4-2684C353B36E/Prisoners(DisclosureOfInformationAboutVictims)Bill

Hunter, J., & Cox, M. (2005). *Forensic Archaeology Advances in Theory and Practice*. Routledge.

Hunter, J., Simpson, B., & Sturdy Colls, C. (2013). *Forensic Approaches to Buried Remains*. Wiley Blackwell.

Indra, L., Errickson, D., Young, A., & Lösch, S. (2022). Uncovering forensic taphonomic agents: Animal scavenging in the European context. *Evolutionary Biology*, *11*(4), 601–627. doi:10.3390/biology11040601 PMID:35453800

Innes, M., Brookman, F., & Jones, H. (2021). “Mosaicking”: Cross construction, sense-making and methods of police investigation. *Policing*, *44*(4), 708–721. doi:10.1108/PIJPSM-02-2021-0028

Jansen-Osmann, P., & Berendt, B. (2005). What makes a route appear longer? An experimental perspective on features, route segmentation, and distance knowledge. *The Quarterly Journal of Experimental Psychology. A, Human Experimental Psychology*, *58*(8), 1390–1414. doi:10.1080/02724980443000638 PMID:16365946

Janzen, G. (2006). Memory for object location and route direction in virtual large-scale space. *Quarterly Journal of Experimental Psychology, 59*(3), 493–508. doi:10.1080/02724980443000746 PMID:16627352

Jeanis, M., & Powers, R. (2017). Newsworthiness of missing persons cases: An analysis of selection bias, disparities in coverage, and the narrative framework of news reports. *Deviant Behavior, 38*(6), 668–683. doi:10.1080/01639625.2016.1197618

Keatley, D., O'Donnell, C., Chapman, B., & Clarke, D. (2022). The psycho-criminology of burial sites: Developing the winthropping method for locating clandestine burial sites. *Journal of Police and Criminal Psychology, 37*(1), 91–100. doi:10.100711896-021-09457-8

Killam, E. (2004). *The Detection of Human Remains* (2nd ed.). Charles C Thomas.

Liebler, C. (2010). Me(di)a Culpa?: The 'Missing White Woman Syndrome' and media self-critique. *Communication, Culture & Critique, 3*(4), 549–565. doi:10.1111/j.1753-9137.2010.01085.x

Liebler, C., Ahmad, W., & Gayle, G. (2020). Not at Risk? News, gatekeeping, and missing teens. *Journalism Practice*, 1–16. doi:10.1080/17512786.2020.1790407

Maddison, D., Ormerod, D., Tonking, S., & Wait, J. (2020). *The Crown Court Compendium Part I : Jury and Trial Management and Summing Up*. Judicial College. https://www.judiciary.uk/wp-content/uploads/2016/06/Crown-Court-Compendium-Part-I-July-2020-1.pdf

Mata Tutor, P., Márquez-Grant, N., Villoria Rojas, C., Muñoz García, A., Pérez Guzmán, I., & Benito Sánchez, M. (2021). Through fire and flames: Post-burning survival and detection of dismemberment-related toolmarks in cremated cadavers. *International Journal of Legal Medicine, 135*(3), 801–815. doi:10.100700414-020-02447-1 PMID:33084995

Ministry of Justice. (2019). *'Claudia's law' to lift families of missing people out of legal limbo.* https://www.gov.uk/government/news/claudia-s-law-to-lift-families-of-missing-people-out-of-legal-limbo

National Crime Agency. (2021). UK Missing Persons Unit. *Data Report, 2019*, 2020.

Ng, K. (2020, February 6). Helen McCourt: 'Give me my child back,' mother tells killer Ian Simms as he is released from prison. *Independent*. https://www.independent.co.uk/news/uk/home-news/helen-mccourt-mother-ian-simms-killer-release-prison-death-a9321281.html

Overbury, T. (1676). A true and perfect account of the examination, confession, trial, condemnation and execution of Joan Perry, and her two sons, John and Richard Perry, for the supposed murder of Will. Harrison, Gent Being one of the most remarkable occurrences which hath h. Early English Books Online, Text Creation Partnership.

Parole Board. (2021). *Disclosure of Information about Victims Member Guidance*. Author.

Pokines, J., Mammano, K., Studebaker-Reed, M., Mowery, J., Patterson, M., Schneider, C., Trapp, B., & Mincher, C. (2018). Success rates of recovering dispersed bones among leaf litter. *Forensic Anthropology*, *1*(4), 189–200. doi:10.5744/fa.2018.0021

Presumption of Death Act (2013).

Presumption of Death (Northern Ireland) Act (2009).

Presumption of Death (Scotland) Act (1977).

Pringle, J. K., & Jervis, J. R. (2010). Electrical resistivity survey to search for a recent clandestine burial of a homicide victim, UK. *Forensic Science International*, *202*(1–3), e1–e7. doi:10.1016/j.forsciint.2010.04.023 PMID:20471188

Prisoners (Disclosure of Information About Victims) Act (2020).

Ruffell, A., & McKinley, J. (2014). Forensic geomorphology. *Geomorphology*, *206*, 14–22. doi:10.1016/j.geomorph.2013.12.020

Ryan, N., Westera, N., Kebbell, M., Milne, R., & Harrison, M. (2020). To know where the bodies are buried: The use of the cognitive interview in an environmental scale spatial memory retrieval task. *Applied Cognitive Psychology*, *34*(3), 565–576. doi:10.1002/acp.3640

Slakoff, D., & Fadella, H. (2019). Media messages surrounding missing women and girls: The "Missing White Woman Syndrome" and other factors that influence newsworthiness. *Criminology, Criminal Justice. Law & Society*, *20*(3), 80–102.

Stillman, S. (2007). 'The missing white girl syndrome': Disappeared women and media activism. *Gender & Development: Media*, *15*(3), 491–502. doi:10.1080/13552070701630665

The Guardian. (2021, October 27). Helen's law: killer refused parole for failing to disclose where body hidden. *The Guardian*. https://www.theguardian.com/society/2021/oct/27/helens-law-killer-refused-parole-for-failing-to-disclose-where-body-hidden

The King v Hindmarsh, [1730] 74 ER; [1792] 168 ER 387.

Thomson, G., & Black, S. (2017). Principles of tool mark analysis and evidential best practice. In S. Black, G. Rutty, S. Hainsworth, & G. Thomson (Eds.), *Criminal Dismemberment: Forensic and Investigative Analysis* (pp. 79–96). CRC Press. doi:10.1201/9781315373126-7

To, D. (2017). Forensic archaeology survey methods, scene documentation, excavation, and recovery methods. In N. Langley & M. Tersigni-Tarrant (Eds.), *Forensic Anthropology: A Comprehensive Introduction* (pp. 35–56). CRC Press.

Ubelaker, D. H., & Wu, Y. (2020). Fragment analysis in forensic anthropology. *Forensic Sciences Research*, *5*(4), 260–265. doi:10.1080/20961790.2020.1811513 PMID:33457044

UK Centre for Ecology and Hydrology. (2022). *Dyfi Bridge 2012*. https://eip.ceh.ac.uk/hydrology/water-resources/#introText

R v Adrian Prout, (2010) Bristol Crown Court, (unreported).

R v Andrew Jones, (2020) Swansea Crown Court (unreported).

R v Bridger, Mark (2013) Mold Crown Court (unreported).

R v Christopher Halliwell, (2016) Bristol Crown Court, (unreported).

R v Davies [2008] EWCA Crim 1055.

R v Mark Bridger, (2013) Mold Crown Court, (unreported).

R v Martin Gerald Baker, (2006) Central Criminal Court, (unreported).

R v Martin Gerald Baker [2008] EWCA Crim 3118.

R v Onufrejczyk [1955] 1 All ER 247; [1955] 1 QB 388.

R v Shirley Banfield and Lynette Banfield [2013] EWCA Crim 1394.

R v Thomas Davison (1934) Old Bailey (unreported).

van Meter, J. G. (1961). Proof of the corpus delicti by circumstantial evidence where the body is never found. *West Virginia Law Review*, *63*(2), 156–161.

Young, J., Higgins, D., & Austin, J. J. (2021). Soil DNA: Advances in DNA technology offer a powerful new tool for forensic science. *Geological Society of London, Special Publications*, *492*(1), 239–247. doi:10.1144/SP492-2017-351

ADDITIONAL READING

Blau, S. (2009). More than bare bones: ethical considerations for forensic anthropologists. In S. Blau & D. Ubelaker (Eds.), *Handbook of Forensic Archaeology and Anthropology* (pp. 457–467). Left Coast Press.

Groen, W., Márquez-Grant, N., & Janaway, R. (Eds.). (2015). *Forensic Archaeology: A Global Perspective*. Wiley Blackwell. doi:10.1002/9781118745977

Hunter, J., & Cox, M. (2005). *Forensic Archaeology Advances in Theory and Practice*. Routledge.

Junkins, E., & O'Carter, D. (2017). Relationships between human remains, graves and the depositional environment. In E. Schotsmans, N. Márquez-Grant, & S. Forbes (Eds.), *Taphonomy of Human Remains: Forensic Analysis of the Dead and the Depositional Environment* (pp. 145–154). John Wiley & Sons. doi:10.1002/9781118953358.ch11

Killam, E. (2004). *The Detection of Human Remains* (2nd ed.). Charles C Thomas.

Litherland, S., Márquez-Grant, N., & Roberts, J. (2012). Forensic Archaeology. In N. Márquez-Grant & J. Roberts (Eds.), *Forensic Ecology Handbook: From Crime Scene to Court* (pp. 23–48). John Wiley and Sons. doi:10.1002/9781118374016.ch3

Wayland, S., Maple, M., McKay, K., & Glassock, G. (2016). Holding on to hope: A review of the literature exploring missing persons, hope and ambiguous loss. *Death Studies*, *40*(1), 54–60. doi:10.1080/07481187.2015.1068245 PMID:26207394

Chapter 9
An Analysis of Biases in US Policing and Subsequent Media Coverage in Response to the Ferguson Shooting of 2014

Liam James Leonard
University of Winchester, UK

EXECUTIVE SUMMARY

This chapter will examine the biases in the policing and subsequent media coverage in response to the shooting of Michael Brown in Ferguson, Missouri, a suburb of St Louis, in 2014. This shooting has become a landmark case that highlight these biases that can have fatal consequences for young African-Americans. The list of cases of police shootings of African-Americans in controversial circumstances is a long and disturbing one and includes victims such as young Tamir Rice, and 12-year-old child shot by police while playing in the playground by his home, also in 2014. The chapter presents an analysis of issues in criminal justice, policing, the courts, and the media which occurred in this case. The shooting of Michael Brown can also be placed alongside the killing of George Floyd in Minneapolis in 2020 as an example of biases in policing, which can have a fatal outcome for African-Americans in the United States.

INTRODUCTION

This chapter provides an analysis of the events surrounding the shooting of Michael Brown in Ferguson, St. Louis in August 2014, and the subsequent media coverage of

DOI: 10.4018/978-1-7998-9668-5.ch009

this event. The goal of this chapter is not to ascertain the guilt of the parties involved in this incident. It does however attempt to present an analysis of the event using Critical Race Theory, as well as a further analysis of the editorial framing agendas of certain media groups which covered the incident.

Critical Race Theory has been the subject of considerable controversy and debate in the United States in recent years. Nonetheless, any serious academic study of contemporary policing of African Americans must acknowledge the scarred history of slavery, the Jim Crow era, the trenchant resistance to basic civil rights for African American by some whites, and a history of hostile policing of that minority group during the Civil Rights struggle in the 1950s and 1960s through to the murder of George Floyd in Minneapolis in 2020. Critical Race Theory puts forward an analysis of the United States as a systemically racist country, through all of that nation's institutions, including the police and large sections of the media.

These media groups were chosen for their online content and editorial policies which reflected the framing of events surrounding the police shooting of Mike Brown, an unarmed youth, in Ferguson, a neighborhood in St Louis. This chapter provides a critical analysis of the coverage provided by media groups such as NBC Online, CNN and the *Washington Post*. Online media outlets were utilized in the research for this chapter, from the evening of the Michael Brown shooting in August 2014 through to the official response of President Barak Obama to the shooting, protests and Grand Jury announcement in November and December 2014. The chapter attempts to provide an understanding of policing and media biases during this coverage, in order to add to the debates on key issues such as media, policing and race in this case and for future analysis.

METHODOLOGY

Assessing Media Valuation Strategies

This chapter employs a critical media analysis developed through an *evaluation strategy*. 'Evaluation strategies' are broad, overarching perspectives on evaluation. The evaluation strategy utilized in this chapter is the qualitative/anthropological model which emphasizes the importance of observation, the need to retain the empirical strengths of the evaluation process, alongside significant aspects of the evaluation process. The chapter also examines the evaluation strategies of both mainstream and alternative media sources in their coverage of the events in Ferguson.

BACKGROUND

On August 9th, 2014, an unarmed eighteen-year-old youth was shot and killed by a police officer in Ferguson, Missouri, a suburb of St. Louis. It is important to note that the youth, Michael Brown, was an African American, while the officer involved in the shooting, was white. In the subsequent days and weeks which followed, crowds of protests would take to the streets of Ferguson to protest about the shooting. The police response to these protests caused further concern for many Americans watching news reports on television and online.

These concerns were heightened by the appearance of militarized armored vehicles and police dressed in military style body armor. For a period of time, the streets of Ferguson began to resemble a besieged city in Iraq or Afghanistan, as the police response took on the appearance of a military occupation. Americans were shocked to see such images in the American heartland. Policing in the United States had seen to reach a disturbing turning point. Another significant aspect of some of the mainstream coverage was the hostile depiction of African Americans in the story, from street protestors to family members and advocates.

We can reflect on the issues that surround the emergence of militarized policing in the United States, in order to explore the issue of race and policing. In addition, the events at Ferguson and other controversial such incidents will be discussed. This methodology will utilize theories of policing, employ a media analysis and develop an issue history to explain the background to problems with policing in African American neighborhoods over many decades, all of which will culminate in the presentation of alternative solutions to problems in community policing nationwide.

By applying a Qualitative Content Analysis of the Evaluation Strategies behind media coverage of the events at Ferguson, the chapter will provide an evaluation of how mainstream and social media reported on what occurred in the St. Louis suburb on the night of Michael Brown's death, and in the weeks subsequent to that event. Meanings will be elucidated from the media event analysis, which will provide findings and establish understandings of the relevant issues surrounding the issues of race and policing and military policing both in St. Louis and across the United States.

The chapter will provide coding frames to assist with the creation of pattern analysis of contributing events in relation to race and militarization as aspects of policing. This framework is part of the "Issue History" which can be developed around such key factors.

MEDIA ANALYSIS: UNDERSTANDING THE "STORYLINE"

The shooting of Michael Brown by police on the 9th of August 2014 in Ferguson was covered by multiple mainstream media outlets across the nation. NBC News featured the Brown shooting by incorporating nearly 300 storylines about events at Ferguson onto its online edition. Therefore, a media analysis based on the coverage of NBC News, as a national media outlet, will provide the first part of this wider investigation.

Public Versus Private

The first NBC report on what occurred at Ferguson is dated August 10, 2014. The dichotomous approach to this story is immediately indicated by the controversial headline "Kill the Cops" which is carried over a photo of local protestors holding their hands up as part of what would be known as the "Don't Shoot" stance taken by participants who wanted to replicate the last stance and words of Michael Brown, as reported by witnesses. The "Don't Shoot" hands up stance would become a central image of the Ferguson protests.

In the report, Ferguson is described as 'a predominantly black suburb north of downtown St. Louis'. After describing how the shooting victim's grandmother found the body in the street near his home, the police response provided was non-committal:

A spokesman with the St. Louis County Police Department, which is investigating the shooting at the request of the local department, confirmed a Ferguson police officer shot the man but didn't give the reason for the shooting (Fieldstadt, 2014).

The report then outlines the response to the incident, stating a crowd gathered outside the Ferguson police station shouting slogans such as "Kill the police". The article ends with a photo of Lewis Head, Michael Brown's stepfather, who holds a sign saying, 'Ferguson Police just executed my unarmed son'. The other main photo is of the crowd confronting police officers who are standing behind a yellow crime scene tape.

Both images establish two of the main narratives of the Ferguson case; one is of the personal tragedy to the Brown family while the other highlights the emotional response of the wider African American community in the area. The coding of the personal and the public aspects of this issue will be among the issues covered in this study. The initial coverage by NBC.com of both aspects sets the tone for the overall coverage of what occurred at Ferguson, and both require scrutiny to provide a fuller understanding of the key issues involved.

This 'public/private' approach is often utilized by media outlets for political coverage such as electoral campaigns. The candidate's public statements are contrasted with private behavior in order to create a moral code filter where moral judgments and condemnations can be applied. This moral filter gives media its power over political events and allows the media to breakdown events for its client audience, with added values such as ideology then included through editorial control.

In the initial NBC.com coverage, the public have been given a public view of the Brown family as poor and marginalized, as the photo of Michael Brown's stepfather holding a torn piece of cardboard with a scrawled inscription, while the public depiction of the Ferguson community was shown to be unruly in the face of a stoic police line. The lines of media coverage had been drawn, and all subsequent coverage would follow along these lines.

Establishing the Media Narrative

The second report dated August 10th used in this analysis combines footage from the police conference with a report on events. This report outlines the police department's version of events surrounding the shooting:

St. Louis County Police Chief Jon Belmar said Michael Brown, of Ferguson, Missouri, was struck "more than just a couple" times by gunshots fired by a Ferguson Police Department officer after a "physical confrontation" that began in a police vehicle and then spilled on to the street. The officer is now on paid administrative leave, Belmar said. The Ferguson Police Department reached out to Belmar immediately following the incident requesting that the St. Louis County Police Department launch an independent investigation, he said (Fieldstadt, 2014).

The police department press conference was reported as a definitive version of events, one which through doubts on eyewitness claims that the victim was shot while surrendering. In addition, footage of protestors provided a demarcation between the police reports and the response of community; in so doing, the media can be seen to be building a framework which favored the authorities and cast doubt on the witnesses' accounts, thereby casting the unruly protestors as responding in a visceral and ultimately lawless fashion.

A further dichotomy is established in the report as police are shown to 'reach out' to Chief Belmar in St. Louis. Conversely, the National Association for the Advancement of Colored People (NAACP) is presented outside of this local 'reaching out' as they called for a wider response from the justice sector:

The shooting has sparked an outcry in the predominantly-black town of about 21,000 — a suburb of the city of St. Louis — and the local chapter of the NAACP have launched their own investigation into the case, appealing to the FBI for help. "We are hurt to hear that yet another teenage boy has been slaughtered by law enforcement," St. Louis County NAACP President Esther Haywood said in a statement (Fieldstadt, 2014).

The Ferguson community is depicted as an outside community to the rest of the city in these reports ('the predominately-black town of about 21,000') while the police are depicted as requiring outside support from the start. Implicitly, the reports are establishing the Ferguson community as a potential threat, to the police and to the security of the St. Louis region. This in some ways provides congruence for the police report which indicated 'a struggle' before Michael Brown was shot and killed, again running against witness statements.

The end result of this form of reporting is one which establishes an understanding that the authorities are telling the truth while the community (victim's family, witnesses, community spokespersons and protestors) must therefore be presenting a version of events which are in some way untrue, rendering any further responses from this group to be somewhat outside the truth and ultimately, outside the law. This is a quintessentially 'hegemonic' response from the media, as outlined by the theorist Antonio Gramsci, in his text *Selections from the Prison Notebooks*. Here, Gramsci outlines the notion that a 'cultural hegemony' through which the manipulations by the cultural institutions of the ruling class reflect the prevailing beliefs, morals and values of that society, and that these then influence the status quo in such a way that only benefits the ruling classes (Gramsci, 1982).

For Gramsci, cultural hegemony can be understood as the manipulation of language in the establishment of relations of power between those in the establishment and the rest of society. In contemporary society, cultural institutions such as the mainstream media which provide the platform for the establishment of hegemony, as television and newspapers set out understandings of social and political events according to the agendas of those in power. While the reports on Ferguson may have done so unintentionally, the modern media industry provides a cultural aspect to the establishment, as a part of what the writers Edward S. Herman and Noam Chomsky have described as 'Manufacturing Consent' (1988). In their book *Manufacturing Consent: The Political Economy of the Mass Media*, Herman and Chomsky argue that the mainstream media in the U.S. are:

...effective and powerful ideological institutions that carry out a system-supportive propaganda function, by reliance on market forces, internalized assumptions, and

self-censorship, and without overt coercion", by means of the propaganda model of communication' (Herman and Chomsky, 1988).

Protesters, Looters, or Rioters?

The third group of reports focused on the community's response to the shooting. Headlines varied from 'Looting Erupts After Vigil for Slain Missouri Teen Michael Brown' to 'Missouri Teen's Fatal Shooting by Cops Sparks Riots' and 'Looters Raid Store After Cop Shoots Teen' (NBCUniversal News Group, 2014a). Accompanying photos show looters ransacking a grocery store.

While looting has often taken place after public protests, there was no attempt made in the reports to differentiate between the protests which emerged spontaneously after Michael Brown's shooting and the opportunistic looting which followed. No one involved in the protests had advocated looting, although anti-police sentiment was openly expressed.

Essentially, the reports had run a thread between the response of the Brown family and Ferguson community which had mobilized in a show of support for them after the shooting, and the criminal behavior of opportunistic looters who had taken advantage of the turmoil in the area. To the outside observer, a large section of the community at Ferguson had been criminalized, despite the fact that no one had at that point been made accountable for the shooting of an unarmed youth in the neighborhood.

Moreover, while there was no direct evidence of a link between the protestors and the looting which came afterwards, the report drew a thread between both events and their participants:

A day of anger over a fatal police shooting of an unarmed black man in suburban St. Louis turned to mayhem as people looted businesses, vandalized vehicles and confronted police... The tensions erupted after a candlelight vigil...Afterward, a convenience store was looted. Several other stores along a main road near the shooting scene were broken into, including a check-cashing store, a boutique and a small grocery store (Salter, 2014).

The reports on looting were interspersed with coverage of the protests. While police chiefs appealed for calm, the FBI were said to be investigating the incident. The family of Michael Brown released a statement saying: 'We need Justice'. As protests continued, police used tear gas against participants. One issue which emerged was the refusal of police the name the officer involved in the shooting. This led to suspicions of a cover up.

By August 18th, the Missouri Governor Jay Nixon had called a State of Emergency and issued a curfew in Ferguson. Police had released a video which appeared to show Michael Brown taking a pack of cigars from a local store, while pushing a store owner aside in the process. The release of this video enraged protestors further, who saw it as an attempt to smear Brown's name in the aftermath of his shooting.

Mainstream media reports stated that 'armored vehicles rolled back onto the streets of Ferguson…as riot police faced off with looters'. The blurring of lines between 'protestors', 'rioters' and 'looters' continued, even when national figures joined the protests:

Protests had started off peacefully in Ferguson on Friday night. Rev. Jesse Jackson linked arms with protesters, leading them in prayer and urging them to "turn pain into power" while fighting back non-violently. Shortly after midnight, crowds got rowdier and looting began to break out (NBCUniversal News Group, 2014b).

The national media contained many images of a militarized police force being deployed at Ferguson in a manner which surprised many observers. As protestors adopted the "Hands Up-Don't Shoot" surrender pose which witnesses said Michael Brown took just before his shooting, the police lines which faced them included militarized vehicles and weaponry which were more readily associated with battles during the Iraq War than with the American heartland. And while many accepted the need for a strong response to looting, the deployment of such a militarized force against Americans in their own neighborhoods was surprising and disturbing to many.

By the 19th of August, after 10 days of protests, the Missouri National Guard had been deployed. Attorney General Eric Helder stated he would travel to Ferguson to try to intervene. This wider response came as the protests continued, and the militarized style policing response intensified. The release of the autopsy on Michael Brown showed the extent of his injuries, angering protesters further.

PORTRAYAL OF EXTERNAL PARTICIPANTS

One aspect of the police response was the arrest of observers, journalists, and others in a heavy-handed crackdown in the Ferguson area. A State Senator was arrested at a protest while two journalists were arrested at a local restaurant for not evacuating quickly enough:

State Senator Jamilah Nasheed, a Democrat from St. Louis, was arrested outside the police station for walking and standing in the street in violation of a city ordinance, according to St. Louis County police, who are helping patrol the streets (McClam, 2014).

Respected Princeton academic and rights advocate Cornel West was arrested along with 49 other protestors on the street and at a local Walmart. Professor West spoke at an Interfaith Rally on October 12th, which drew an attendance of 2,000 people. The meeting also featured contributions from ordinary protestors who voiced their objection to the Brown shooting.

It is also interesting to examine the coverage given to external participants by certain media groups. *The Guardian Online* presented coverage of the arrest of two journalists early in the protests on August 13th and 14th, 2014. Jon Swaine for The Guardian outlined the arrest of the journalists as follows:

Two reporters were arrested, and teargas was fired at demonstrators in Ferguson, Missouri, on Wednesday, five nights after an unarmed black teenager was shot dead by an officer from the town's predominantly white police force. The Washington Post condemned the detention of its journalist, Wesley Lowery, as "illegal" and an "assault on the freedom of the press to cover the news". The Huffington Post attacked the arrest of its reporter, Ryan J. Reilly, as "militant aggression". Reilly said that the "police resembled soldiers more than officers" (Swaine, 2014).

It is worth noting the different slant taken by the traditionally liberal leaning *Guardian*, (a US edition of a British newspaper) in comparison with the more conservative *NBC Online* coverage discussed earlier. Here, the Guardian seems to have captured the prevailing mood of both Americans who were shocked at the militarized appearance of the police deployed at Ferguson and the concerns expressed by both the *Washington Post* and the *Huffington Post* at the treatment of their reporters at the hands of this police force.

It is also interesting to note that the Guardian stresses the fact that Michael Brown was 'an unarmed teen' and that Ferguson's police were 'predominately white'. This coverage is very different to *NBC Online's* depiction of unruly protestors and out of control looters.

The Guardian's Jon Swaine witnessed the arrest of two reporters, and described it as follows:

The two reporters were taken in cuffs from a McDonald's in downtown Ferguson and placed in an unmarked white police van. "They're reporters," shouted one member of the public, who had also been in the restaurant. Lowery and Reilly both tweeted about being asked to leave the restaurant moments before they were seen being arrested. Asked why he was being detained, the first reporter shouted: "For videotaping them." When I approached a police line in an effort to confirm the reporters' identities, I was threatened with arrest and told to retreat (Swaine, 2014).

Marty Baron, executive editor of the *Washington Post*, condemned the arrests in a statement, where he said "there was absolutely no justification for his arrest" and said the organization was appalled by the conduct of the officers involved. Lowery was illegally instructed to stop taking video and followed police instructions, Baron said, after which he was slammed into a machine and handcuffed. "That behaviour was wholly unwarranted and an assault on the freedom of the press to cover the news," Baron said. "The physical risk to Wesley himself is obvious and outrageous (Swaine, Roberts, and Glenza, 2014).

The Guardian also provided some insight to these events by publishing excerpts from Wesley Lowery's Twitter account. These excerpts provide the reader with an understanding of what transpired in the chaos of Ferguson in the aftermath of the shooting and protests:

Officers decided we weren't leaving McDonalds quickly enough, shouldn't have been taping them. Officers slammed me into a fountain soda machine because I was confused about which door they were asking me to walk out of... Was waiting to be taken away, large black man SCREAMING for help in back of police truck. They refused his several calls for paramedics."I'm dying. I'm dying. Please call help he screamed." They mocked him. Got no explanation at any point why in custody other than "trespassing" - at a McDonalds where we were customers. I'm emotional, but need to note: Ryan and I are fine. ...Have seen people in Ferguson hurt by gas/ rubber bullets. This wasn't that (Swaine, 2014).

The Guardian can also be distinguished from the coverage of *NBC Online* due to its utilization of academic perspectives of the events at Ferguson. The British criminologist Tim Newburn provides a discussion of how Ferguson differs from previous British race related protest. In his article, Newburn contrasts the 2011 shooting by British police of Mark Duggan, and unarmed black teenager from London, with that of Michael Brown in Ferguson. Newburn cites a report commissioned by the London School of Economics and *the Guardian* called 'Reading the Riots' that provided the following findings:

Beyond the shooting itself, significant alienation among young people and deep distrust of, and hostility towards, the police were key factors in the rioting in all the cities in which disorder occurred (Newburn, 2014).

Despite the similarities in both cases, where young unarmed black men were shot by police, followed by a period of unrest, Newburn outlines the differences in the UK and US incidents. What becomes crucial from Newburn's perspective was the outbreak of 'an information war' in both cases, almost from the moment the shootings took place.

Initially, the police released details, including stills from a surveillance camera, of a convenience store robbery that had occurred just before the shooting, suggesting that Brown had been involved. Details of the initial autopsy on Michael Brown were then made public, including the suggestion that he had traces of cannabis in his bloodstream.

As family and friends had felt in the Duggan case, it appeared that strenuous efforts were being taken to divert attention from the shooting itself. The rioting, though it has not as yet spread beyond Ferguson, has exhibited many of the elements that were evident in England in 2011: attacks on police, the looting of local stores, the widespread destruction of property, and complaints about police harassment (Newburn, 2014).

Nonetheless, Newburn outlines some distinctive aspects to both events. While he sees Ferguson as being very much about race, it was only partially so in the UK after Duggan was shot. (Duggan was part Afro-Caribbean and part Irish, both communities which have traditionally suffered at the hands of the UK police). In the aftermath of a series of shootings of black youth in the US such as Trayvon Martin killing in February 2012, the killing of Michael Brown, another unarmed African American youth, was seen to be a tipping point in community relations with the police across the United States.

Newburn sees real similarities between Ferguson and the UK's largest riots by the Afro-Caribbean community in South London, Birmingham and Liverpool in the early 1980s. These riots had contributory factors which combined race and policing, all issues which had been instrumental in the events in Ferguson.

The manner in which predominately white police forces had policed black communities in 2011 London and 2014 St. Louis shaped the responses of local communities angered by the killing of unarmed youths from their neighborhoods. Newburn also sees differences in the response of the UK police and the militarized force which descended on Ferguson, and notes that the Missouri Highway Patrol had brief success in calming the situation:

As illustrated by the brief interlude in Ferguson last week when the highway patrol managed briefly to quell the disorder, a combination of firm but proportionate policing with serious engagement with the community is generally viewed as holding out the greatest promise of success (Newburn, 2014).

While comparative studies are interesting, local factors are often the most telling. One person stood out in the Ferguson case in a manner which had a local resonance. In the midst of the chaotic scenes of militarized policing and angry protestors at Ferguson, a hero in short sleeves emerged. Captain Ron Johnston provided the type of leadership and common-sense community policing that St. Louis and the nation was crying out for. Captain Johnston was an African American and a lifelong St. Louis resident, and a distinguished member of the Missouri Highway patrol.

After weeks of near-apocalyptic scenes on the streets of Ferguson, the sight of Captain Johnston working with protest leaders to restore calm in the face of what seemed to be an invasion was one of the remarkable images of a tumultuous late summer in Missouri. Johnston marched with protestors, restoring a lost sense of justice to their cause. At that moment, Johnston seemed to embody a type of policeman which all communities could relate to, and all policemen should aspire to be.

Online Survey Debates

While the mainstream media examined the issue in a traditional manner, the online discussion was sometimes more nuanced. This section will examine media discussions about online surveys on Ferguson. The sites involved are YouGov and the Pew Research Center, with the results being discussed on Huffington Post. According to the Pew Research Survey, there is a marked difference in the responses of black and white people to the Ferguson shooting and aftermath:

"Blacks are about twice as likely as whites to say that the shooting of Michael Brown "raises important issues about race that need to be discussed" (Pew Research Center, 2014).

The survey also outlined variations in the black and white population in relation to the police response and investigation to the shooting. The survey of 1000 people taken in the aftermath of the shooting, demonstrates certain differences in both sets of the population on many of the key questions surrounding the incident. The survey asks whether:

Important issues about race or whether the issue of race is getting more attention than it deserves: 44% think the case does raise important issues about race that require discussion, while 40% say the issue of race is getting more attention than it deserves (Pew Research Center, 2014).

By about four-to-one (80% to 18%), African Americans say the shooting in Ferguson raises important issues about race that merit discussion. By contrast, whites, by 47% to 37%, say the issue of race is getting more attention than it deserves (Pew Research Center, 2014).

While many in the African American population were concerned about the Brown shooting in the aftermath of similar deaths of young African Americans such as Trayvon Martin, many whites seem to think that too much focus was being placed on race. This understanding was clearly influenced by the media coverage of the Ferguson incident and serves as a reminder of the need for balanced coverage of incidents involving race and policing.

This racial divide can also be seen in relation to the question of whether the police went too far in their response to the Ferguson shooting, though the deploying of a militarized force with heavy armored vehicles for instance:

Fully 65% of African Americans say the police have gone too far in responding to the shooting's aftermath. Whites are divided: 33% say the police have gone too far, 32% say the police response has been about right, while 35% offer no response.

Three quarters of African American respondents had little confidence in the judicial process. This can be compared with roughly one third of whites who responded, this sector felt the justice system was fair and could be trusted. Therefore, the challenge remains to those in the justice system; how can this gulf in confidence be overcome?

In relation to the Brown shooting, the Pew survey found that there was a political as well as racial divide in the responses received. For those who replied from both races, 68% of those who identified themselves as Democratic voters found that the Brown case raises important issues about race, while 61% of those who identified themselves as Republicans felt the Ferguson incident has gotten too much attention in the media.

These finding reveal a racial and political divide which is centered on the media coverage of events such as the Ferguson shooting and its aftermath. According to Robert Jones in *The Atlantic*:

the Pew Research Center poll found that overall the country is divided over whether Brown's shooting "raises important issues about race that need to be discussed" (44 percent) or whether "the issue of race is getting more attention than it deserves" (40 percent). However, black Americans favor the former statement by a four-to-one margin (80 percent vs. 18 percent) and at more than twice the level of whites (37 percent); among whites, nearly half (47 percent) believe the issue of race is getting more attention than it deserves (Jones, 2014).

Figure 1. Pew Research Center Survey August 14th -17th, 2014

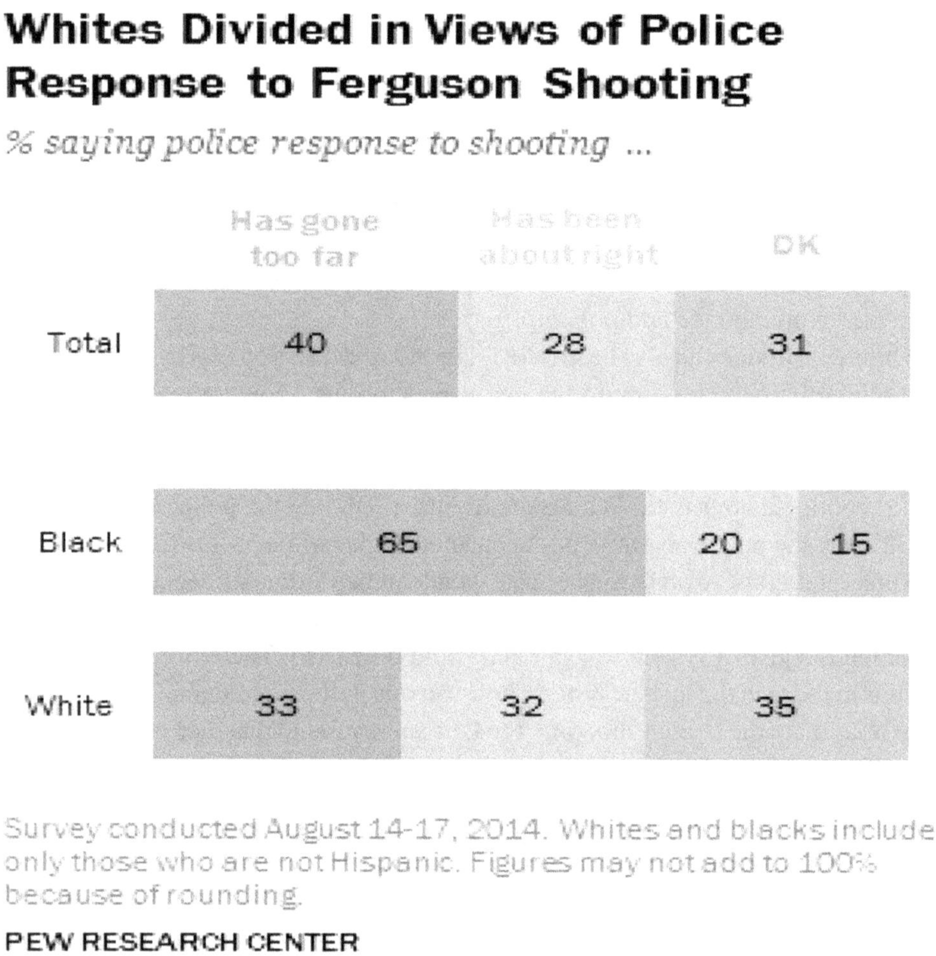

Issues with The Grand Jury

In the aftermath of the shooting and subsequent unrest, the St. Louis Prosecutor, Robert P. McCulloch had the option of bypassing a Grand Jury hearing and brining the case straight to trial. However, he chose instead to call a Grand Jury. In most cases, a Grand Jury is comprised of twelve people selected from an existing jury pool to meet *in camera*, (closed court) on a weekly basis for duration of six months.

The jury meets to hear evidence and form an opinion on whether criminal charges are warranted in a particular case. In most cases, it takes nine votes to issue an

Figure 2. Pew Research Center Survey August 14th -17th, 2014

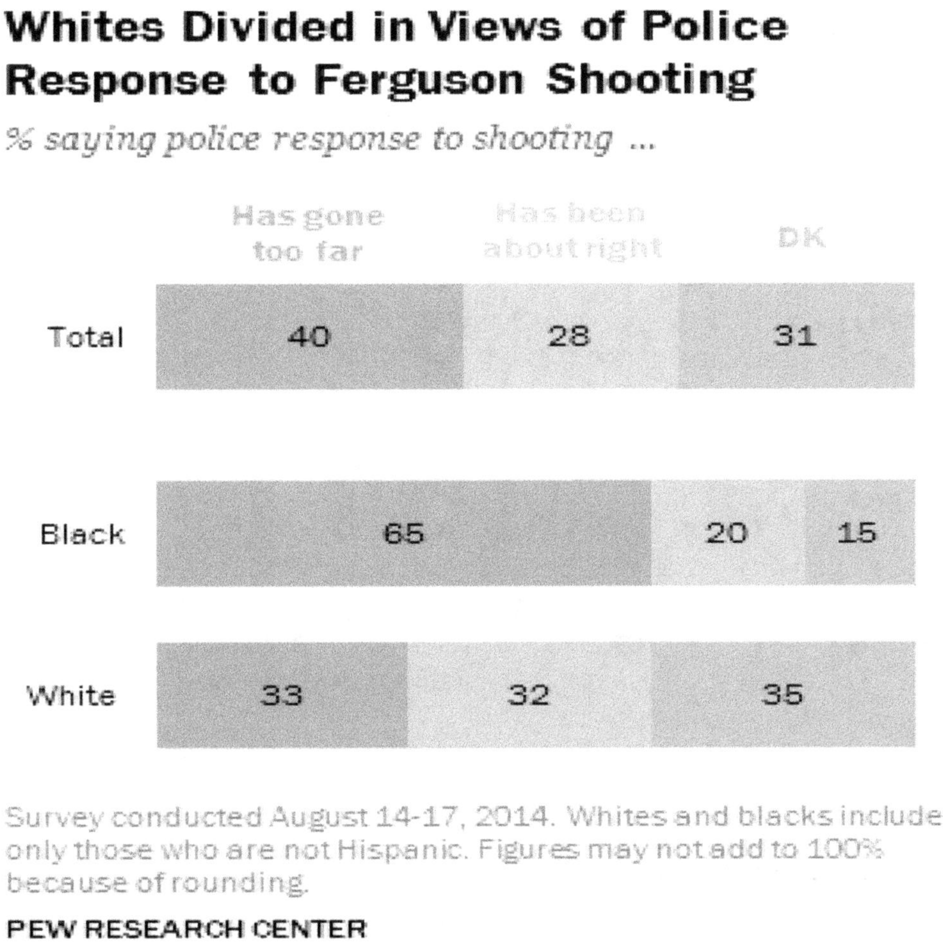

indictment, which subsequently sends a defendant to a public trial. St. Louis Today outlined the procedure surrounding the Grand Jury in this case:

St. Louis County Prosecuting Attorney Robert P. McCulloch can bypass a grand jury and take a case to trial by filing a complaint that goes first to a preliminary hearing, a public proceeding in which a judge decides if there should be a trial. Often, his office files a charge first and then obtains an indictment to replace it, avoiding the preliminary hearing. McCulloch chose to take the full investigation of Wilson's use of deadly force to the grand jury.

Figure 3. Pew Research Center Survey August 14th -17th, 2014

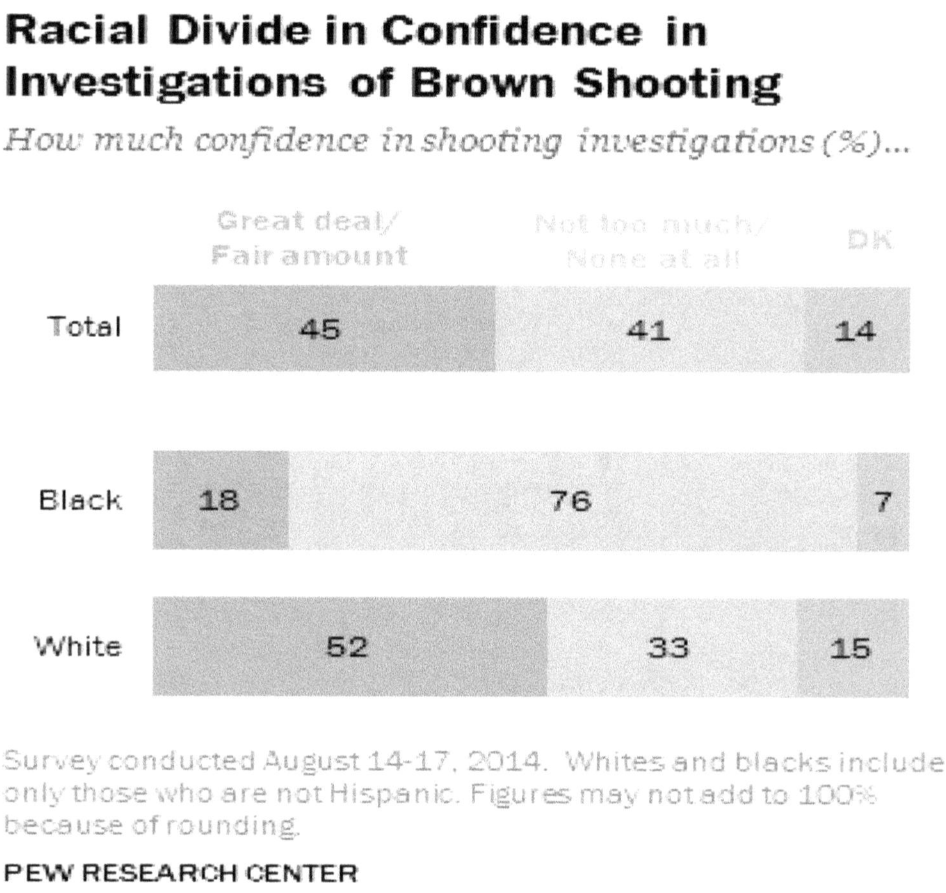

He announced weeks ago that he would present all the evidence gathered, leaving to grand jurors the decision of what to do. His spokesman, Ed Magee, said Monday it is a somewhat unusual circumstance in that the office is not asking the grand jury to endorse a charge already filed. He said prosecutors will help the grand jury navigate legal issues and draw its own conclusion about what to do with Wilson. Wilson is entitled but not obligated to testify. If he does, he must leave his attorney at the door (Byers, 2014).

The Grand Jury panel was comprised on nine whites and three blacks, and this jury had been sworn in earlier in the summer of 2014, before the shooting. The jury was not sequestered during the hearing. There were petitions to have Prosecutor

Figure 4. Pew Research Center Survey August 14th -17th, 2014

Most Republicans Say Race Is Getting Too Much Attention in Teen Shooting

% saying police shooting of African-American teen ...

	Raises important issues about race	Race getting too much attention	DK	N
	%	%	%	
Total	44	40	15=100	1000
White	37	47	16=100	718
Black	80	18	2=100	106
Hispanic	50	25	24=100	107
18-29	55	34	11=100	170
30-49	41	43	16=100	242
50-64	44	39	17=100	266
65+	40	44	16=100	279
College grad+	51	41	8=100	372
Some college	40	42	18=100	281
HS or less	43	39	18=100	339
Republican	22	61	17=100	247
Independent	40	46	14=100	354
Democrat	68	21	11=100	292

Survey conducted August 14-17, 2014. Whites and blacks include only those who are not Hispanic. Figures may not add to 100% because of rounding.

PEW RESEARCH CENTER

McCulloch step down from the Brown shooting case, due to a perception of his closeness with the St. Louis police department. CNN also report concerns about the impartiality of some of those selected to participate on the jury. Nonetheless,

McCulloch prevailed and on September 16th, Officer Wilson testified to the Grand Jury.

Many media outlets expressed concerns about the grand jury system and the potential for some bias preventing cases such as that of the Brown shooting going to trial. Grand Juries are a somewhat unusual aspect of the United States justice system, with origins dating back to pre-Independence British rule. In fact, Britain (England/Wales and Scotland), along with its former colonies in Canada, Ireland, Australia and New Zealand have all ceased to use the grand jury system, which had originated in the 12th century. In the United States, the use of Grand Juries is part of the 5th Amendment which reads:

The Fifth Amendment to the U.S. Constitution, adopted in 1791, includes a grand jury clause that reads, "No person shall be held to answer for a capital, or otherwise infamous crime, unless on a presentment or indictment of a grand jury." All federal capital crimes and federal crimes punishable by imprisonment for more than one year must therefore be presented to a federal grand jury, unless the accused waives this right. The federal grand jury does not determine whether the accused is guilty; rather, it decides if there is "probable cause" to believe that the accused has committed a crime. By codifying the grand jury in the Fifth Amendment, the framers intended to protect people "against hasty, malicious and oppressive prosecution (Cordell, 2014).

Some states use grand juries along with a 'preliminary hearing' system. The preliminary hearing allows for cross-examination of witnesses. Grand juries on the other hand do not allow for evidence or cross-examinations. Unlike preliminary hearings which are open to the public, grand juries are held in private. This creates inherent problems, according to Cordell:

In high-profile, controversial cases, where officers use lethal force, prosecutors face a dilemma. If they don't file charges against officers, they risk the wrath of the community; if they do file charges, they risk the wrath of the police and their powerful unions. By opting for secret grand jury proceedings, prosecutors pass the buck, using grand jurors as pawns for political cover. The Michael Brown and Eric Garner cases are examples of how prosecutors manipulate the grand jury process (Cordell, 2014).

In the Ferguson case, the Grand Jury's role was to decide whether or not there was a case to answer against Officer Wilson, and whether a crime had been committed. It did not decide on his innocence or guilt; this would have been the role of a new jury if the case had gone to trial. The Telegram provided this description of the Grand Jury in the Ferguson case:

The grand jury is composed of 12 people "selected at random from a fair cross-section of the citizens," according to Missouri law. The jury is 75 percent white: six white men, three white women, two black women and one black man. St. Louis County overall is 70 percent white, but about two-thirds of Ferguson's residents are black. Brown was black. The officer is white (Telegram & Gazette, 2014).

The St. Louis County Grand Jury had been coming to the end of a standard four month term, and had been hearing routine cases once a week during that time. The jury sat with the Prosecutor and a witness. While grand juries often here an abridged version of the evidence at hand, in the Ferguson case more detailed evidence was presented, along with testimonies of witnesses and participants in the incident. A former chief medical examiner for the City of New York, Dr. Michael Baden, who performed one of three autopsies on Michael Brown, also gave evidence.

Once the St. Louis County Grand Jury had completed its deliberations on the Ferguson case after three months, its verdict was announced. There would be no trial in the case of the shooting of Michael Brown. While protests erupted nationally, the media attempted to shed light on the grand jury process in this case.

The Washington Post interviewed Ed Magee, spokesman for Prosecuting Attorney Robert McCulloch, alongside other legal experts in order to help with a greater understanding of the process which had taken place. Here is a selection of questions from that interview:

Q: Did the jury's ruling on whether to indict Wilson for the Aug. 9 fatal shooting of Brown have to be unanimous?

A: No. In Missouri, there are 12 members on a grand jury and nine must vote in favor of an indictment for there to be one.

What standard is used to determine whether Wilson should be indicted?

Jurors have to decide whether there is probable cause to believe Wilson committed a crime. The standard is lower than a jury trial in criminal court, where jurors must determine whether there is proof beyond a reasonable doubt that a crime was committed.

Will there still be a trial in criminal court?

No. The grand jury was convened to determine if Wilson should face criminal charges for the shooting. No indictment means no trial.

If new evidence surfaces in the case, can a new grand jury be convened?

There is no statute of limitations on a homicide, so if new evidence emerged, it would be reviewed and the case would possibly go to a new grand jury.

Does the grand jury decision have any bearing on the Justice Department's criminal investigation into Wilson?

No. The Justice Department probe will continue on its own course. However, the FBI — which is investigating for the Justice Department — and the St. Louis

County Police Department cooperated with one another, sharing all evidence gathered during their investigations. People familiar with the investigation have told The Post that the Justice Department is unlikely to file charges against Wilson. It is looking at whether Wilson violated Brown's civil rights in the fatal shooting.

What about the Justice Department's broad civil rights investigation into the Ferguson Police Department?

The federal government will also continue looking at whether the Ferguson Police Department is engaged in widespread civil rights violations that require reforms (Kindy, 2014).

Other answers provided in the interview included confirmation that jurors could not go public with details of the hearing while witnesses could, the Brown family could take a civil case, but the lack of a prosecution would count against this, and that Officer Brown was stepping down from the Ferguson Police Department.

The shooting was subject to three separate investigations. The first was undertaken by the St. Louis County Police Department. The second was that of the Federal Bureau of Investigations (FBI). In the third investigation, the Department of Justice Civil Rights investigation was called in order to verify whether any police department policies or federal or state laws had been violated. According to now retired Attorney General Eric Holder: 'The problems exposed by Ferguson threaten the entire nation'. Holder spoke of the broken bonds between communities and the police that were meant to serve them:

Broadly speaking, without mutual understanding between citizens... whose rights must be respected...and law enforcement officers ...who make tremendous and often-unheralded personal sacrifices every day to preserve public safety...there can be no meaningful progress," Holder said in prepared remarks. "Our police officers cannot be seen as an occupying force disconnected from the communities they serve. Bonds that have been broken must be restored. Bonds that never existed must now be created (Holder as quoted in Shackford, 2014).

Holder referred to Brown's death as a 'tragedy' and looked for a 'national conversation' about criminal justice and law enforcement in the aftermath of the Brown shooting[1].

REFERENCES

Byers, C. (2014, September 16). Grand jury now has until January to decide whether to charge Ferguson officer. *St. Louis Post Dispatch.* Retrieved from https://www.stltoday.com/news/local/crime-and-courts/grand-jury-now-has-until-january-to-decide-whether-to-charge-ferguson-officer/article_aa4111fc-2952-54c9-8316-76c4867dea48.html

Chomsky, N., & Herman, E. (1988). *Manufacturing consent: The political economy of the mass media*. Pantheon Books.

Cordell, L. H. (2014, December 9). Grand Juries Should Be Abolished. *Slate*. Retrieved from https://slate.com/news-and-politics/2014/12/abolish-grand-juries-justice-for-eric-garner-and-michael-brown.html

Fieldstadt, E. (2014, August 11). *Teen killed by Missouri officer after 'physical confrontation': Police*. Retrieved from https://www.nbcnews.com/storyline/michael-brown-shooting/teen-killed-missouri-officer-after-physical-confrontation-police-n177206

Gramsci, A. (1982). *Selections from the Prison Notebooks*. Lawrence and Wishart.

Jones, R. (2014, August 21). Self-Segregation: Why It's So Hard for Whites to Understand Ferguson. *The Atlantic*. Retrieved from https://www.theatlantic.com/national/archive/2014/08/self-segregation-why-its-hard-for-whites-to-understand-ferguson/378928/

Kindy, K. (2014, November 24). How the Ferguson grand jury process works. *The Washington Post*. Retrieved from https://www.washingtonpost.com/politics/how-the-ferguson-grand-jury-process-works/2014/11/24/46599f9a-73f9-11e4-a589-1b102c2f81d0_story.html

Leonard, L. (Ed.). (2017) Environmental Criminology: Spatial Analysis and Regional Issues, Advances in Sustainability and Environmental Justice. Emerald Group Publishing.

McClam, E. (2014, October 21). *State senator Jamilah Nasheed arrested in latest Ferguson protest*. Retrieved from https://www.nbcnews.com/storyline/michael-brown-shooting/state-senator-jamilah-nasheed-arrested-latest-ferguson-protest-n230411

NBCUniversal News Group. (2014a, August 11). *Looters raid store after cop shoots unarmed Missouri teen*. Retrieved from https://www.nbcnews.com/storyline/michael-brown-shooting/looters-raid-store-after-cop-shoots-unarmed-missouri-teen-n177516

NBCUniversal News Group. (2014b, August 16). *Michael Brown killing: Police in Ferguson fire tear gas amid looting*. Retrieved September 30, 2022, from https://www.nbcnews.com/storyline/michael-brown-shooting/michael-brown-killing-police-ferguson-fire-tear-gas-amid-looting-n182196

Newburn, T. (2014, August 20). The Ferguson riots may seem similar to those in UK in 2011 – but there are stark contrasts. *The Guardian*. Retrieved from https://www.theguardian.com/commentisfree/2014/aug/20/ferguson-missouri-not-so-far-from-tottenham-toxteth

Pew Research Center. (2014, August 18). *Stark racial divisions in reactions to Ferguson Police shooting*. Pew Research Center - U.S. Politics & Policy. Retrieved from https://www.pewresearch.org/politics/2014/08/18/stark-racial-divisions-in-reactions-to-ferguson-police-shooting/

Salter, J. (2014, August 11). *Vandalism, looting after vigil for Missouri man*. AP News. Retrieved from https://apnews.com/article/business-shootings-police-michael-brown-vandalism-f9de54875a4d450683e07bfd0691df14

Shackford, S. (2014, December 2). Holder Says Feds to End Racial Profiling. Unless He's Declaring an End to the Drug War, No. *Reason*. Retrieved from https://reason.com/2014/12/02/holder-says-feds-to-end-racial-profiling/

Swaine, J. (2014, August 14). Ferguson police arrest reporters amid rage over Michael Brown shooting. *The Guardian*. Retrieved from https://www.theguardian.com/world/2014/aug/14/ferguson-police-arrest-reporters-as-unrest-continues-over-michael-brown-shooting

Swaine, J., Roberts, D., & Glenza, J. (2014, August 14). Missouri governor removes St Louis police from Ferguson protest duty. *The Guardian*. Retrieved from https://www.theguardian.com/world/2014/aug/14/obama-ferguson-police-excessive-force-michael-brown#:~:text=%E2%80%9CThat%20behavior%20was%20wholly%20unwarranted,arrest%20of%20reporter%20Wesley%20Lowery

Telegram & Gazette. (2014, November 24). Answers to questions about the Ferguson grand jury. *The Worcester Telegram & Gazette*. Retrieved from https://www.telegram.com/story/news/state/2014/11/24/answers-to-questions-about-ferguson/35873516007/

ENDNOTE

1 Some of the material in this chapter was the subject of the author's study included in Leonard, L. (Ed) (2017) *Environmental Criminology: Spatial Analysis and Regional Issues*, Advances in Sustainability and Environmental Justice, Emerald Group Publishing, Bingley.

Chapter 10
The Aileen Wuornos Case: Bending the Criminal Binary of Monsters and Martyrs

Christine Bussey
Judson College, USA

EXECUTIVE SUMMARY

During an era in which serial killers simultaneously terrified and titillated the American public, Aileen Wuornos stood out in what had largely been, and continues to be, a boys' club. However, unlike her male counterparts, Wuornos incited revulsion rather than enthrallment. Indeed, even feminist advocacy groups, which had championed the right of abused women to defend themselves, were silent when it came to Wuornos's prosecution, incarceration, and execution. To understand this abdication requires consideration of the ways in which understandings of crime, specifically those involving women, are dichotomized. Two decades after the execution of Aileen Carol Wuornos, have these same binaries been bent?

INTRODUCTION

Though executed by the State of Florida two decades ago, Aileen Carol Wuornos, "America's Most Notorious Female Serial Killer," lives on through social discourse, particularly that generated by an ever-growing tome of cinematic portrayals. To date, the most memorable of these is likely Charlize Theron's Oscar-winning performance of Wuornos in the 2003 biographical crime drama *Monster*. However, the specter of Wuornos has undoubtedly reached viewers through other movie genres, including documentary and horror/thriller, as well as via telejournalism.

DOI: 10.4018/978-1-7998-9668-5.ch010

Amidst these characterizations, a discernible dichotomy emerges in the telling of Wuornos' murderous saga. To be sure, the preponderance of accounts underscores the primordial viciousness she exacted on her victims, depicting Wuornos as an unconscionable brute refusing to duly assume responsibility for her barbarity. Yet, other depictions attempt to humanize her, providing context for her heinous acts by emphasizing the cruel life circumstances she faced and the resulting trauma she endured. This chapter undertakes discussion of Wuornos' criminal existence within the societal imagination as either monster or martyr.

ANALYTICAL FRAMEWORK

Feminist criminology offers insight into the monster/martyr criminal binary to which accounts of Wuornos' criminal violence skew. For much of its disciplinary history, criminology evaded serious contemplation of female criminality. When women's criminality was contemplated, women offenders were characterized as aberrant, having defied what was believed to be their inherent femininity. For example, Cesare Lombroso, "Father of Modern Criminology," opined in the nineteenth century that woman's natural disposition was wholly incompatible with criminality and that a female offender was "more terrible than any man" (Lombroso and Ferrero, 1895, p. 151).

Lombroso's contention that women's de facto nature was incompatible with the purported masculinity of crime ossified within American penology. Indeed, presumptions regarding women's innate femininity gave rise to paternalistic lenience shown by the criminal justice system, a microcosm of the larger patriarchal society in which it functioned. Women's lessened culpability stemmed from perceptions of their physical and mental capabilities, as well as their inability to eschew emotion. For example, when incarceration grew nationally as means of social control, it was widely supposed that women could not survive the austerity of imprisonment. Separate carceral facilities for women emerged, equipped with programming designed to cultivate femininity, which was deemed lacking or absent in women who broke the law. However, the criminal justice system's presumptive chivalry did not extend to the "evil woman," one who flouted conventional femininity; instead, undeserving of mercy, the female offender received harsher treatment (Belknap, 2020). The "evil woman's" societal affront is two-fold, having violated both the law and the dictates of her prescribed gender role. The resounding absence of support for Wuornos, even from feminist advocacy groups, as she faced prosecution, sentencing, and execution, suggests that the ostensible masculinity of her criminal acts, coupled with her unfeminine presentation, eliminated her eligibility for any modicum of chivalrous consideration.

The woman offender who is deserving of chivalry and the evil woman who isn't problematize another criminological dyad: victim and offender. With few exceptions, such as the affirmative defense of self-defense, these categories cannot merge. Yet, reality challenges this calcification. While victims do not always become perpetrators, "it is the rare serious perpetrator who was not also a victim" (Smith, 2004, p. 369). As Young (1996) observes, the battered woman who kills her abuser embodies "both victimhood (she is a battered woman) and criminality (she commits homicide)" (p. 24). This "dual value" within the criminal justice system prompts a crisis of interpretation: Is she an offender or a victim, a monster or a martyr? The inconsistencies within Wuornos' own accounts of her crimes complicate her designation as victim.

MAIN FOCUS OF THE CHAPTER

Issues, Controversies, Problems

When it comes to recounting the murders committed by Aileen Carol Wuornos, there exists little consensus beyond the body count. In 1991, she confessed on videotape to killing six men whom she had lured to secluded locations along Florida's Highway 75. A seventh victim was named, but his body was never recovered. Despite being resoundingly referred to as the first "female serial killer," historical research suggests that this dubious distinction is incorrect. Sociologist and criminologist Eric Hickey estimates that, from 1800-1988, nearly three dozen female serial killers existed within the United States (Chesler, 1992). Debate also exists as to whether Wuornos was actually a serial killer. American psychotherapist Phyllis Chesler (1992) notes that Wuornos did not exemplify the characteristics emblematic of serial killers: she wasn't addicted to pornography; she didn't eroticize her hatred; she didn't stalk prostitutes (she was a prostitute); and she plead self-defense, at least initially, which is a rarity among serial killers.

Discrepancies further arise as to what animated her murderous spree (Diamond, 2019). Many of the inconsistencies in understanding her motivations came from Wuornos herself. Though several individuals corroborated some of what she claimed to have done, she often "misstated the truth" or "clearly produced fabrications" (Shipley & Arrigo, 2004, p. 95). Wuornos obfuscated "'what happened' by shaping her account in different ways at different times" (Diamond, 2019, p. 2). Discrepancies also appear in academic analyses of her crimes. Chesney-Lind and Eliason (2006) write that "most testimony suggests she killed men who threatened violence against her in an extreme form of post-traumatic stress disorder," which these scholars contend "transformed from the framework of battered woman syndrome to a predatory serial killer by the media" (p. 37). In contrast, based on their synthesis of Wuornos' own reporting and the available forensic evidence, Shipley and Arrigo (2004) challenge the contention that Wuornos perceived being lethally threatened by her victims, including her first, Richard Mallory, who had served nearly a decade in prison for assault with an attempt to rape. However, Chesler (1992) finds Wuornos' trial testimony detailing Mallory's attack compelling and further notes that "the jury never got to hear any evidence about violence towards prostitutes in general, or about Mallory's history of violence towards women in particular" (p. 948). [1] Moreover, despite widespread incredulity that Wuornos could have killed in self-defense six times, her lifelong history of suffering abuse may very well have engendered true belief that her life had been endangered by these men (Ibid).

To recognize Wuornos' killings as acts of self-defense requires both conventional understanding of this affirmative defense, as well as how Dr. Lenore Walker's pioneering research on the "learned helplessness" experienced by abuse victims expanded conceptualization of this defense. In American jurisprudence, the doctrine of self-defense privileges a person to defend themselves through the use of force reasonably necessary to counter an apparent threat of imminent and unlawful violence from another. The person claiming self-defense cannot be the initial aggressor and must "reasonably believe" that they are facing immediate threat of harm. The degree of force used cannot exceed the amount necessary to neutralize the threat. Wuornos' killings do not seamlessly comport with the dictates of this legal doctrine. Most problematic is ascertaining whether she "reasonably believed" that each of her victims posed an imminent lethal threat to her. In her lone trial, that for the killing of Richard Mallory, she provided what seemed compelling testimony as to her reasonable belief that using deadly force was necessary. However, another legal doctrine, that of imperfect self-defense, could have applied and would have mitigated against imposition of a death sentence. Imperfect self-defense does not require reasonability of the defendant's belief, only sincerity in the defendant's belief. Reasonability of belief is assessed in accordance with a reasonable person standard.

METHODS AND CRIMINOLOGICAL THEORY

The methods used for this chapter included a case study methodology, which explored the Wuornos case, investigation, trial and subsequent outcomes. Some media analysis and a survey of relevant literature was incorporated into this approach. In the main, the theories used were criminological, and feminist theory was also utilized here. We can outline the case study approach in the following manner. A case study incorporates the collection and presentation of detailed information about a particular case, including the key issues, details and areas of focus surrounding the case and investigation, and any subsequent trial and legal outcome. Media analysis is also utilized for case studies. A case study generated 'Grounded Theory', from which an analysis of the case is built. According to Glaser, Strauss, and Strutzel (1968), there are four main 'Elements of Grounded Theory'. There are as follows:

- **Fit:** This has to do with how closely concepts fit with the incidents they are representing, and this is related to how thoroughly the constant comparison of incidents to concepts was done.
- **Relevance:** A relevant study deals with the real concern of participants, evokes or captures the attention, and is not only of academic interest.
- **Workability:** The theory works when it explains how the problem is being solved with much variation.
- **Modifiability:** A modifiable theory can be altered when new relevant data is compared to existing data (ibid).

Therefore, a Grounded Theory is never simply 'right or wrong', it just has more or less fit, relevance, workability and modifiability, according to Glaser, Strauss, and Strutzel. The application of grounded theory to a case such as the one studies here allows for the development of a framework of analysis which is beneficial to generating outcomes, all of which underpins the case and therefore creates new understandings of the existing information on the case, its investigation, legal proceedings and outcomes. It also allows for the incorporation of other perspectives from outside the criminal justice system, such as political or media perspectives. According to Yin (2009), the Case Study Method can 'satisfy the three tenets of the qualitative method: describing, understanding, and explaining'.

Wider perspectives emerge from these three key tenets, which can then be used to support findings derived from the main issues of focus and units of analysis in the case study itself. Furthermore, Yin outlines three important facets of the case study approach:

Exploratory case studies, fieldwork, and data collection may be undertaken before research questions and hypotheses, but the framework of the study must in place. Selecting cases is a difficult process, but offers the opportunity to maximize what can be learned. Explanatory cases are suitable for doing causal studies. The utilization outcomes were explained by three rival theories: a knowledge-driven theory, a problem-solving theory, and a social-interaction theory.

Problem-solving theory follows the same path, but originates not with a researcher, but with an external source identifying a problem. The social-interaction theory claims that researchers and users belong to overlapping professional networks and are in frequent communication).

Descriptive cases require that the investigator begin with a descriptive theory. This facilitates comparative studies, 'active learning', and cause-effect relationships. The descriptive theory must cover the depth and scope of the case study (Yin, 2009).

CRIMINOLOGICAL THEORY

For a case study of this type, criminological theory provides the backdrop for the analysis of the case. Criminology examines the criminal justice system, its processes and outcomes. It also can incorporate wider sociological perspectives such as feminism. Essentially, criminology examines power and control in society, with a focus on law, order, crime and justice. We also examine the behavior of criminals through this approach. For instance, Sutherland's own theory of 'Differential Association' contends that criminal behavior is itself a learned through conditioning and social interaction with those who re-enforce criminality through peer-pressure. These re-enforces pass on criminal behavior, attitudes and avoidance procedures in a process of developing deviant norms in a context where non-deviant norms are largely absent. In this way, deviant criminality becomes functional in so much as it becomes a function of the deviant subculture which emerges from the absent of positive normative behavior and socialization.

This perspective included a concern with behavioral factors as part of an attempt to understand and rehabilitate criminals into a process of managing crime and criminal behavior. Punishing transgressive behavior superseded any concern with understanding or reforming such behavior as a result of this cultural shift. From a theoretical perspective, this cultural move towards punitive managerialism led to a need to re-assess sociological understandings of peer-influence and socialization conditioning. In other words, theorists began to question whether crime could be understood through the 'nature versus nurture' debate. Did someone commit a crime due to impulsive and selfish tendencies, or did criminal behavior originate in peer-pressure and negative socialization? Why do some children from marginal backgrounds become criminals while others go on to achieve 'successful' lifestyles?

We can also explore concepts of control and social control through the case study approach.

Writing in his seminal work Crime Control as Industry (2016), Nils Christie outlines his vision of how western societies were facing increased unrest due to unequal wealth distribution and lack of access to properly paid work. After a sustained period of neo-liberalism and rationalization throughout the western world,

Christie's prediction of rising crime rates in relatively wealthy states came to pass. However, the responses to this increase in crime have been varied from nation to nation. In Christie's case, the rise of the 'crime control industry' is a response that combines social control with a growth industry based on processing members of certain sections of society through a course of action that includes arrest, remand, trial and imprisonment at a time when the emphasis on rehabilitation appears to have diminished.

The globalization of criminal activity has provided a backdrop towards the growth of what Christie termed 'the crime control industry'. States which were used to dealing with identifiable local threats from indigenous crime gangs have had to adapt to the onset of a multinational crime sector, where those orchestrating crimes have access to global networks of cohorts, materials and customers. Some of the more audacious criminal figures have been known to make contact with the media through mobiles, as the cult of personality has come to include crime figures who attempt to embody the lifestyle depicted in television programs, movies and documentaries, which are very popular with the public at large. One example of this is the movie based on the Wuornos case, titled *Monster,* and starring Charlize Theron as Wuornos, and Christina Ricci as her companion and accomplice.

CONCLUSION

Two decades have passed since Aileen Carol Wuornos was executed for, what are resoundingly described as, the serial murders she committed. A discernible dichotomy exists as to whether the lethal violence she exacted skewed more heretical or heroic. As to the former, the innate masculinity of her crimes violated what many deem the natural law of prescribed gender roles, thereby calling for her sustained demonization in the retelling of her story. However, a counternarrative, one characterizing her more as an anti-heroine who ultimately "fought back" against the systems that failed her, challenges the conceptualization of her as a "monster." This latter understanding of Wuornos' crimes derives from expanded comprehension of what it means to, within the legal context, act in self-defense.

REFERENCES

Belknap, J. (2020). *The invisible woman: Gender, crime, and justice*. Sage Publications.

Chesler, P. (1992). A woman's right to self-defense: The Case of Aileen Carol Wuornos. *John's L. Rev.*, *66*, 933.

Chesney-Lind, M., & Eliason, M. (2006). From invisible to incorrigible: The demonization of marginalized women and girls. *Crime, Media, Culture*, *2*(1), 29–47. doi:10.1177/1741659006061709

Christie, N. (2016). *Crime control as industry: Towards gulags, western style.* Routledge. doi:10.4324/9781315512051

Diamond, S. (2019). "A Flower in a Hard Rain": Melodramatic Storytelling by, and About, Aileen Wuornos. *Anthurium A Caribbean Studies Journal, 15*(2).

Glaser, B. G., Strauss, A. L., & Strutzel, E. (1968). The discovery of grounded theory; strategies for qualitative research. *Nursing Research*, *17*(4), 364. doi:10.1097/00006199-196807000-00014

Lombroso, C., & Ferrero, G. (1895). The female offender (Vol. 1). D. Appleton.

Shipley, S., & Arrigo, B. (2004). *The Female Homicide Offender: Serial Murder and the Case of Aileen Wuornos*. Pearson Prentice Hall.

Smith, A. (2004). The monster in all of us: When victims become perpetrators. *Suffolk UL Rev.*, *38*, 367.

Yin, R. K. (2009). *Case study research: Design and methods* (Vol. 5). sage.

Young, A. (1996). *Imagining Crime Textual Outlaws and Criminal Conversations.* Academic Press.

KEY TERMS AND DEFINITIONS

Battered Woman Defense: An expansion of the affirmative self-defense, incorporating understanding of Battered Woman Syndrome.

Battered Woman Syndrome: A set of psychological symptoms experienced by women victimized by domestic violence that instills a sense of learned helplessness. Dr. Lenore Walker's research in the 1970s and 80s is credited for recognition of BWS in the mental health and legal fields.

Chivalry Hypothesis: The presumption that women comporting with conventional gender norms will be treated more leniently by the criminal justice system than men, as well as those women who defy such norms.

Evil Woman Hypothesis: The presumption that women acting in defiance of conventional gender norms will be treated more severely by the criminal justice system than men who engage in comparable acts or women who comport with such norms.

Feminist Criminology: A subfield of criminology that addresses the questions of (1) whether theories explaining male criminality aptly apply to female criminality and (2) why criminal behavior has historically and overwhelmingly manifested as a male phenomenon.

Imperfect Self-defense: An affirmative defense in which the accused's honest but unreasonable belief in the necessity of using force mitigates the punishment imposed.

Self-Defense: An affirmative defense in which the accused's honest and reasonable belief in the necessity of using force absolves them of culpability.

ENDNOTE

1 Chesler (1992) discusses multiple witnesses who offered accounts of Mallory's violence towards women: Jackie Davis (former girlfriend), Chastity Lee Marcus (an exotic dancer and prostitute), and Nancy Peterson (another ex-girlfriend). For various reasons, none of which involved witness refusal, these women did not testify for the defense.

Chapter 11
A Rural Community's Mobilization and Media Strategies in Response to a Contested Infrastructural Project

Liam James Leonard
Arden University Manchester, UK

EXECUTIVE SUMMARY

The chapter will examine the mobilization and social media response of a rural community in Ireland to the imposition of a gas pipeline on their farms, in the western coastal region of that jurisdiction. This analysis will include a discussion of the concept of 'rural sentiment' as a factor in the mobilization of community campaigns against infrastructural projects which are perceived as a threat to existing ways of life in regional areas. The chapter will also explore key theoretical concepts for this community-based responses to environmental degradation in rural areas, including critical criminology, green criminology rural criminology and resource curse theory and ask whether the campaign was ecopopulist, with issues of social and environmental justice at its core. The 'crime' here was in relation to the disruption of nature and community life in a rural area by a corporate entity, backed by the state. The case analysis will be achieved through a case study approach.

DOI: 10.4018/978-1-7998-9668-5.ch011

INTRODUCTION

Land grabbing is described as a process involving 'outsiders–nation-states as well as corporations – colluding with local domestic elites to radically alter existing land ownership and land uses' (White, 2012, p.1). This article will examine one such process, which pitted a rural Irish community against corporate actors and state agencies in an attempt to protect their families and land from the imposition of an onshore gas pipeline and processing plant. This form of dispute has been demonstrated to have 'social justice issues' at its core (Carrington and Pereira, 2011). This campaign of opposition would lead to the imprisonment of local activists, known as 'the Rossport 5', the establishment of an activist community group '(Shell to Sea') which was opposed to the ecological degradation caused by the pipeline in an area which had been set out as a conservation area due to its scenic beauty and biodiversity. The article utilizes White's understanding of 'activity which diminishes social equity in the provision of healthy sustainable environments' (White, 2012, p.1) as 'eco-crime' in order to locate this case within the rural criminology/green criminology nexus.

The article's framework incorporates a number of competing actors, each of which takes a position on the pipeline project based on their dominant paradigms. For the corporate entities involved the development represents an opportunity for profit making from resources embedded in the North Atlantic off the Irish coastline. The Irish state was promoting a form of accelerated development which would bring jobs to rural areas. Although agriculture and fishing had traditionally provided employment for some in the local community, emigration rates remained high in the region. The state was committed to the introduction of large-scale infrastructural projects as part of the prevailing neo-liberal policies favored by the coalition government which was in power from the earliest days of this pipeline dispute, through to the economic crisis which followed the collapse of the Irish banking system in 2008. In addition, a coalition of groups opposed to the pipeline emerged in support of the local farmers who were imprisoned for refusing to sign a document in which they would guarantee to stay away from the pipeline, despite its proximity or incursion on to their lands.

This dispute occurred in line with a tradition of rural and suburban communities who have mobilized to resist infrastructural projects by the state or corporate actors, ranging from campaigns against nuclear power and toxic industries in the 1980s through to 'anti-roads' campaigns against motorways in the 1990s (Leonard, 2006, 2008). This mobilization, by the 'Shell to Sea' campaign against the Corrib Gas pipeline operated by corporate multinationals, throws up a number of questions about risk society, ecological modernization, state policy and community movement responses to all of these issues, which will be interrogated in this chapter.

THEORETICAL FRAMEWORK

The theoretical framework for this chapter will include the perspectives of Green Criminology, Critical Criminology and Rural Criminology. Critical Criminology provides a critique based on the political economy of a rural community which opposed corporate and state entities during the gas pipeline dispute. It also allows for a critique of the oppressive manner in which the Irish criminal justice system was used against the community protest group which emerged in resistance to the pipeline and development. Green Criminology and Rural Criminology provides scope for a rural perspective on this dispute, based on the potential for the degradation of a rural community and its environment due to the pipeline and installation development. The rural community in the County Mayo of Ireland has fought for recognition of community rights since the Land League agitation of the late 1800s, and many involved in the gas pipeline dispute feel they are continuing in a local tradition of community rights advocacy.

As the local community is an indigenous 'Gaeltacht' or traditional Irish speaking area, it has indigenous origins which have set it apart from those who have tried to impose perceived injustices such as mass evictions, removal of farming and fishing rights and industrial development by the state under British or Irish rule, or corporate entities. I argue that this form of rural response as having its origins in a type of 'rural sentiment' (Leonard, 2008). The study will utilize 'Resource curse theory' (Aughty, 1993) to demonstrate the inability of a post-colonial country such as Ireland to utilize its resources without the intervention of corporate multinationals, who don't have local interests at heart. The chapter will also use social movement framing theory to indicate how the protesters were able to extend their risk frame by increasing the sense of shared grievance surrounding local identity, sense of place and sense of exploitation by the corporate multinationals involved in the development of the gas pipeline.

A Political Economy of Resource Exploitation

The political economy of resource exploitation in this case involves the Irish state, who sold off their nation's resources for one of the lowest royalties ever negotiated with the multinational corporate sector. Over time, a number of Tribunals of Inquiry have been established to investigate the political class in Ireland over recent decades (Leonard 2014). From both the critical and rural criminology perspective, the actions of the Irish state in establishing 'sweetheart deals' with corporate entities creates problematic themes, such as rural resource exploitation and the use of national criminal justice systems to uphold these deals against the interest of the local communities involved.

According to Ruggiero and South:

Power misused or used for profit to the exclusion of all else is likely to cause harm. Business and government interests exploit both environmental resources and human labour. But even more damaging is that, although all this may apply to market economies in general, hegemonic discourses around 'growth and freedom' have, during the last few decades, intensified the potential destructiveness of enterprise. In this respect, neo-liberal doctrines contradict their very axioms: namely, that the full costs of transactions must be borne by the involved parties (Ruggiero and South 2013).

Successive Irish governments have had allegations of corruption against them, and there were many concerns voiced about the nature of the deals done between the state and multinational corporations in relation to off-shore resource exploration (Leonard 2006, 2008, 2014). In the case of the gas resources off the Irish coast, the deals signed off by the state provided royalties lower than many developing nations received for their oil or gas, with the gas only being piped to major cities. Many locals were as concerned about the nature of the deal being entered into by their government as they were about local community and environmental issues caused by the pipeline. Carrington and Pereira (2011) in their study of similar conflicts in Australia argue that this type of dispute between a concerned community and both state and corporate agencies can be seen as a social justice issue. Szsaz (1998) has termed this form of environmental justice dispute as 'ecopopulist', where campaigns can extend their movement framing beyond their backyardist or 'NIMBY' (Not In My Backyard) origins, by establishing a wider protest framework which incorporates social and political concerns (Leonard, 2006).

CASE STUDY ANALYSIS

This section of the study will present a case study built from an 'issue history' (Szasz, 1994), based on the framing processes of the 'Shell to Sea' social movement. My research into this case began in 2003 and the campaign continues to the present day. I undertook a case study approach to the Corrib Gas dispute, building material archives and my findings publishing in journals and books over the intervening years. According to Yin (2008), the Case Study method can 'satisfy the three tenets of the qualitative method: describing, understanding, and explaining'. My previous studies on community movements had also drawn on the case study approach:

Case studies provide multi-perspective analyses. This means that the researcher considers not just the voice and perspective of the actors, but also of the relevant groups of actors and the interaction between them. This one aspect is a salient point in the characteristic that case studies possess. They give a voice to the powerless and voiceless (Feagin, Orum, & Sjoberg, 1991; Leonard, 2005).

This analysis of social or environmental justice campaigns includes forms of case study methods such as the 'exploratory', 'explanatory' and descriptive' (Yin, 2008); or 'intrinsic', 'instrumental' or 'collective' (Stake, 1995; Leonard, 2005). Exploratory case studies provide holistic examinations of the background to salient cases of environmental justice such as that of the 'Shell to Sea' campaign. With explanatory case studies providing an understanding of the significant criteria surrounding environmental or social justice's process and mobilizations, observations are then combined with the gathering of documentary evidence to provide a deeper understanding of critical and rural criminology in theory and in practice.

In addition, this study of the 'Shell to Sea' campaign applies descriptive forms of theory that is then developed further to contextualise existing understandings of social and environmental justice into an Irish framework. This case studies stems from an in-depth investigation over many years, as opposed to sampling research, according to Yin (2008) and Stake (1995) (Leonard, 2005). Yin (2008) has identified six sources of evidence available to the case study researcher.

These include 'documentation'; 'the use of archival records'; 'interviews'; 'direct observation'; 'participant observation' and 'physical artefacts.' The research was able to utilize these during the fieldwork on the 'Shell to Sea' case study, combining the data and findings of each source of information to address wider understandings of social and environmental justice in policy and practice. This research sets out to identify the key unit of analysis (the Shell to Sea case study) and in so doing create further understandings of the concepts of critical, green and rural criminology and the realities of state and corporate policy and practice, through the 'Shell to Sea' case study being analysed.

Case Study Background

In Ireland, the first years of this century were characterized by a period of rapid development and large-scale infrastructural projects. One such development was located in Ballinaboy, County Mayo. In 2001, multinationals with state contracts planned to construct a gas pipeline from the Corrib Field, which lay 100 miles offshore, and onshore across the farmlands of the area. Planning permission was also acquired for a processing-plant on a 400-acre site near local farmlands at Rossport. In 2002, an amendment to state law allowed commercial industries access to private lands with a Compulsory Acquisition Order (CPO). A CPO was issued for land on the planned route of the pipe – over the objection of the owners; and five of these farmers ('The Rossport Five') were eventually to spend 94 days in prison in 2005.

The projected pipeline, which was planned to run alongside the homes of the Rossport families – was seen as a dangerous hazard to homes and the community nearby. The load of such a pipeline would be carried at a pressure five times greater than that allowed in Irish domestic gas pipes. The local community would derive no economic benefit, since the gas was to be pumped to larger cities like Galway and Dublin. The response from the local framing community was one of opposition to the pipeline and plant. The motivations of rural protestors run deep. Their 'Shell to Sea' campaign originated from a primordial concern for their local hinterlands. Green philosophical responses are more likely to be found emerging from the indigenous sub consciousness of native populations such as those in rural areas such as Rossport, in North County Mayo, as part of a community's subliminal relationship with its surroundings. For the 'Shell to Sea' protestors, their lives and the land reclaimed from the sea by their forbears are as one, forging a relationship that is as 'green' as it gets. While academics, industrialists and the state present themselves as environmentalists, it is the native wisdom of the rural community in Mayo which can be seen as truly eco-centric, due to their primary concern for 'The Land' (Leonard, 2006).

From a critical criminology viewpoint, there is some degree of oppression in this case. The landowners had been summoned to the Irish High Court on four separate occasions at great personal cost. The High Court Action taken against the Rossport residents restrained the named defendants from refusing to allow pipe-laying on their lands. They had sought evidence of the CAOs before they would allow entry to their lands. This evidence was held back for up to two and a half years. A further attempt to gain entry to the lands at Rossport was followed by the summoning of five local men to the High Court. The men were all charged with breaching the interim order of the court after the men confirmed that they could not abide by the terms of the Court Order. In a statement to the court one defendant summed up the men's position "the farms form the basis of the identity of the people. Monetary compensation cannot compensate for undermining the social identity of the people" (Leonard 2007).

The five farmers were jailed for contempt of court, despite one of the defendants stating from his prison cell that Articles 40 and 43 of the Irish Constitution demand that the State protect the fundamental rights and property of every citizen. With their incarceration the 'Rossport 5', as they became known, would become the news story of the summer of 2005. The national press held daily updates of the campaign and the men and their family's acquired celebrity status. As they were taken away to prison local supporters surrounded the men's land to prevent Shell from gaining access. The campaign took on a new momentum as trade unionists, anti-globalization activists and environmentalists began to support the campaign.

The campaign received widespread support. One example of this was from a west of Ireland parliamentarian who would go on to become President of Ireland. Michael D. Higgins of the Labour Party supported the 'Shell to Sea' campaign at a rally in Galway in 2005, stating:

I was involved in the Resource Protection Campaign in 1973. At that time, Energy Minister Justin Keating, signed away the licenses for bounty-payment. There is now an absence of moral courage well the people of the left said that our resources shouldn't be taken from us.

These five men in jail are a reflection on law and morality because they wanted to protect their families. The injunction is flawed because the state hadn't given permission for the pipeline. These men have contempt for an injunction that is based on a lie.

The government should ask for the injunction to be lifted. There is a need for a change of consciousness. We must show solidarity for the men and their magnificent families. They have but one small demand--that the gas is cleaned at sea. (Micheal D. Higgins, Labour Party President and current Irish President, 2005, Leonard, 2006).

Higgins makes references to 'moral courage' in his speech, framing the campaign as a contest about social morality and the collective conscience that had been breached by Shell's aggressive response to resistance. In a Durkheiman way, Higgins was connecting this issue with the collective moral conscience inviting others to join the protest as it violated their moral rights was built around a moral frame. The English television station Channel 4 ran a news item which questioned the plans for an onshore pipeline and terminal in Rossport. The report claimed that locals had faced pressure to sign over their property and that the deal with the Royal Dutch Shell company was 'unprecedented in Europe'.

Records were produced in the report which raised allegations of political interference and pressure being brought to bear on the local County Council's planning committee while it was also revealed that the then ruling Irish political party *Fianna Fáil* received donations from two of the companies involved in the Corrib Field operation. The Channel 4 report was critical of the manner in which Ireland's national resources were being given away without any revenue making its way back to the Irish taxpayer, with the Corrib deal giving a poorer return than similar deals signed in Nigeria (Leonard, 2008). That autumn, the connection between Ireland and Nigeria was strengthened by the appearance of Dr. Owens

Wiwa, brother of the murdered author and anti-oil industry activist Ken Saro Wiwa, who backed the campaign against Shell when he visited Ireland. The campaign now had a transnational context, stretching from Norway to Nigeria.

Winter 2005 also saw the release of a report on the Corrib gas issue by the Centre for Public Inquiry (CPI). The report claimed that the National Planning Board was subjected to 'external pressure' on the issue, a claim the Board denied (Leonard 2006). The report's executive summary put forward a number of findings. These included criticism of the state's handling of resources and royalties, its regulatory framework surrounding the introduction of the Compulsory Acquisition Orders (CAOs) and the gas pipeline, the location of the pipeline and terminal and the supervision of work carried out at the site. The report was also critical of the access provided for Shell executives to senior politicians, including the Taoiseach (Connolly and Lynch, 2005). The Centre for Public Inquiry (CPI) would also become embroiled in a political row due to accusations made by then Justice Minister Michael McDowell about the political connections of the Centre's Executive Director, Frank Connolly. An independent report released in conjunction with the CPI's findings claimed that if the onshore pipeline ruptured it could cause 'high fatalities' (Kiprewitz, 2005, p.6). The Corrib pipeline was irregular 'due to its operational pressure, lack of historical data in the system evaluation, proximity to people and dwellings and deficiencies in the demonstration of maximum pipeline pressure' (Kiprewitz, 2005, p.6).

While 'Shell to Sea' welcomed the CPI report the subsequent politically motivated closure of the Centre threw a cloud over its findings, further demonstrating the degree of complexity and political intrigue which surrounded this issue. Throughout the winter of 2007 a series of clashes between police and protestors who wanted to prevent further work on the pipeline and terminal at Erris made national news. However, this once localized campaign had caught the imagination of the Irish public and those activists beyond who felt a common sense of moral violation by the bullying tactics of Shell and Statoil, with networks extending from Norway to Nigeria. The campaign continues to gain support, and the 'Shell to Sea' campaign was awarded the Goldman environmental prize in recognition of the effectiveness of their campaign. The twists and turns of this dispute have challenged the thinking of those involved, while shaping the wider understandings of the issues involved. Ultimately, the success of 'Shell to Sea's' protest has been its impact in changing the cultural discourse of a changing Ireland comes to embrace the concerns of this small West of Ireland community (Leonard, 2008).

The Irish Department of Justice requested that Atlantic Philanthropies, which funded the Centre for Public Inquiry, cease it support for that organization, with the Centre closing as a result. This form of political involvement again raised issues about the moral framework surrounding the Corrib Gas pipeline issue, from green and critical criminology perspectives.

The main framing strategies of the 'Shell to Sea' campaign emerged around this combination of local populism and a wider expression of cultural nationalism alongside traditional campaign focus points such as health and safety concerns:

- The dangers and risk posed by the pipeline.
- Local duty to defend families and property.
- The unsavory behavior of the multinational and the state.
- The misrepresentation of facts on the issue.
- The prioritization of corporate profits over local concerns (Leonard 2008).

Taking a rural criminology perspective, the risk frame highlighted the dangers posed by the onshore gas pipeline which was planned to run alongside the homes of many families in Rossport. The then Minister of State confirmed in a written reply in the *Dáil* (Irish parliament) to concerned deputies that such a pipeline would be unparalleled in Ireland, Europe or elsewhere. The rated pressure of the pipeline would exceed that used by *An Bord Gas* (The Irish Gas Board) nearly five times while the gas that would be transported through the pipeline with unrefined oil and water could cause blockages and be risk prone with obstructions occurring far from the gas field where they could be treated. A further concern raised by the campaigners was the lack of any material benefit for the local community that was bearing the brunt of these risks as all of the gas would be piped through the county into larger cities such as Galway and Dublin. In this way the campaigners were able to extend their risk frame by increasing the sense of shared grievance surrounding local identity, sense of place and sense of exploitation which was running high throughout the county. For the 'Shell to Sea' campaigners this approach would have the double negative effect of having all profits repatriated to the multinationals while the chance to develop the west's gas supply would also be lost to the country's sprawling urban area.

Shell attempted to serve their state-backed Compulsory Acquisition Orders (CAOs) on locals in the Rossport area in January 2005. By March the company had applied to the High Court for restraining orders against local landowners the five men and some of their neighbors. Subsequently shell began excavating peat from the proposed refinery site around nearby Ballinaboy and the Erris Peninsula. Amid chaotic scenes diggers began to sink into the bog while heavy vehicles crashed on the inadequate roads surrounding the area. Locals were unable to get past heavy machinery on the one narrow road into the area. As the multinationals planned for 70 truck movements a day during construction confrontations became inevitable. Local residents turned for help to sympathetic local politicians, who claimed that the 'people of Erris who have been compelled to have the Corrib gas upstream pipeline adjacent to their homes are scared out of their minds' (Connolly and Lynch, 2005, p.43).

From both the green and critical criminology perspective, the justice system's response was oppressive. The Irish High Court Action taken against the Rossport residents restrained the named defendants from refusing to allow pipe-laying on their lands. The landowners had been summoned to the High Court on four separate occasions at great personal cost. The landowners had sought evidence of the CAOs in due course before they would allow entry to their lands. This evidence was held back for up to two and a half years. A further attempt to gain entry to the lands at Rossport was followed by the summoning of five local men to the Irish High Court. These local men were all charged with breaching the interim order of the court after the men confirmed to the court that they could not abide by the terms of the Court Order (Connolly and Lynch, 2005, p.45). In a statement to the court, one of the defendants summed up the men's position in the following statement 'The farms form the basis of the identity of the people. Monetary compensation cannot compensate for undermining the social identity of the people' (Connolly and Lynch, 2005, p.45).

The five were jailed for contempt of court despite, as one of the defendants would state from prison, the fact that the constitution under Articles 40 and 43 demand that the State protect the fundamental rights and property of every citizen. With their incarceration the 'Rossport 5' would become a national and international news story. Many national and local newspapers held daily updates of the campaign and the men, and their families took on celebrity status. As the men were taken away to prison local supporters surrounded the men's land to prevent workmen from gaining access. The campaign took on a new momentum.

Campaign Mobilization and Use of Media

The imprisoning of the 'Rossport 5', as they became known, changed the minds of many locals who had previously favored the terminal. The 'Shell to Sea' campaign began to mobilize on a wider level as picketing, rallies and rallies were extensively stepped up. The significant alliances which the families had forged took up the campaign as key figures from local trade unions, politics and colleges organized the committee. Another mobilization strategy of the campaign following the men's imprisonment was the placing of pickets on Shell or Statoil service stations around the country. In addition, a series of rallies were held nationwide that drew thousands of ordinary people who wished to express their concern about the imprisoning of the five men. Shell's terminals were also the target of organized blockades by environmentally minded 'ecowarriors', while ecological societies from the University sector were also prominent at many of the campaign's events. A 'Solidarity camp' was established as a campsite vigil by these groupings. The camp is still active. This wider support base gave rise to a mobilization of support unparalleled in previous environmental campaigns. Support for the Rossport 5 came from all levels of Irish society including local political groups, trade unions and the anti-globalization network, as well as artists and musicians. This cross section of support allowed 'Shell to Sea' to extend their framing process to incorporate a much wider remit as oppositional politics and cultural discourse were embraced.

This progression from a single issue 'backyard' dispute into an extensive form of ecopopulist dissent corresponds broadly with 'the transition from NIMBY to ecopopulism' (Szasz, 1994). This is a strategy or object which environmental campaigners had attempted to create over the various campaigns of the last four decades (Leonard 2008). The fulcrum of this evolution was, undoubtedly, the imprisonment of the five men. However, while similar fates have been meted out to protestors in recent years it must be said that the 'Rossport 5's' eloquent statements in defense of their actions during their 94 days in Cloverhill Prison won a great deal of public support for their cause. Even though the men were fully committed to their cause they were shocked at their treatment claiming that they were only seeking justice:

We were put in prison for protecting ourselves. They said we broke the law but we only broke an injunction that shouldn't have been there. We never did any harm. We were just trying to protect our families and rather than listen to us they put us into prison for 94 days (Leonard 2008).

While the camp at Rossport continued to attract sympathizers and grassroots activists from around the country and abroad the Shell to Sea protests continued with events occurring at an almost daily rate. A 'National Day of Protest' was called against Shell and Statoil. Organized pickets occurred at stations across Ireland. A national petition was also organized as thousands put their signature or e-mailed in messages of support to the 'Shell to Sea' website (http://www.shelltosea.org). Their webpage provided the campaign with a powerful tool in the highly computer-literate Ireland. Grassroots bloggers and activist websites gave prominence to the campaign and links between protestors across the globe were established via the internet. It could be said that this new communication technology provided the links to environmental circuits which existed nationally and globally. Internet technologies opened up possibilities for environmental campaigners such as 'Shell to Sea' that also facilitated their ability, not just to gain media coverage but to shape the news and influence the public perception of the debate. Such power is unwieldy unless applied well and 'Shell to Sea' ran a compelling campaign. The 'Shell to Sea' website was a mobilizing resource in itself providing updates and messages. Moreover, it set out a series of strategies which activists would support, such as suggesting participation through:

- Inviting activists to Rossport and the Mayo Solidarity Camp to learn more about the issue.
- Supporting the Shell to Sea All-Ireland speaking tour
- Financial donation and Fundraising
- Contacting the Media, Letters to the Press
- Getting Unions, community groups, religious groups, etc, to support the campaigns.
- Poster and Flyer distribution, with posters ready for downloading from the Shell to Sea website
- Organizing meetings, protests and blockades and boycotting Shell and Statoil
- Signing or distributing the Shell to Sea petition which was also online and could be downloaded
- Asking radio stations to play some of the songs written and recorded for the campaign such as "The Rossport 5 song". A DVD was also distributed by the campaigners. \
- Contacting government ministers, including the Taoiseach, with e-mail addresses being provided.
- Contacting the Norwegian ambassador or government directly with e-mail addresses supplied (Leonard, 2008).

The provision of this array of campaign strategies on the 'Shell to Sea' site allowed the campaign to circumvent established media outlets and provided the widest range of involvement for the public from petition signing to the organization of blockades. By mobilizing their campaign in this extensive manner 'Shell to Sea' became a resource in itself as the centerpiece to a burgeoning grassroots eco-movement which encompassed locals, environmentalists, students and political activists in a manner not witnessed since Ireland's anti-nuclear protests in the early 1980s (Leonard, 2008).

One response from the state to the controversy was the announcement of a safety review of the Corrib gas pipeline by the Natural Resources Ministry. This department stated that officials had inspected Shell's onshore site and that in his opinion a serious breach of the consents given to Shell had occurred. In the hope of resolving the dispute the Minister ordered the dismantling of the length of gas pipeline that had already been assembled at the site. Shell announced that it would lay off 128 workers at the site if the protest continued (Leonard, 2008). The state's initiative included the establishment of a technical group to monitor the Corrib gas project which included senior civil servants, geographers, engineers, and legal experts (Leonard, 2008). As the men completed their first month in prison, Shell was coming under increased pressure to lift their injunction to allow the men to go free, particularly in the wake of the breach of its technical consents. Legal attempts were made to free the men due to the fact that Ministerial consent had been given for preparatory work only, rather than the construction and installation at the site. Opposition leaders also called for the men's release. 'Shell to Sea' spokespersons cautiously welcomed the Minister's intervention although the campaign noted the timing of the announcement on the eve of a major rally in support of the men and in the week of their latest court hearing. A National Rally in Dublin attracted over 2,000 people. Pickets were arranged in diverse locations such as the Norwegian embassy in Brussels and at political events. Over 1,000 people picketed outside Shell petrol stations that month (Leonard, 2006).

Further criticism of the state's policies was highlighted in a local news feature on the issue by an American energy regulator. All concerned parties including the protestors, industry and the political sector were constrained by the lack of 'uniform safety requirements for gas pipelines', a policy which was 'at odds with international practice' (Leonard, 2007). The article contrasted safety regulators in the United States for gas pipelines that emanated from two government agencies including an Office of Pipeline Safety with what was called 'a frightening lapse' in the Irish regulatory framework. Pipelines in the United States are also protected by a 'certificate of public convenience and necessity' (Leonard, 2007), words which would have a ring of irony to the imprisoned Rossport men. Public enquiries and written submissions were an integral part of the licensing system in the United States. As the men spent their 50th day in jail they must have found such regulatory discrepancies to be very questionable. While Shell and Statoil negotiated with Mayo County Council on the issue the men offered to engage in dialogue with representatives of the corporate multinationals if the Court injunction against them was lifted. Executives from the multinationals claimed the injunction was a matter for the courts but welcomed the men's statement, nonetheless. Shell claimed it would be open to legal challenges if it relinquished the injunction, something which was rejected by many. One strategic response of the men in prison was their claim that Shell's refusal to lift the injunction was preventing them from preparing their case for the full hearing on the issue and that as Shell had suspended work on the site the injunction now made no sense. The men accused Shell of not being interested in dialogue and said that they were obliged to defend their families as the state had refused to do so. According to the protestors, the industries involved 'were more interested in their strategy than the law' (Leonard, 2008). The protestors accused the multinationals of 'vindictiveness' for not withdrawing the injunction claiming that they could not impede work at the site while it was non-operational. Community groups from Mayo called for the injunction to be released while the Irish Labour Party stated that the continued imprisonment of the men was 'bordering on becoming a national disgrace' (Leonard, 2008).

Another significant development in the extension of the campaign was the pressure which was brought to bear on Statoil and the Norwegian government. Pickets were held at Norwegian embassies and in September 2005 family members and 'Shell to Sea' supporters went to Norway where they met with representatives of Statoil and the government while supporters picketed the Norwegian embassy in Dublin. 'Shell to Sea' were seen to make the point that the Norwegian taxpayer would benefit from 36% of any revenue from the Corrib Field while the Irish taxpayer would receive no benefits at all. The protestors were also keen to exploit the political opportunity which arose from the Norwegian general election campaign that was underway at the time. A further extension of the campaign's international frame was the links created with the Nigerian resource activists including the brother of Ken Saro-Wiwa, Dr. Owens Wiwa, who joined the march to the Dáil in support of the Rossport 5. The march coincided with the men's appearance at the High Court as they approached 94 days in prison.

On the 30th of September 2005 the Irish High Court President freed the Rossport 5 to cheers from their families and supporters. The court stated that the injunction 'no longer served any useful purpose'. The Rossprt 5's legal council asked the court to also remove the order of committal claiming it to be 'coercive' and that the men should not face further sanction in the future. However, while the men offered an apology for breaking the court order, they refused to give an undertaking on any future activities. In a further development the High Court indicated to all representatives of the multinationals that he wanted these companies to address its breach of the Minister's licenses but that he would not deal with that issue while the men languished in prison (Leonard, 2006).

As the men walked free with their jubilant supporters, they vowed that their campaign would go on. The issue was set to continue the following month as Shell stated its intention to pursue the matter of a permanent injunction against the Rossport 5 and any other objectors to the pipeline. The safety review established by the state was also scheduled for that month. The state announced plans to appoint a mediator to negotiate with both parties. The men made a triumphant appearance at the 'Shell to Sea' rally in Dublin alongside supportive politicians and Dr. Wiwa. As they returned to Mayo traditional bonfires lit the way along their route back to Rossport. According to the 'Rossport 5' their campaign showed that 'Irish people expect a higher state of democracy, and they expect more of their government in relation to people's safety and welfare' (Leonard, 2008). The men also indicated their willingness to return to prison if necessary. Prominent campaign supporters indicated that the extension of the campaign into Norway during their general election had played a significant part in building the momentum that led to the men's release. The newly elected administration was believed to have instigated the meeting between senior Statoil executives and the Irish government the week before the men's release in the wake of the visit of 'Shell to Sea' to Norway. The protestors said that this meeting with Statoil and the Norwegian authorities revealed that 'they did not know what was happening and were shocked by it' (Leonard, 2008). It was felt that the men would have remained in prison but for his Norwegian trip and subsequent intervention. 'Shell to Sea' supporters had met to work out the best way to get the men released. As the Norwegian government owned 71% of Statoil, it was decided to bring the campaign to Oslo, extending the geographical bounds of the campaign further).

Campaigners were able to plan the trip with the help of Norwegian journalists and trade unionists whom the group had developed links with during the campaign. They supplied 'Shell to Sea' with valuable details, contacts and lists of who to meet during their time in Oslo, maximizing the impact of their mission. They were able to get national exposure on Norwegian television as a result at a time when Dublin City Council were threatening to prosecute anyone who put up posters advertising 'Shell to Sea's' Dublin rally. The most significant meetings during their trip were with Norwegian Oil and Energy Minister and Senior Vice President of Statoil who would meet with Noel Dempsey a week after the Shell to Sea mission (Leonard, 2008). While the men celebrated with families and supporters, they continued to plan the next phase of their campaign. They insisted that the Irish government should participate in any talks between the families and Shell claiming that 'the state cannot remain neutral in this'. The men thanked the public who had supported them with up to 150 cards while they were in prison. The men won further support from the public for their eloquence and resolve on their release including the manner in which they highlighted conditions facing the inner-city youth who were their prison mates in Cloverhill prison. The men claimed they got no special treatment in the prison but were well treated by their fellow prisoners.

In October 2005 one of the protestors who had been imprisoned attended the Minister's Safety review where the state outlined a 'post hoc' justification of the government's strategy for the terminal. The men were critical of the hearing stating that it was 'an attempt to retrospectively suggest that consultation had occurred' (Leonard, 2008). Members of the Shell to Sea campaign and the other members of the Rossport 5 did not attend due to the constraints of the outstanding injunction. The review heard evidence that some of the initial objections to the project may not have been forwarded to the state's technical advisory group (Leonard, 2006). Other evidence at the review included a submission from a retired US Naval engineer who stated that a pipeline explosion would devastate everything within 250 yards of the pipeline releasing 'the equivalent of 3,500 tonnes of TNT. The absence of many of the 'Shell to Sea' campaigners at the hearing was compensated for by the submissions of expert allies such as environmental and fisheries groups. At the Irish High Court, the campaign accused the state of using the mediation process as a ploy. The campaign stated that the Minister had helped the multinationals to lift their injunction to 'take the spotlight off the serious safety issues we were highlighting'. The campaign continued throughout this period with the five men making appearances at rallies and meetings across the country. The Solidarity Camp at Rossport continued to be a fulcrum of activity while up to 20,000 people had signed the petition organized by the protest group. 31 of the 34 landowners affected by the acquisition orders for the pipeline had taken the side of the men by that stage of the campaign (Leonard 2006).

The winter of 2005 also saw the release of a report on the Corrib gas issue by the Centre for Public Inquiry (CPI). The report's executive summary put forward a number of findings. These included criticism of the state's handling of resources and royalties, its regulatory framework surrounding the introduction of the Compulsory Acquisition Orders (CAOs) and the gas pipeline, the location of the pipeline and terminal and the supervision of work carried out at the site. The report was also critical of the access provided for Shell executives to senior politicians (Connolly and Lynch 2005). The Centre for Public Inquiry (CPI) would also become the centre of a political row due to accusations made by the Justice Ministry about the alleged activities of the Centre's Executive Director. An independent report released in conjunction with the CPI's findings claimed that the onshore pipeline could rupture causing 'high fatalities' (Kiprewitz, 2005, p.6). The Corrib pipeline was irregular 'due to its operational pressure, lack of historical data in the system evaluation, proximity to people and dwellings and deficiencies in the demonstration of maximum pipeline pressure' (ibid). While 'Shell to Sea' welcomed the CPI report the subsequent political row surrounding the Centre threw a cloud over its findings, further demonstrating the degree of complexity and political intrigue which surrounded this issue.

The government's own safety review's preliminary findings recommended limiting the gas pressure for the pipeline, while the multinationals rejected the accusation that hydrogen sulphide or 'sour gas', which had similar qualities to cyanide, would be released or corrode the pipeline. The industry claimed that it would be 'unlikely' that concentrations of the toxic substance would reach dangerous levels at the site. 'Shell to Sea' acknowledged the report but their website promised a major escalation in their campaign of opposition including requests for 'gifts' such as night-vision goggles and bolt-cutters for cutting fencing. 'Shell to Sea' also announced that a major rally was planned to coincide with attempts by Shell to recommence work at the site. A Roadshow was organized with the intention of building the Rossport Solidarity Camp by holding meetings at various points around the country. This series of meetings was organized to facilitate the mobilization of the second phase of Shell to Sea's campaign promoting the Solidarity Camp for people who wished to participate in the protest and who would be able to provide logistical expertise. While the camp was originally a spontaneous demonstration of support for the Rossport 5, Shell to Sea were prepared to extend their campaign into a much broader project of activism that could extend out to embrace the anti-globalization grassroots movements with which it had opened up links. This intent can be seen from the following posting on the 'Shell to Sea' website:

This is a major opportunity to defeat an environmentally hazardous development and the struggle thus far has already been an inspiration to many people around the country. Victory will have a significant radicalising affect, not just on a remote corner of Mayo, but across the island ("Building Rossport Solidarity Camp Meeting In Cublin", n.d.).

Rural Community Responses and 'Rural Curse Theory' Analysis

The 'Shell to Sea' campaign continues. While the dispute at Rossport was initially about Shell's onshore pipeline being located near a number of local homes and farms, it has long since moved away from that single issue and has come to represent a range of social and political concerns and about the corporate power of resource extraction companies and the asymmetrical relationships with land holders to compel their compliance and deference. These responses have come to mean different things to those involved while attempts to comprehend the events at Rossport can be seen to be almost as intrusive as Shell's pipeline. While many in North Mayo harbor fears about the imposition of the pipeline this fear does not always extend to a full understanding of whether the pipeline is safe or not, nor what economic benefits it may or may not bring. According to the campaign many locals 'simply do not want it'. The pipeline represents an unwelcome intrusion into their land and community. It is this very sense of place that the 'Shell to Sea' campaigners wish to protect and the threat posed by outsiders has reawakened a determined resistance in the North Mayo community that has its roots in an identity born of the past with little concern for notions of 'progress'. Ironically, the Irish government would have been keen to repeat the economic growth of both the host nations of the corporate groups involved, in both the Netherlands (Shell) and Norway (Statoil). Both nations displayed 'Resource curse' theory issues (Aughty, 1993), such as 'the Norwegian Paradox' and the 'Dutch Disease', both of which demonstrate the varying outcomes faced by small to medium countries which develop their economic resources. In the context of the globalized world, there are many pros and cons from resource development. Ireland stands to gain almost no royalties for the disruptive gas facility in Rossport, except for a few hundred local jobs during its development.

CONCLUSION

A moral framework has been set in North Mayo, one that values family and community over economic growth. This form of moral framing has a subconscious element to it which has been instinctively unleashed in many Irish disputes over time. A subsequent sacrifice to defend the blood lines rooted in the hinterlands has been witnessed over many centuries in Irish history and has become a primary aspect in the development of *rural sentiment* (Leonard 2008). From a critical criminology perspective, the Rossport men near one hundred days in Mountjoy prison and the traumatic effect this injustice had on family and neighbors can be seen as a heavy handed response by the Irish justice system to the concerns of a local community. This trenchant stance has been acknowledged by the multinationals who have appointed local spokespersons to try and comprehend the depth of feeling directed against them. Alternative routes for the pipeline have been suggested to try to meet peoples' concerns. The dispute continued to gain headlines as protestors and police clashed at the site in recent years, with allegations of police abuse of protestors making headline news. The 'Shell to Sea' campaign was recognized as the protestors were awarded the Goldman Environmental prize. The award was a timely acknowledgement of the efforts of the Rossport families in the protection of their local community and environment and establishes the case within the frameworks set out by White (2013) as an environmental justice issue and (Carrington and Pereira, 2011) as a rights and social justice issue. The 'Shell to Sea' case also displays elements of the 'geographies of crime' set out by Carrington, McIntosh and Scott (2010) in their study of mining disputes.

The 'Shell to Sea' campaign has raised the complex issue of a community response to an infrastructural project based on both a sense of grievance about the intrusion of the project in the area and fears about the safety of the gas pipeline. The response of the North Mayo community has emerged from a historically derived sense of place which has been articulated as part of a wider discursive framing process that links cultural nationalism with community-based environmentalism. Politically the issue can be traced back to the long-standing state policy of selling off resources while facilitating land acquisitions by partners. Local political response has been mixed with some supporting the 'Shell to Sea' campaign while mainstream councillors and national representatives were ambivalent or chose to favour onshore development. From an 'ecopopulist' perspective the rural or agrarian politics of the past has been rekindled while the 'Shell to Sea' campaign has developed an international support network from Ireland to Norway and Nigeria. This clearly establishes the campaign as going 'beyond NIMBY' as Szsaz (1998) has established.

The shift in policy direction undertaken by successive neo-liberal Irish governments led to a move towards a primarily ecological modernisation orientated policy framework (as set out by the European Union). The emphasis on economic growth over environmental protection or concerns for communities has subsequently become a priority. This has been exacerbated by the Eurozone crisis and bailout of the Irish economy by the International Monetary Fund (IMF) since 2008 (Leonard and Botetzagias, 2011). Ultimately, the costs of economic growth have led to greater environmental degradation and an undermining of significant aspects of the nation's heritage. In particular, rural communities have borne the cost of Ireland's transition from a rural agrarian society into an industrialised and globalised economy, leading to the Corrib Gas dispute reflecting elements of 'resource curse' theory. While communities have demonstrated a commitment to retaining some aspect of the traditional values and heritage of the 'Emerald Isle', the state's policy of prioritising rapid infrastructural development in order to underpin private consumption and multinational investment over local community services may prove to be ill advised as fluctuations on the global markets continue. As the cycle of the 'Celtic Tiger' gave way to the era of IMF sponsored austerity in the wake of the post 2008 economic crisis, the ecological values and concerns of these local communities may provide a new direction for the post economic boom austerity era.

REFERENCES

Aughty, R. (1993). *Sustaining Development in Mineral Economies: The Resource Curse Thesis*. Routledge.

Building Rossport Solidarity Camp Meeting in Dublin. (n.d.). Retrieved from http://www.shelltosea.com/node/635

Carrington, K., McIntosh, A., & Scott, J. (2010). Globalization, frontier masculinities and violence: Booze, blokes and brawls. *British Journal of Criminology*, *50*(3), 393–413. doi:10.1093/bjc/azq003

Carrington, K., & Pereira, M. (2011). Assessing the social impacts of the resources boom on rural communities. *Rural Society*, *21*(1), 2–20. doi:10.5172/rsj.2011.21.1.2

Connolly, F., & Lynch, R. (2005). *The Great Corrib gas controversy*. Center for Public Inquiry.

Feagin, J. Orum, A., & Sjoberg, G. (Eds.). (1991). A Case Study for Case Study. Chapel Hill, NC: University of North Carolina Press.

Kiprewitz, R. (2005). *The Proposed Corrib Onshore System: An Independent Analysis*. CPI.

Leonard, L. (2005). Greenhouse Press Ecopolitics Series: Vol. 1. *Politics Inflamed: GSE and the campaign against Incineration in Ireland*. Greenhouse Press with Drogheda Choice.

Leonard, L. (2006). *Green nation: the Irish environmental movement. Drogheda*. Emerald Publishing.

Leonard, L. (2007). *The environmental movement in Ireland*. Springer Science & Business Media.

Leonard, L. (2007). Moral Framing in a Resource Dispute: The" Shell to Sea" Campaign in North Mayo. *Studies: AN Irish Quarterly Review*, *95*(380), 375–386.

Leonard, L. (2008). Rapid development & community mobilization in the Republic of Ireland. *Community Development (Columbus, Ohio)*, *39*(3), 59–74. doi:10.1080/15575330809489669

Leonard, L. (2011). *Community campaigns for sustainable living: health, waste & protest in civil society*. Emerald Group Publishing. doi:10.1108/S2041-806X(2011)7

Leonard, L. (2014). Cultural Criminology, Governmentality and the Liquidity of the Failing State: The View from Ireland. *Critical Criminology*, *22*(2), 293–306. doi:10.100710612-013-9217-0

Leonard, L., & Botetzagias, I. (2011). *Sustainable politics and the crisis of the peripheries*. Emerald Group Publishing.

Ruggiero, V., & South, N. (2013). Toxic state-corporate crimes, neo-liberalism and green criminology: The hazards and legacies of the oil, chemical and mineral industries. *International Journal for Crime. Justice and Social Democracy*, *2*(2), 12–26. doi:10.5204/ijcjsd.v2i2.115

Stake, R. (1995). *The Art of Case Research: Design and Methods*. Sage.

Szasz, A. (1994). *Ecopopulism: Toxic waste and the movement for environmental justice*. U of Minnesota Press.

White, R. (2012). Land theft as rural eco-crime. *International Journal of Rural Criminology*, *1*(2), 203–217. doi:10.18061/1811/53698

White, R. (2013). Resource extraction leaves something behind: Environmental justice and mining. *International Journal for Crime. Justice and Social Democracy*, *2*(1), 50–64. doi:10.5204/ijcjsd.v2i1.90

Yin, R. (2009). *Case Study Research: Design and Methods*. Sage.

Chapter 12
A Penchant for Murder:
The Case Study of John Wayne Gacy

Gianna M. Strube
Independent Researcher, USA

EXECUTIVE SUMMARY

John Wayne Gacy is a name that lives in infamy in the study of American serial killers. His fiendish means of murder and his countless victims make Gacy a fascinating subject when attempting to understand the pathology of a serial killer. This chapter will examine contextual factors encompassing Gacy's murders and the psychological factors that may have contributed to his offending, including paraphilia. Certain theoretical principles of homicide will be used to analyze John Wayne Gacy's murder motivations such as the frustration-aggression theory, psychosexual aggression, and the social control theory. This chapter will also include information from the media, courts, character involvement, and general case notes. Media analysis is important because many serial killers reach out to the media and want that recognition and the attention they so crave. Although the media attention can also cause more problems by creating broadcasts and giving away secrets about the investigation, putting it in the hands of the killer.

INTRODUCTION

John Wayne Gacy. Jr was one of the most dreaded serial killers in Chicago during the 70s. While most other serial killers of the time worked in isolation, Gacy happened to be a social figure who inculcated a very different picture of himself in public. This paper will cover certain aspects of Gacy from a criminal aspect, such as a

DOI: 10.4018/978-1-7998-9668-5.ch012

brief profile, details of the crime, aspects of the trial, media, the defense strategy, and the final outcome.

GACY PROFILE

Gacy was born to parents of Danish and Polish heritage in 1942 in Chicago, IL. He was the second child of his parents with two sisters. The children had a strict Catholic background, having attended Catholic school in North Chicago (Bell & Bardsley, 2001). While his childhood was normal, there were a few accidents and health problems that Gacy suffered from. Those include a severe blow to his head as a child while playing on a swing set that also had a probable effect on his physical and mental health in later years (Taylor, 2003). His father was a highly abusive alcoholic and often ended up beating his wife and children for trivial reasons (Sullivan & Maiken, 2012).

Gacy's first minor crime occurred when he stole a toy truck from a store for which his father ended up beating him with a belt and called him a 'queer' (Cahill, 2011, p.26). As he grew up, he worked various odd jobs, including that of a mortuary attendant, and subsequently completed a business degree from Northwestern Business College. This helped him land a job in sales. His first marriage failed after he was convicted by a grand jury and ended up serving time for an act of sodomy with a teenage boy (Taylor, 2003). After release, he remarried and tried to lead a normal life by getting into politics and community affairs, but went back to his old ways by committing assault on a teenage boy and later graduating to murder.

Crimes Committed

After his release on the sodomy charge, Gacy started a new crime spree. Even before this new crime pattern, Gacy had already been convicted and imprisoned for sexual assault on a boy. He lured some into his car by impersonating an officer, or to his house with the offer of a job, a place to party, or even money. Once he had his victim in his space, Gacy coaxed them with drugs or alcohol or a sick magic trick, during which he'd handcuff them and dangle the key in front of their face. On January 2, 1972, he met 15-year-old, Timothy Jack McCoy, at the Chicago Greyhound bus terminal. He convinced the boy to spend the night at his home and ended up murdering him. Gacy, then, disposed of the body by burying it in the crawl space and covering the grave with concrete. (Cahill, 2011, p.101) In an interview in 1980, Gacy mentioned his thoughts on his first killing, "That's when I realized that death was the ultimate thrill." (p.349) Soon after this killing, Gacy took a short break and commenced killing around January 1974 and continued this pattern on a sustained basis until he was caught in 1978 after the disappearance of 15-year-old Robert Piest. (OCPA) In this instance, Gacy might have never been caught had Piest's mother not alerted the police about his disappearance and about the fact that he had left home to meet Gacy for a job. Robert Piest's body was found in the Des Plaines River on April 9, 1979, and identified by his dental records with an autopsy revealing torture before death. (Sullivan & Maiken, 2012, p.362) The only survivors of Gacy's elaborate killing spree were Donald Vorhees and Robert Donnelly, who experienced severe torture and sexual assault but managed to survive the ordeal.

The worst part of this series of murders was that most of the young boys who lost their lives did so after sustained brutal torture and sexual assault from Gacy. He performed at parties and hospitals as "Pogo the Clown," but his penchant for murder was no joke. By the time he was caught, Gacy the "Killer Clown" had amassed at least 33 victims. In order to dispose of the bodies, Gacy buried them in the crawl space under the house and later in the Des Plaines River when he discovered that he could not accommodate any more bodies in the crawl space. (Cahill, 2011, p.219) Most of the boys who disappeared were from his contracting company (PDM), although the police could never ascertain the identity of a few victims. (Amirante and Broderick, 2015, p.104)

THE TRIAL: PROSECUTION AND DEFENCE STRATEGIES

As per the Office of the Prosecuting Attorney for Clark County (2012), John Gacy was charged with 33 murders with a bulk of the victims being teenage boys. Although the trial commenced in Cook County, the jury selection occurred largely from Rockford, Illinois since the judge was of the opinion that a jury of the same county would be inherently biased due to resulting press coverage. (Amirante and Broderick, 2015, p.241)

At the trial, Gacy's attorneys Sam Amirante and Robert Motta were primarily focused on proving that Gacy was insane. In doing so, the court confined Gacy to over 300 hours of supervision at the Menard Correctional Center. (Cahill, 2011, p.261) The intention of the defense requesting this supervision was to determine if Gacy was mentally competent to stand trial as well as to determine the stand that the defense should take during the trial. To convince the state and the doctors, Gacy told them, "There are four Johns. John the contractor, John the clown, and John the politician. The fourth person went by the name of Jack Hanley. Jack was the killer and did all the evil things." (OCPA, 2012) While Gacy had tried to convince the doctors that he suffered from possible multiple personality disorder, his advocates preferred to take the stand of 'Not Guilty by Reason of Insanity.' (p.316) In accordance with this stand, Gacy's counsel produced a number of medical experts to testify to the defense's stand of Gacy's insanity (pp.320-321). Of these, at least three well-known experts testified that one could classify Gacy as a paranoid schizophrenic with multiple personality disorder. The evidence against Gacy, including the testimonies of Voorhees and Donnelly, was overwhelming due to which the defense strategy had to solely rely on the insanity plea to save Gacy.

On the other hand, the prosecution's case (represented by Prosecutor Terry Sullivan) was that Gacy was in sound mental health and in total control of his actions. (Sullivan & Maiken, 2012, p.250) Further, the case made out by the prosecution was strong since the State presented evidence in the form of witnesses to highlight the premeditation that was visible in the killings. In addition, the prosecution also presented medical experts who refuted the defense's claims of Gacy suffered from multiple personality disorder and insanity. To enhance the case, the prosecution also succeeded in convincing two of Gacy's employees to testify before the court that they had been hired by Gacy to dig trenches in the crawl space under his house, although they did not know the real reason for these trenches. (Cahill, 2011, p.181)

During the testimony of Dr. Stein, the Cook County Medical Examiner the methods of death were revealed. The medical examiner testified that thirteen victims had died of asphyxiation six due to ligature strangulation and one due to multiple stab wounds to the chest, while in about nine to ten cases the reason for death could not be ascertained. (Sullivan & Maiken, 2012, p.322) However, Stein affirmed that all the deaths occurred due to homicide. In response to this testimony, the defense attempted to show that all the 33 deaths might have been caused due to possible erotic asphyxia, although Stein refuted these claims with appropriate evidence (p.323). The testimony of a few survivors of Gacy's killing spree such as Donald Voorhees, Robert Donnelly, and Jeffery Rignall also stood in favor of the prosecution. In particular, during the testimony, Rignall described the attacks that Gacy perpetrated on him as "beastly and animalistic." (Amirante & Broderick, 2015, p.290) Most of the surviving victims were scarred for life and the prosecution could highlight these aspects in a very precise way to the jury.

In the final arguments, the state detailed out the case and the gravity of the offense as well as the depravity of the accused in perpetuating these ghastly crimes with particular reference to Gacy as "the worst of all murderers." (Amirante & Broderick, 2015, p.324) The prosecution also, in the final note, considered the manner in which Gacy had almost got away with the crimes had the last of these murders not been properly investigated. As opposed to the prosecution stand, the defense counsel Amirante and Motta stuck to their stand and argued against the testimony provided by the state's doctors on Gacy's mental health. In doing so, the defense strategy was primarily aimed at the jury by painting the picture of a "man driven by compulsions he was unable to control." (Sullivan & Maiken, 2012, p.363) In line with the defense strategy, the counsel kept referring to the testimony of doctors who spoke on the side of the defense. Further, the defense also used the testimonies of Jeffery Ringall and other survivors to highlight the fact that Gacy's beastly and animal-like behavior pointed to insanity. Finally, the defense made a plea that Gacy should be declared insane so that his brain and behavior would provide valuable input to the medical and criminal faculty. To further counter this argument, the state prosecutor William Kunkle continued the rebuttal argument by referring to the defense's insanity plea as a façade and gave numerous instances of Gacy's ability to act logically and control his actions. Finally, at the close of the argument, Kunkle pulled out photos of 22 victims of the Gacy killings and displayed them to the jury while requesting the members to "show the same sympathy this man showed when he took these lives and put them there." (Sullivan & Maiken, 2012, p.368)

Final Results

The jury unanimously declared Gacy guilty on 12 counts of murder with an initial execution date set for June 2, 1980. (Amirante & Broderick, 2015, p.387) Upon sentencing, Gacy was moved to the Menard Correctional Facility in Chester, IL, and he stayed there for almost 14 years. During this period, Gacy studied law books and attempted to file numerous appeals in various higher courts, including the US Supreme Court, all of which were turned down. (Cahill, 2011, p.351) The Illinois Supreme Court finally set his execution date for May 10, 1994, with death by lethal injection. Even before the execution, Gacy in a true psychopathic style did not express any remorse, and his last words before being executed were "Kiss my Ass." (OCPA, 2012) The media coverage was everywhere, that being on the radio, the newspaper, documentaries, and news stations. His name was everywhere, leading more people to become paranoid and to keep their children off the streets. This 'innocent' clown was convicted on many accounts and to this day all the bodies and names have still not been revealed.

CONCLUSION

But on general principle, a person who neither cared for human life nor human dignity definitely should not be let off on the premise of insanity. The important fact is that Gacy had no remorse for his acts even till the very end and for this very reason Gacy is a poster boy for those who advocate the death penalty. The aesthetic value of John Wayne Gacy's work is affected by his mortality. It is not his artistic 'skills' as an outsider artist that causes his work to be popular or even aesthetically pleasant, is it the controversy that surrounds his work. His name alone is what causes his work to sell at such outlandish prices. It is the collectors of 'murderbilia' that purchase his work based on associating Gacy's own mortality with this work rather than appreciating it for whatever aesthetic value his work may have. The idea of reaching into the mind of a killer by owning basically, a piece of him. Is his morality evident in his work? Yes, although he attempts to hide his insidious side by trying to 'bring joy to' viewers with his creepy friendly clown alter ego, you can't help linking his past to what this man really was with the heinous crimes that he committed and that does have influence on his work when evaluating it.

REFERENCES

Amirante, S. L., & Broderick, D. (2015). *John Wayne Gacy: Defending a Monster*. Simon and Schuster.

Bell, R., & Bardsley, M. (2001). *John Wayne Gacy Jr*. The Crime Library.

Cahill, T. (2011). *Buried dreams: Inside the mind of a serial killer*. Premier Digital Publishing.

Office of the Clark County Prosecuting Attorney, Clark County, Indiana (OCPA). (2012). *John Wayne Gacy – Record #237*. Author.

Sullivan, T., & Maiken, P. T. (2012). *Killer Clown: The John Wayne Gacy Murders*. Pinnacle Books.

Taylor, T. (2003). *The Clown that Killed*. Prairie Ghosts.

Compilation of References

ActC. J. (2003). (2003). https://www.legislation.gov.uk/ukpga/2003/44/contents

Amirante, S. L., & Broderick, D. (2015). *John Wayne Gacy: Defending a Monster*. Simon and Schuster.

Andrew, C., & Mitrokhin, V. (2000). *The Mitrokhin Archive: The KGB in Europe and the West*. Penguin. doi:10.1080/03071840008446488

Associated Press. (1966). *CAN757: File Footage of Moors Murder Case Pre Trial*. https://www.youtube.com/watch?v=wrt2dJXb9Q

Astor, D. (1990, Jan. 2). Why the Moors Murders are Kept Alive. *The Guardian*, p. 15.

Attorney General says 'Perverted Sexual Element' was Involved in the Moors Killings. (1966, Apr. 21). *The Times,* p. 10.

Aughty, R. (1993). *Sustaining Development in Mineral Economies: The Resource Curse Thesis*. Routledge.

Bailey, E. (1997). Du Plantier maintains silence on his wife's brutal murder. *Irish Examiner*. Available at: https://www.irishnewsarchive.com/free_search/?pub=IEX&search_olive=eoin%20bailey&yearFrom=1996&toYear=1997

Bailey, B., Farber, D., & Lee, S. (1999). Summer of Sam. *The Journal of American History, 86*(3), 1447. doi:10.2307/2568751

Barnes, G. (1990, February 2). Brady's a Liar Says Evil Myra. *The Mirror (Stafford, Tex.)*.

Bates, A. (1999). The Newsworthiness of Crime. *British Journal of Forensic Practice, 1*(2), 22–27. doi:10.1108/14636646199900012

BBC News. (2000). *Hindley: I Wish I'd Been Hanged*. https://www.news.bbc.co.uk/1/hi/uk/661139.stm

Beauregard, E., & Bouchard, M. (2010). Cleaning up your act: Forensic awareness as a detection avoidance strategy. *Journal of Criminal Justice, 38*(6), 1160–1166. doi:10.1016/j.jcrimjus.2010.09.004

Beauregard, E., & Martineau, M. (2014). No body, no crime? The role of forensic awareness in avoiding police detection in cases of sexual homicide. *Journal of Criminal Justice*, *42*(2), 213–220. doi:10.1016/j.jcrimjus.2013.06.007

Belknap, J. (2020). *The invisible woman: Gender, crime, and justice*. Sage Publications.

Bellotti, A. (2021, July 6). Vile Criminals who Bonded Behind Bars – Including Rose West and Myra Hindley's Love Affair. *The Mirror (Stafford, Tex.)*.

Bell, R., & Bardsley, M. (2001). *John Wayne Gacy Jr*. The Crime Library.

Berryman, H. (2002). Disarticulation pattern and tooth mark artifacts associated with pig scavenging of human remains: A case study. In M. H. Sorg & W. D. Haglund (Eds.), *Advances in Forensic Taphonomy: Method, Theory, and Archaeological Perspectives* (pp. 487–495). CRC Press.

Bertoldi, C. (2009, Feb. 19). Violata la casa degli orrori: macabri riti nella stanza di Mez. Incursione notturna nella villetta del delitto della studentessa [House of Horrors violated: macabre rituals in Mez's room. Night raid on the student's crime cottage]. *Il Giornale*. https://www.ilgiornale.it

Bettels, K., Grimstead, D., Allsop, C., Chaussée, A., Bolton-King, R., Sturdy Colls, C., Chapman, B., Keatley, D., Tilley, E., Turner, J., Spence, S., & Marquardt, A. (2022). (in press). Finding the missing and unknown: Novel educational approaches to warming up cold cases. *Science & Justice*. Advance online publication. doi:10.1016/j.scijus.2022.03.007

Beyond Pity. (1997, Feb. 6). *The Sun*, p. 6.

Bickle, G., & Peterson, R. D. (1991). The impact of gender-based family roles on criminal sentencing. *Social Problems*, *38*(3), 372–394. doi:10.2307/800605

Birch, H. (1993). If looks could kill: Myra Hindley and the iconography of evil. *Moving targets: Women, murder and representation*, 32-61.

Birch, H. (1995). A special kind of evil. *The Independent, 23*.

Bitton, Y., & Dayan, H. (2019). "The Perfect Murder": An exploratory study of staged murder scenes and concealed femicide. *British Journal of Criminology*, *59*(5), 1054–1075. doi:10.1093/bjc/azz015

Black, L. (2009). *The representation of female offenders in Irish newspapers* [MA Thesis]. University College Dublin.

Blom-Cooper, L., & Morris, T. (1999). Life until death: Interpretations of section 1 (1) of the Murder (Abolition of the Death Penalty) Act 1965. *Criminal Law Review (London, England)*, 899–905.

Bluestone, G. (2021). *Hype: How Scammers, Grifters, and Con Artists Are Taking Over the Internet—and Why We're Following*. Harlequin.

Boltanski, L., & Thevenot, L. (1999). The Sociology of Critical Capacity. *European Journal of Social Theory*, *2*(3), 359–377. doi:10.1177/136843199002003010

Bonger, W. (1916). *Criminality and economic conditions* (1st ed.). Creative Media Partners.

Boss, P. (1999). *Ambiguous Loss: Learning to Live with Unresolved Grief.* Harvard University Press.

Boss, P. (2006). *Loss Trauma and Resilience: Therapeutic Work with Ambiguous Loss.* Norton.

Botelho, G. (2012, May 23). *What happened the night Trayvon Martin died.* CNN. https://www.cnn.com/2012/05/18/justice/florida-teen-shooting-details/index.html

Brent, H. (2021). *Ian Bailey told French prosecutors to 'Pog mo Thoin' when they demanded he face trial in France.* Available at: https://www.irishpost.com/news/ian-bailey-told-french-prosecutors-to-pog-mo-thoin-when-they-demanded-he-face-trial-in-paris-215300

Brooke, C. (2013, July 20). Myra Hindley, the Former Nun and their Lesbian Trysts in Prison after Table Tennis. *Daily Mail.* https://www.pressreader.com/uk/scottish-daily-mail/20130720/282329677548152

Brunson, R. K., & Miller, J. (2006). Young black men and urban policing in the United States. *British Journal of Criminology, 46*(4), 613–640. doi:10.1093/bjc/azi093

Building Rossport Solidarity Camp Meeting in Dublin. (n.d.). Retrieved from http://www.shelltosea.com/node/635

Bungey, S., & Forde, J. (2021). *West Cork Podcast: the unsolved murder of Sophie Toscan Du Plantier* [podcast series]. The West Cork Podcast. https://www.westcorkpodcast.com/about

Byers, C. (2014, September 16). Grand jury now has until January to decide whether to charge Ferguson officer. *St. Louis Post Dispatch.* Retrieved from https://www.stltoday.com/news/local/crime-and-courts/grand-jury-now-has-until-january-to-decide-whether-to-charge-ferguson-officer/article_aa4111fc-2952-54c9-8316-76c4867dea48.html

Cahill, T. (2011). *Buried dreams: Inside the mind of a serial killer.* Premier Digital Publishing.

Campbell, D. (1997, Oct. 29). 83pc Oppose Hindley's Release. *The Guardian*, p. 9.

Capponi, A. (2009, Dec. 6). Amanda e Raffaele guardati a vista. Gli Usa contro la giustizia italiana [Amanda and Raffaele closely watched. USA against Italian justice]. *Corriere della Sera.* https://www.corriere.it

Carlizzi, G. (2008). *Meredith Kercher. Un delitto imperfetto* [Meredith Kercher. An imperfect crime]. Mond & Editori.

Caroppo, L. (2021, Aug. 23). Mostro, la pistola da Vinci a un avvocato. E Pacciani è stato sicuramente ucciso [Monster, the gun from Vinci to a lawyer. And Pacciani was definitely killed]. *La Nazione.* https://www.lanazione.it

Carrabine, E. (2011). Images of torture: Culture, politics and power. *Crime, Media, Culture, 7*(1), 5–30. doi:10.1177/1741659011404418

Carrington, K., McIntosh, A., & Scott, J. (2010). Globalization, frontier masculinities and violence: Booze, blokes and brawls. *British Journal of Criminology*, *50*(3), 393–413. doi:10.1093/bjc/azq003

Carrington, K., & Pereira, M. (2011). Assessing the social impacts of the resources boom on rural communities. *Rural Society*, *21*(1), 2–20. doi:10.5172/rsj.2011.21.1.2

Carr, N., & Holt, S. (2010). Outrageous Provocation? The Media Reporting of Domestic Violence in Ireland. In P. Share & M. Corcoran (Eds.), *Ireland of the Illusions: A Sociological Chronicle, 2007–2008* (1st ed.). IPA.

Catalfamo, C. (2006). Stand your ground: Florida's castle doctrine for the twenty-first century. *Rutgers JL & Pub. Pol'y*, *4*, 504.

Cesario, J., Johnson, D. J., & Terrill, W. (2019). Is there evidence of racial disparity in police use of deadly force? Analyses of officer-involved fatal shootings in 2015–2016. *Social Psychological & Personality Science*, *10*(5), 586–595. doi:10.1177/1948550618775108

Chaney, C., & Robertson, R. V. (2013). Racism and police brutality in America. *Journal of African American Studies*, *17*(4), 480–505. doi:10.100712111-013-9246-5

Chaussée, A. (2019). The language of forensic archaeology: Discourses in field and in court. In K. Moran & C. Gold (Eds.), Forensic Archaeology: Multidisciplinary Perspectives (pp. 75–89). Springer Nature.

Chesler, P. (1992). A woman's right to self-defense: The Case of Aileen Carol Wuornos. *John's L. Rev.*, *66*, 933.

Chesney-Lind, M., & Eliason, M. (2006). From invisible to incorrigible: The demonization of marginalized women and girls. *Crime, Media, Culture*, *2*(1), 29–47. doi:10.1177/1741659006061709

Chibnall, S. (1977). *Law-and-order News: An Analysis of Crime Reporting in the British Press* (1st ed.). Psychology Press.

Chomsky, N., & Herman, E. (1988). *Manufacturing consent: The political economy of the mass media*. Pantheon Books.

Chopin, J., Beauregard, E., & Bitzer, S. (2020). Factors influencing the use of forensic awareness strategies in sexual homicide. *Journal of Criminal Justice*, *71*(April), 101709. doi:10.1016/j.jcrimjus.2020.101709

Christie, N. (1986). The Ideal Victim. In E. A. Fattah (Ed.), *From Crime Policy to Victim Policy* (1st ed.). Palgrave Macmillian. doi:10.1007/978-1-349-08305-3_2

Christie, N. (2016). *Crime control as industry: Towards gulags, western style*. Routledge. doi:10.4324/9781315512051

Clerk Accused of Three Murders. (1965, Dec. 3). *The Times*, p. 17.

CNN. (2021, February 17). *Trayvon Martin Shooting Fast Facts*. CNN. https://www.cnn.com/2013/06/05/us/trayvon-martin-shooting-fast-facts/index.html

Coady, D. (2006). *Conspiracy Theories. The Philosophical Debate*. Routledge.

Cohen, S. (2002). *Folk Devils and Moral-Panics* (3rd ed.). Routledge.

Cohn Aizenman, H. (2012). Pretrial publicity in post-trayvon martin world. *Criminal Justice*, *27*(3), 12–17.

College of Policing. (2021). *Missing Persons*. https://www.app.college.police.uk/app-content/major-investigation-and-public-protection/missing-persons/#risk-assessment-and-response

Connolly, F., & Lynch, R. (2005). *The Great Corrib gas controversy*. Center for Public Inquiry.

Cordell, L. H. (2014, December 9). Grand Juries Should Be Abolished. *Slate*. Retrieved from https://slate.com/news-and-politics/2014/12/abolish-grand-juries-justice-for-eric-garner-and-michael-brown.html

Coroners and Justice Act, (2009).

Corrieri, B., & Márquez-Grant, N. (2019). Using nutrient foramina to differentiate human from non-human long bone fragments in bioarchaeology and forensic anthropology. *Homo*, *70*(4), 255–268. doi:10.1127/homo/2019/1113 PMID:31701996

Corte di Assise di Appello di Perugia [Court of Assizes of Appeal of Perugia]. 4/2011.

Corte di Assise di Perugia [Court of Assizes of Perugia]. 7/2009.

Corte di Cassazione [Court of Cassation]. 422/2013.

CPS. (2018). *The Code for Crown Prosecutors* (8th ed.). Crown.

Crews, G., Montgomery, R., & Garris, W. (1996). Satanic, Occult, and Ritualistic violence in America. *Violence in America.*, *1*(1), 33–53.

Cummins, I., Foley, M., & King, M. (2019). *Serial killers and the media: The Moors Murders legacy*. Springer. doi:10.1007/978-3-030-04876-1

Davenport, A., & Harrison, K. (2011). Swinging the blue lamp: The forensic archaeology of contemporary child and animal burial in the UK. *Mortality*, *16*(2), 176–190. doi:10.1080/13576275.2011.560706

Day, E. (2015, July 19). #Blacklivesmatter: The birth of a new Civil Rights Movement. *The Guardian*. https://www.theguardian.com/world/2015/jul/19/blacklivesmatter-birth-civil-rights-movement

De Lucia, C. (2016, April 19). How the Chester Chronicle Covered the Infamous Moors Murders Trial. *Chester Chronicle*. Retrieved from https://www.cheshire-live.co.uk/news/history/how-chester-chronicle-covered-infamous-11209509

Desai, S. R. (2019). Humanizing Trayvon Martin: Racial profiling, implicit biases, and teacher education. *Urban Education*, *54*(8), 1031–1057. doi:10.1177/0042085916646609

Diamond, S. (2019). "A Flower in a Hard Rain": Melodramatic Storytelling by, and About, Aileen Wuornos. *Anthurium A Caribbean Studies Journal, 15*(2).

Dick, P. (2005). Dirty work designations: How police officers account for their use of coercive force. *Human Relations, 58*(11), 1363–1390. doi:10.1177/0018726705060242

Domínguez-Solera, S., & Domínguez-Rodrigo, M. (2009). A taphonomic study of bone modification and of tooth-mark patterns on long limb bone portions by suids. *International Journal of Osteoarchaeology, 19*(3), 345–363. doi:10.1002/oa.987

Donelson, R. (2017). Blacks, Cops, and the State of Nature. *Ohio St. J. Crim. L., 15*, 183.

Douglas Brown, K. (2015). *Stand your ground: Black bodies and the justice of God.* Orbis Books.

Dowd, N. E. (2021). Black Lives Matter: Trayvon Martin, the Abolition of Juvenile Justice and# BlackYouthMatter. *University of Florida Journal of Law and Public Policy, 31*(43), 43–57.

Dower, J. (2021). *Sophie: A murder in West Cork* [documentary series]. Netflix.

Doyle, R., & Barnes, G. C. (2020). Targeting missing persons most likely to come to harm among 92,681 cases reported to Devon and Cornwall Police. *Cambridge Journal of Evidence-Based Policing, 4*(3–4), 160–177. doi:10.100741887-020-00051-2

Dubsky, A., & Christensen, A. (2018). Can intentionally compacting a clandestine grave make it more difficult to detect with a soil probe? *Journal of Forensic Identification, 68*(1), 147–156.

Dugatkin, L. A. (1992). The evolution of the "con artist". *Ethology and Sociobiology, 13*(1), 3–18. doi:10.1016/0162-3095(92)90003-M

DyerT. (2022). *Media conglomeration, Local News, and Capital Market consequences.* Available at: https://papers.ssrn.com/sol3/papers.cfm?abstract_id=4055618 doi:10.2139/ssrn.4055618

Elliza, J. (2000). *Seeing Things: Television in the Age of Uncertainty.* I.B. Tauris. doi:10.5040/9780755604784

Emmott, B. (2011, Oct. 5). Ecco perché il delitto di Perugia è diventato un caso unico [That's why the crime of Perugia has become a unique case]. *La Stampa.* https://www.lastampa.it

Engel, R. S., Sobol, J., & Wordon, R. E. (2000). Further exploration of the demeanor hypothesis: The interaction effects of suspects' characteristics and demeanor on police behavior. *Justice Quarterly, 17*(2), 235–258. doi:10.1080/07418820000096311

Ericson, R., Baranek, P., & Chan, J. (1989). Negotiating Control: A Study of News Sources. Open University Press.

Evis, L. (2016). *Forensic archaeology: the application of comparative excavation methods and recording systems.* Archaeopress Publishing Ltd. doi:10.2307/j.ctvxw3nq9

Fabregat, E., & Beck, T. J. (2019). On the erasure of race in control culture discourse: A case study of Trayvon Martin's role in the Black Lives Matter Movement. *Social Identities*, *25*(6), 759–774. doi:10.1080/13504630.2019.1572502

Feagin, J. Orum, A., & Sjoberg, G. (Eds.). (1991). A Case Study for Case Study. Chapel Hill, NC: University of North Carolina Press.

Ferguson, C. (2021). *Detection Avoidance in Homicides Debates, Explanations and Responses*. Routledge. doi:10.4324/9780367266851

Ferguson, C., & McKinley, A. (2020). Detection avoidance and mis/unclassified, unsolved homicides in Australia. *Journal of Criminal Psychology*, *10*(2), 113–122. doi:10.1108/JCP-09-2019-0030

Ferguson, C., & Petherick, W. (2016). Getting away with murder: An examination of detected homicides staged as suicides. *Homicide Studies*, *20*(1), 3–24. doi:10.1177/1088767914553099

Ferguson, S. C., & McClendon, J. H. (2013). Indignity and death: Philosophical commentary on white terror, black death, and the Trayvon Martin tragedy. In G. Yancy & G. Jones (Eds.), *Pursuing Trayvon Martin: Historical contexts and contemporary manifestations of racial dynamics* (pp. 41–58). Lexington Books.

Ferriter, D. (2004). *The transformation of Ireland: 1900-2000* (1st ed.). Profile Books.

Fieldstadt, E. (2014, August 11). *Teen killed by Missouri officer after 'physical confrontation': Police*. Retrieved from https://www.nbcnews.com/storyline/michael-brown-shooting/teen-killed-missouri-officer-after-physical-confrontation-police-n177206

Ford, R. (1994, Dec. 8). Hindley asks for mercy after 28 years in prison. *The Times,* p. 9.

Franceschetti, P. (2014). *Considerazioni sul delitto Meredith* [Considerations on the crime Meredith]. https://petalidiloto.com

Franceschini, E. (2020, Feb. 7). Morto il padre di Meredith Kercher, la studentessa uccisa a Perugia [Meredith Kercher's father died, the student killed in Perugia]. *La Repubblica.* https://www.repubblica.it

Fuery, K. (2017). *New media: Culture and image*. Bloomsbury Publishing.

Fulcher, S. (2017). *Catching a Serial Killer*. Ebury Press.

Fulton, S., & Martin, T. (2017). *Rest in power: the enduring life of Trayvon Martin*. Spiegel & Grau.

Fyfe, J. J. (2002). Too many missing cases: Holes in our knowledge about police use of force. *Justice Research and Policy*, *4*(1-2), 87–102. doi:10.3818/JRP.4.1.2002.87

Garland, D. (2000). The culture of high crime societies: Some preconditions of recent law and order policies. *British Journal of Criminology*, *40*(3), 347–375. doi:10.1093/bjc/40.3.347

Garner, J. H., Maxwell, C. D., & Heraux, C. G. (2002). Characteristics associated with the prevalence and severity of force used by the police. *Justice Quarterly*, *19*(4), 705–746. doi:10.1080/07418820200095401

Garofano, N., & Russell, P. (2011). *Assassini per caso. Luci e ombre del delitto di Perugia* [Assassins by chance. Lights and shadows of the crime of Perugia]. Rizzoli.

Gerbner, G. & Gross, L. (1976). Living With Television: The Violence Profile. *Journal of Communication, 26*(2), 172-194.

Gerbner, G., & Gross, L. (1972). Living with television: The violence profile. *Journal of Communication*, *26*(2), 173–199. PMID:932235

Gialuz, M. (2019). La violazione dei diritti fondamentali nuoce alla ricerca della verità: La Corte di Strasburgo condanna l'Italia per il procedimento nei confronti di Amanda Knox [Violation of fundamental rights harms the quest for truth: the Strasbourg Court condemns Italy for the proceedings against Amanda Knox]. *Diritto Penale Contemporaneo*, *2*, 155–168.

Gibson, K. (2022). Inventing Anna True Story: Everything to Know About Anna Delvey, Including Her Crimes and Where She Is Now. *People Magazine*.

Glaser, B. G., Strauss, A. L., & Strutzel, E. (1968). The discovery of grounded theory; strategies for qualitative research. *Nursing Research*, *17*(4), 364. doi:10.1097/00006199-196807000-00014

Gold, S. D. (2014). *Son of Sam Case: Simon & Schuster Inc. v. Members of United States Crime Victims Board*. Cavendish Square Publishing, LLC.

Graeff, E., Stempeck, M., & Zuckerman, E. (2014). The battle for 'Trayvon Martin': Mapping a media controversy online and off-line. *First Monday*, *19*(2). Advance online publication. doi:10.5210/fm.v19i2.4947

Gramsci, A. (1982). *Selections from the Prison Notebooks*. Lawrence and Wishart.

Grant, L. (1997, May 28). The Time for Atonement. *The Guardian*, p. A11.

Gray, S. (2017). "Blue Lives Matter" laws: The extension of hate crime statutes to include law enforcement. *Kentucky Law Journal (Lexington, Ky.)*.

Graziano, L., Schuck, A., & Martin, C. (2010). Police misconduct, media coverage, and public perceptions of racial profiling: An experiment. *Justice Quarterly*, *27*(1), 52–76. doi:10.1080/07418820902763046

Greaves, S. (1985, May 29). Hindley Decision Backed by Poll. *The Times*, p. 12.

Greenfield, H. (1988). Special studies: Bone consumption by pigs in a contemporary Serbian village: implications for the interpretation of prehistoric faunal assemblages. *Journal of Field Archaeology*, *15*(4), 473–479. doi:10.1179/jfa.1988.15.4.473

Greenhalgh, M., & Shalev Greene, K. (2021). *Impact of Police Cuts on Missing Person Investigations*. https://pure.port.ac.uk/ws/portalfiles/portal/28691081/Final_version.pdf

Greer, C. (2019). *Crime and Media: A Reader* (1st ed.). Routledge. doi:10.4324/9780367809195

Guardianship (Missing Persons) Act (2017).

Gurnham, D. (2003). The moral narrative of criminal responsibility and the principled justification of tariffs for murder: Myra Hindley and Thompson and Venables. *Legal Studies*, *23*(4), 605–623. doi:10.1111/j.1748-121X.2003.tb00230.x

Hall, S., Critcher, C., Jefferson, T., Clarke, J., & Roberts, B. (1978). *Policing the Crisis: Mugging, the State and Law and Order* (1st ed.). Macmillan. doi:10.1007/978-1-349-15881-2

Hamel, J., Dufour, S., & Fortin, D. (1993). *Case Study Methods*. Sage Publications. doi:10.4135/9781412983587

Harrison, K., Dawson, L., & Mackinnon, G. (2016). Interdisciplinary approaches to the search and location of buried bodies. In H. Kars & L. van den Eijkel (Eds.), Soil in Criminal and Environmental Forensics (pp. 201–212). Springer.

Heidensohn, F. (1985). *Women and Crime* (1st ed.). Macmillan Education UK.

Hindley, M. (1980). *Petition to the Home Secretary*. Academic Press.

Hindley's Gaol Love for Former Nun. (1972, Apr. 2). *The Guardian*, p. 7.

HM Advocate v David Gilroy [2013] HCJAC 18.

HM Advocate v David Gilroy, (2012) Edinburgh High Court of Justiciary (unreported).

HM Advocate v Edward Cairney and Avril Jones, (2019) Glasgow High Court of Justiciary, (unreported).

HM Advocate v Thomas Pryde, (2010) Glasgow High Court of Justiciary (unreported).

Hodges, A. (2015). Ideologies of language and race in US media discourse about the Trayvon Martin shooting. *Language in Society*, *44*(3), 401–423. doi:10.1017/S004740451500024X

Holmes, T. (2017). Professional Criminals and White-Collar Crime in Popular Culture. In Oxford Research Encyclopedia of Criminology and Criminal Justice. doi:10.1093/acrefore/9780190264079.013.215

Home Office. (1792). *Criminal Registers of Prisoners in Middlesex and the City*. London Lives 1600-1800. https://www.londonlives.org/browse.jsp?div=NAHOCR70005CR700050193

Horsman, G. (2016). Unmanned aerial vehicles: A preliminary analysis of forensic challenges. *Digital Investigation*, *16*, 1–11. Advance online publication. doi:10.1016/j.diin.2015.11.002

House of Lords Hansard. (2020). *Prisoners (Disclosure of Information About Victims) Bill*. https://hansard.parliament.uk/Lords/2020-07-01/debates/5FEFEC9B-F6D7-4648-9CF4-2684C353B36E/Prisoners(DisclosureOfInformationAboutVictims)Bill

Hume, H. (2022, Jan. 22). Infamous Moors murderer Myra Hindley's final days spent rotting in a Suffolk prison. *Suffolk Live.*

Hunter, J., & Cox, M. (2005). *Forensic Archaeology Advances in Theory and Practice.* Routledge.

Hunter, J., Simpson, B., & Sturdy Colls, C. (2013). *Forensic Approaches to Buried Remains.* Wiley Blackwell.

Indra, L., Errickson, D., Young, A., & Lösch, S. (2022). Uncovering forensic taphonomic agents: Animal scavenging in the European context. *Evolutionary Biology, 11*(4), 601–627. doi:10.3390/biology11040601 PMID:35453800

Inglis, T., & McKeogh, C. (2012). The double bind: Women, honour and sexuality in contemporary Ireland. *Media Culture & Society, 34*(1), 68–82. doi:10.1177/0163443711427200

Innes, M., Brookman, F., & Jones, H. (2021). "Mosaicking": Cross construction, sense-making and methods of police investigation. *Policing, 44*(4), 708–721. doi:10.1108/PIJPSM-02-2021-0028

Irish Examiner Reporter. (1998). *Gardai deny second murder trial claim.* Available at: https://www.irishnewsarchive.com/free_search/?pub=IEX&search_olive=Sophie%20Toscan%20Du%20Plantier&yearFrom=1998&toYear=1998

Irish Examiner Reporter. (1999). Family speak of anguish over killer of woman still being at large. *Irish Examiner.*

Irish Examiner Reporter. (2000). *A gruesome account of the Sophie Toscan Du Plantier murder.* Available at: https://www.irishnewsarchive.com/free_search/?pub=IEX&search_olive=Sophie%20Toscan%20Du%20Plantier&yearFrom=1996&toYear=2000

Jacobs, L. A., Kim, M. E., Whitfield, D. L., Gartner, R. E., Panichelli, M., Kattari, S. K., Downey, M. M., McQueen, S. S., & Mountz, S. E. (2021). Defund the police: Moving towards an anti-carceral social work. *Journal of Progressive Human Services, 32*(1), 37–62. doi:10.1080/10428232.2020.1852865

Jansen-Osmann, P., & Berendt, B. (2005). What makes a route appear longer? An experimental perspective on features, route segmentation, and distance knowledge. *The Quarterly Journal of Experimental Psychology. A, Human Experimental Psychology, 58*(8), 1390–1414. doi:10.1080/02724980443000638 PMID:16365946

Janzen, G. (2006). Memory for object location and route direction in virtual large-scale space. *Quarterly Journal of Experimental Psychology, 59*(3), 493–508. doi:10.1080/02724980443000746 PMID:16627352

Jeanis, M., & Powers, R. (2017). Newsworthiness of missing persons cases: An analysis of selection bias, disparities in coverage, and the narrative framework of news reports. *Deviant Behavior, 38*(6), 668–683. doi:10.1080/01639625.2016.1197618

Jefferson-Bullock, J., & Exum, J. J. (2020). That is Enough Punishment: Situating Defunding the Police Within Antiracist Sentencing Reform. *The Fordham Urban Law Journal, 48,* 625.

Jewkes, Y. (2011). *Media and Crime* (2nd ed.). Sage.

Johnson, R. (2011). Suspect mental disorder and police use of force. *Criminal Justice and Behavior*, *38*(2), 127–145. doi:10.1177/0093854810388160

Jones, R. (2014, August 21). Self-Segregation: Why It's So Hard for Whites to Understand Ferguson. *The Atlantic*. Retrieved from https://www.theatlantic.com/national/archive/2014/08/self-segregation-why-its-hard-for-whites-to-understand-ferguson/378928/

Justifiable Use of Force. Fla. Stat. Title XLVI, Chapter 776 (2021). http://www.leg.state.fl.us/statutes/index.cfm?App_mode=Display_Statute&URL=0700-0799/0776/0776ContentsIndex.html

Kandelia, S. (2011). Life meaning life: Is there any hope of release for prisoners serving whole life orders? *Journal of Criminal Law*, *75*(1), 70–87. doi:10.1350/jcla.2011.75.1.684

Kang, J. (2005). Trojan horses of race. *Harvard Law Review*, *118*, 1490–2005.

Katz, J. (1987). What makes crimenews'? *Media Culture & Society*, *9*(1), 47–75. doi:10.1177/016344387009001004

Kavanagh, T. (1997, May 22). Straw: I'll Never Let Evil Myra Walk Free. *The Sun*, p. 25.

Kay, J., & Gay, M. (1985, Mar. 2). 15 Years More for Evil Myra. *The Sun*.

Kay, J., Saxty, G., & Hartley, C. (2000, Mar. 31) Uniquely Evil Myra. *The Sun*.

Keatley, D., O'Donnell, C., Chapman, B., & Clarke, D. (2022). The psycho-criminology of burial sites: Developing the winthropping method for locating clandestine burial sites. *Journal of Police and Criminal Psychology*, *37*(1), 91–100. doi:10.100711896-021-09457-8

Keightley, A. (2017). *Ian Brady: The Untold Story of the Moors Murders*. Robson Books.

Killam, E. (2004). *The Detection of Human Remains* (2nd ed.). Charles C Thomas.

Kindy, K. (2014, November 24). How the Ferguson grand jury process works. *The Washington Post*. Retrieved from https://www.washingtonpost.com/politics/how-the-ferguson-grand-jury-process-works/2014/11/24/46599f9a-73f9-11e4-a589-1b102c2f81d0_story.html

Kiprewitz, R. (2005). *The Proposed Corrib Onshore System: An Independent Analysis*. CPI.

Konnikova, M. (2017). *The Confidence Game: Why we fall for it... Every time*. Penguin.

Lane, K., Williams, Y., Hunt, A. N., & Paulk, A. (2020). The Framing of Race: Trayvon Martin and the Black Lives Matter Movement. *Journal of Black Studies*, *51*(8), 790–812. doi:10.1177/0021934720946802

Lawson, T. F. (2012). Fresh cut in an old wound a critical analysis of the Trayvon martin killing: The public outcry, the prosecutors' discretion, and the stand your ground law. *University of Florida Journal of Law and Public Policy*, *23*(3), 271–310.

Lee, C. (2013). Making race salient: Trayvon martin and implicit bias in not yet post-racial society. *North Carolina Law Review*, *91*(5), 1555–1612.

Legewie, J. (2016). Racial profiling and use of force in police stops: How local events trigger periods of increased discrimination. *American Journal of Sociology*, *122*(2), 379–424. doi:10.1086/687518

Leonard, L. (Ed.). (2017) Environmental Criminology: Spatial Analysis and Regional Issues, Advances in Sustainability and Environmental Justice. Emerald Group Publishing.

Leonard, L. (2005). Greenhouse Press Ecopolitics Series: Vol. 1. *Politics Inflamed: GSE and the campaign against Incineration in Ireland*. Greenhouse Press with Drogheda Choice.

Leonard, L. (2006). *Green nation: the Irish environmental movement. Drogheda*. Emerald Publishing.

Leonard, L. (2007). Moral Framing in a Resource Dispute: The" Shell to Sea" Campaign in North Mayo. *Studies: AN Irish Quarterly Review*, *95*(380), 375–386.

Leonard, L. (2007). *The environmental movement in Ireland*. Springer Science & Business Media.

Leonard, L. (2008). Rapid development & community mobilization in the Republic of Ireland. *Community Development (Columbus, Ohio)*, *39*(3), 59–74. doi:10.1080/15575330809489669

Leonard, L. (2011). *Community campaigns for sustainable living: health, waste & protest in civil society*. Emerald Group Publishing. doi:10.1108/S2041-806X(2011)7

Leonard, L. (2014). Cultural Criminology, Governmentality and the Liquidity of the Failing State: The View from Ireland. *Critical Criminology*, *22*(2), 293–306. doi:10.100710612-013-9217-0

Leonard, L., & Botetzagias, I. (2011). *Sustainable politics and the crisis of the peripheries*. Emerald Group Publishing.

Levi, M. (2006). The media construction of financial white-collar crimes. *British Journal of Criminology*, *46*(6), 1037–1057. doi:10.1093/bjc/azl079

Liebler, C. (2010). Me(di)a Culpa?: The 'Missing White Woman Syndrome' and media self-critique. *Communication, Culture & Critique*, *3*(4), 549–565. doi:10.1111/j.1753-9137.2010.01085.x

Liebler, C., Ahmad, W., & Gayle, G. (2020). Not at Risk? News, gatekeeping, and missing teens. *Journalism Practice*, 1–16. doi:10.1080/17512786.2020.1790407

Lim, H., Fridell, L. A., & Lee, H. (2014). The impact of supervision and neighborhood context on police use of less-lethal force: A multi-level analysis. *Journal of Police Studies*, *14*, 155–182.

Liska, E., & Baccaglini, W. (1990, August). Feeling Safe by Comparison: Crime in the Newspapers. *Social Problems*, *37*(3), 360–37. doi:10.2307/800748

Lombroso, C., & Ferrero, G. (1895). The female offender (Vol. 1). D. Appleton.

Lum, C., Koper, C. S., & Wu, X. (2021). Can We Really Defund the Police? A Nine-Agency Study of Police Response to Calls for Service. *Police Quarterly*.

Maddison, D., Ormerod, D., Tonking, S., & Wait, J. (2020). *The Crown Court Compendium Part I : Jury and Trial Management and Summing Up*. Judicial College. https://www.judiciary.uk/wp-content/uploads/2016/06/Crown-Court-Compendium-Part-I-July-2020-1.pdf

Madison, E. (2015). Media Portrayals of the Trayvon Martin Tragedy. *Cultural Studies « Critical Methodologies, 15*(4), 278–282.

Mason, G. (2020). Blue Lives Matter and Hate Crime Law. *Race and Justice*.

Mastronardi, V. M., & Castellini, G. (2009). *Meredith. Luci e ombre a Perugia* [Meredith. Lights and shadows in Perugia]. Armando.

Mata Tutor, P., Márquez-Grant, N., Villoria Rojas, C., Muñoz García, A., Pérez Guzmán, I., & Benito Sánchez, M. (2021). Through fire and flames: Post-burning survival and detection of dismemberment-related toolmarks in cremated cadavers. *International Journal of Legal Medicine, 135*(3), 801–815. doi:10.100700414-020-02447-1 PMID:33084995

McClam, E. (2014, October 21). *State senator Jamilah Nasheed arrested in latest Ferguson protest*. Retrieved from https://www.nbcnews.com/storyline/michael-brown-shooting/state-senator-jamilah-nasheed-arrested-latest-ferguson-protest-n230411

McCluskey, J. D., & Terrill, W. (2005). Departmental and civilian complaints as predictors of police coercion. *Policing, 28*(3), 513–529. doi:10.1108/13639510510614582

Mcfadden, B. (2020, Sept. 21). How Twisted Serial Killers Myra Hindley and Rose West Became Lesbian Lovers in Jail. *Daily Star*.

McLaughlin, E. C., Lynch, J., & Simon, D. (2019, December 5). *George Zimmerman sues Trayvon Martin's parents and others for more than $100 million*. CNN. https://www.cnn.com/2019/12/04/us/george-zimmerman-lawsuit-trayvon-martin-mother/index.html

Mendelsohn, R. (1947). Victimology and contemporary society's trends. *Victimology, an International Journal, 1*(1), 8-28.

Meringolo, J. C. (2010). The media, the jury, and the high-profile defendant: A defense perspective on the media circus. *New York Law School Law Review, 55*, 981.

Ministry of Justice. (2019). *'Claudia's law' to lift families of missing people out of legal limbo*. https://www.gov.uk/government/news/claudia-s-law-to-lift-families-of-missing-people-out-of-legal-limbo

Moors Trial: Recording Played in Court. (1966, Apr. 27). *The Guardian*, p. 4.

Myra Hindley and Thompson and Venables. (n.d.). *Legal Studies, 23*(4), 605–623.

National Crime Agency. (2021). UK Missing Persons Unit. *Data Report, 2019*, 2020.

NBCUniversal News Group. (2014a, August 11). *Looters raid store after cop shoots unarmed Missouri teen*. Retrieved from https://www.nbcnews.com/storyline/michael-brown-shooting/looters-raid-store-after-cop-shoots-unarmed-missouri-teen-n177516

NBCUniversal News Group. (2014b, August 16). *Michael Brown killing: Police in Ferguson fire tear gas amid looting*. Retrieved September 30, 2022, from https://www.nbcnews.com/storyline/michael-brown-shooting/michael-brown-killing-police-ferguson-fire-tear-gas-amid-looting-n182196

Newburn, T. (2014, August 20). The Ferguson riots may seem similar to those in UK in 2011 – but there are stark contrasts. *The Guardian*. Retrieved from https://www.theguardian.com/commentisfree/2014/aug/20/ferguson-missouri-not-so-far-from-tottenham-toxteth

Ng, K. (2020, February 6). Helen McCourt: 'Give me my child back,' mother tells killer Ian Simms as he is released from prison. *Independent*. https://www.independent.co.uk/news/uk/home-news/helen-mccourt-mother-ian-simms-killer-release-prison-death-a9321281.html

Nix, J., Campbell, B. A., Byers, E. H., & Alpert, G. P. (2017). A bird's eye view of civilians killed by police in 2015: Further evidence of implicit bias. *Criminology & Public Policy*, *16*(1), 309–340. doi:10.1111/1745-9133.12269

O'Connell, M. (1999). Is Irish Public Opinion towards Crime Distorted by Media Bias? *European Journal of Communication*, *14*(1), 191–212. doi:10.1177/0267323199014002003

O'Donnell, I. (2005). Crime and justice in the Republic of Ireland. *European Journal of Criminology*, *2*(1), 99–131.

O'Mahony, S. (2019). From shebeens to supervised injecting centres: The socio-historical construction and portrayal of addiction in modern Ireland. *Irish Journal of Sociology*, *27*(2), 153–197. doi:10.1177/0791603519835437

O'Sullivan, C. (2008). The Nun, the Rape Charge, and the Miscarriage of Justice: The Case of Nora Wall. *The Northern Ireland Legal Quarterly*, *59*(1), 305.

Odell, R., & Gregg, W. (2006). *Murderers' Row: An International Murderers' Who's Who*. The History Press.

Office of the Clark County Prosecuting Attorney, Clark County, Indiana (OCPA). (2012). *John Wayne Gacy – Record #237*. Author.

Oliver, M. B., & Armstrong, G. B. (1995). Predictors of viewing and enjoyment of reality-based and fictional crime shows. *Journalism & Mass Communication Quarterly*, *72*(3), 559–570. doi:10.1177/107769909507200307

Olson, L. (2017). Blue lives have always mattered: The usurping of hate crime laws for an unintended and unnecessary purpose. *St Mary's Law Review on Race and Social Justice*, *20*, 13–55.

Overbury, T. (1676). A true and perfect account of the examination, confession, trial, condemnation and execution of Joan Perry, and her two sons, John and Richard Perry, for the supposed murder of Will. Harrison, Gent Being one of the most remarkable occurrences which hath h. Early English Books Online, Text Creation Partnership.

Paoline, E. III, & Terrill, W. (2007). Police education, experience, and the use of force. *Criminal Justice and Behavior*, *34*(2), 179–196. doi:10.1177/0093854806290239

Paoline, E., & Terrill, W. (2004). Women police officers and the use of coercion. *Women & Criminal Justice*, *15*(3-4), 97–119. doi:10.1300/J012v15n03_05

Parole Board. (2021). *Disclosure of Information about Victims Member Guidance*. Author.

Peelo, M., Francis, B., Soothill, K., Pearson, J., & Ackerley, E. (2004). Newspaper reporting and the public construction of homicide. *British Journal of Criminology*, *44*(2), 256–275. doi:10.1093/bjc/44.2.256

Peffley, M., & Hurwitz, J. (2013). Persuasion and resistance: race and the death penalty in America. In H. T. Greene & S. Gabbidon (Eds.), *Race and crime: a text/reader* (1st ed., pp. 355–366). Sage.

Pettigrew, M. (2016a). Public, Politicians, and the Law: The Long Shadow and Modern Thrall of Myra Hindley. *Current Issues in Criminal Justice*, *28*(1), 51–66. doi:10.1080/10345329.2016.12036056

Pettigrew, M. (2016b). Myra Hindley: Murderer, Prisoner, Policy Architect. The Development of Whole Life Prison Terms in England & Wales. *International Journal of Law, Crime and Justice*, *47*, 97–105. doi:10.1016/j.ijlcj.2016.09.001

Pew Research Center. (2014, August 18). *Stark racial divisions in reactions to Ferguson Police shooting*. Pew Research Center - U.S. Politics & Policy. Retrieved from https://www.pewresearch.org/politics/2014/08/18/stark-racial-divisions-in-reactions-to-ferguson-police-shooting/

Pleasance, H. (2011). Lost Children, the Moors & Evil Monsters: The photographic story of the Moors murders. *Image & Narrative*, *12*(4), 18–38.

Pokines, J., Mammano, K., Studebaker-Reed, M., Mowery, J., Patterson, M., Schneider, C., Trapp, B., & Mincher, C. (2018). Success rates of recovering dispersed bones among leaf litter. *Forensic Anthropology*, *1*(4), 189–200. doi:10.5744/fa.2018.0021

Pressler, J. (2018). *Maybe she had so much money she just lost track of It*. New York Magazine.

Presumption of Death (Northern Ireland) Act (2009).

Presumption of Death (Scotland) Act (1977).

Presumption of Death Act (2013).

Pringle, J. K., & Jervis, J. R. (2010). Electrical resistivity survey to search for a recent clandestine burial of a homicide victim, UK. *Forensic Science International*, *202*(1–3), e1–e7. doi:10.1016/j.forsciint.2010.04.023 PMID:20471188

Prisoners (Disclosure of Information About Victims) Act (2020).

Protest Over Hindley's Transfer Cost. (1968, Feb. 3). *The Guardian*, p. 3.

Quinlan, C. (2011). *Inside: Ireland's women's prisons, past and present* (1st ed.). Irish Academic Press.

R v Adrian Prout, (2010) Bristol Crown Court, (unreported).

R v Andrew Jones, (2020) Swansea Crown Court (unreported).

R v Bridger, Mark (2013) Mold Crown Court (unreported).

R v Christopher Halliwell, (2016) Bristol Crown Court, (unreported).

R v Davies [2008] EWCA Crim 1055.

R v Mark Bridger, (2013) Mold Crown Court, (unreported).

R v Martin Gerald Baker [2008] EWCA Crim 3118.

R v Martin Gerald Baker, (2006) Central Criminal Court, (unreported).

R v Onufrejczyk [1955] 1 All ER 247; [1955] 1 QB 388.

R v Secretary of State for the Home Department; Ex Parte Hindley [1998]

R v Secretary of State for the Home Department; Ex Parte Hindley [2000]

R v Shirley Banfield and Lynette Banfield [2013] EWCA Crim 1394.

R v Thomas Davison (1934) Old Bailey (unreported).

Rawlings, P. (1995). True Crime. In *Papers from then British Criminology Conference*. Loughborough University.

Ressler, R. K., Burgess, A. W., Douglas, J. E., Hartman, C. R., & D'Agostino, R. B. (1986). Sexual killers and their victims: Identifying patterns through crime scene analysis. *Journal of Interpersonal Violence*, *1*(3), 288–308. doi:10.1177/088626086001003003

Rickford, R. (2016). Black lives matter: Toward a modern practice of mass struggle. *New Labor Forum*, *25*(1), 34–42. doi:10.1177/1095796015620171

Risse, M., & Zeckhauser, R. (2004). Racial profiling. *Philosophy & Public Affairs*, *32*(2), 131–170. doi:10.1111/j.1088-4963.2004.00009.x

Ritchie, J. (1988). *Myra Hindley: Inside the Mind of a Murderess*. Angus & Robertson Publishers.

Ruffell, A., & McKinley, J. (2014). Forensic geomorphology. *Geomorphology*, *206*, 14–22. doi:10.1016/j.geomorph.2013.12.020

Ruggiero, V., & South, N. (2013). Toxic state-corporate crimes, neo-liberalism and green criminology: The hazards and legacies of the oil, chemical and mineral industries. *International Journal for Crime. Justice and Social Democracy*, *2*(2), 12–26. doi:10.5204/ijcjsd.v2i2.115

Russell-Brown, K. (1998). *The color of crime: Racial hoaxes, white fear, Black protectionism, police harassment and other macroaggressions*. New University Press.

Ryan, N., Westera, N., Kebbell, M., Milne, R., & Harrison, M. (2020). To know where the bodies are buried: The use of the cognitive interview in an environmental scale spatial memory retrieval task. *Applied Cognitive Psychology, 34*(3), 565–576. doi:10.1002/acp.3640

Salter, J. (2014, August 11). *Vandalism, looting after vigil for Missouri man.* AP News. Retrieved from https://apnews.com/article/business-shootings-police-michael-brown-vandalism-f9de5487 5a4d450683e07bfd0691df14

Saxty, D. (1998, Nov. 6). Myra One Step Closer to Hell. *The Sun*, p. 17.

Saxty, D. (1999, Feb. 10). Never Forget Evil of Myra. *The Sun.*

Schlesinger, P. (1977). Newsmen and their Time-Machine. *The British Journal of Sociology, 28*(3), 336–350. doi:10.2307/589998

Schone, J. M. (2000). The Hardest Case of All: Myra Hindley, Life Sentences, and the Rule of Law. *International Journal of the Sociology of Law, 28*(4), 273–289. doi:10.1006/ijsl.1999.0125

Seigel, M. (2017). The dilemma of 'racial profiling': An abolitionist police history. *Contemporary Justice Review, 20*(4), 474–490. doi:10.1080/10282580.2017.1383773

Sellin, T. (1937). *Crime in the depression* (1st ed.). Ayer Co Publishers.

Sellin, T. (1938). *Culture, conflict and crime.* Social Science Research Council. doi:10.1086/217919

Serrano, N. (2022). *Five Ways Podcasts Are Redefining Black Representation.* (Online). Available at: https://www.adweek.com/partner-articles/5-ways-podcasts-are-redefining-black-representation/

Shackford, S. (2014, December 2). Holder Says Feds to End Racial Profiling. Unless He's Declaring an End to the Drug War, No. *Reason.* Retrieved from https://reason.com/2014/12/02/holder-says-feds-to-end-racial-profiling/

Sheridan, J. (2021). *Murder at the cottage: The search for justice for Sophie Toscan Du Plantier* [documentary series]. Now TV, Sky Crime.

Sheridan, M. (2014). *The Murder of Sophie: how I hunted and haunted the West Cork killer* (1st ed.). Gadfly Press.

Shipley, S., & Arrigo, B. (2004). *The Female Homicide Offender: Serial Murder and the Case of Aileen Wuornos.* Pearson Prentice Hall.

Shostack, G. L. (1990). Stand up for ethics. *The Journal of Business Strategy, 11*(3), 48–50. doi:10.1108/eb039376

Simkin, S. (2013). 'Actually evil. Not high school evil': Amanda Knox, sex and celebrity crime. *Celebrity Studies, 4*(1), 33–45. doi:10.1080/19392397.2012.750107

Slakoff, D., & Fadella, H. (2019). Media messages surrounding missing women and girls: The "Missing White Woman Syndrome" and other factors that influence newsworthiness. *Criminology, Criminal Justice. Law & Society, 20*(3), 80–102.

Smith, A. (2021). *Breaking News: The Presence Of Framing In Partisan Cable News Network's Coverage Of Officers Murdering Black Victims* [Master Thesis]. University of Central Florida.

Smith, A. (2004). The monster in all of us: When victims become perpetrators. *Suffolk UL Rev.*, *38*, 367.

Smith, E. (1923). *Confessions of a Confidence Man: A Handbook for Suckers*. Scientific American Publishing.

Smith, M. R., & Petrocelli, M. (2001). Racial profiling? A multivariate analysis of police traffic stop data. *Police Quarterly*, *4*(1), 4–27. doi:10.1177/109861110100400100l

Smith, P. K. (2015). Black lives matter: A new movement takes shape. *International Socialist Review*, 96.

Solomon, J., Kaplan, D., & Hancock, L. E. (2021). Expressions of American White Ethnonationalism in Support for "Blue Lives Matter". *Geopolitics*, *26*(3), 946–966. doi:10.1080/14650045.2019.1642876

Solomon, J., & Martin, A. (2019). Competitive victimhood as a lens to reconciliation: An analysis of the black lives matter and blue lives matter movements. *Conflict Resolution Quarterly*, *37*(1), 7–31. doi:10.1002/crq.21262

Sontag, S. (2004). *Regarding the Pain of Others*. Picador.

Stake, R. (1995). *The Art of Case Research: Design and Methods*. Sage.

Stanford, P. (2002, Nov. 16). Myra Hindley. *The Guardian*.

Stillman, S. (2007). 'The missing white girl syndrome': Disappeared women and media activism. *Gender & Development: Media*, *15*(3), 491–502. doi:10.1080/13552070701630665

Storrs, E. (2004). Our Scapegoat: An Exploration of Media Representations of Myra Hindley and Rosemary West. *Theology and Sexuality*, *11*(1), 9–28. doi:10.1177/135583580401100103

Sullivan, T., & Maiken, P. T. (2012). *Killer Clown: The John Wayne Gacy Murders*. Pinnacle Books.

Surette, R. (1998). *Media, crime, and criminal justice: Images and realities* (1st ed.). Wadsworth Publishing.

Swaine, J. (2014, August 14). Ferguson police arrest reporters amid rage over Michael Brown shooting. *The Guardian*. Retrieved from https://www.theguardian.com/world/2014/aug/14/ferguson-police-arrest-reporters-as-unrest-continues-over-michael-brown-shooting

Swaine, J., Roberts, D., & Glenza, J. (2014, August 14). Missouri governor removes St Louis police from Ferguson protest duty. *The Guardian*. Retrieved from https://www.theguardian.com/world/2014/aug/14/obama-ferguson-police-excessive-force-michael-brown#:~:text=%E2%80%9CThat%20behavior%20was%20wholly%20unwarranted,arrest%20of%20reporter%20Wesley%20Lowery

Sympathy for a She-Devil? (1994, Dec. 11). *The Observer*, p. 20.

Szasz, A. (1994). *Ecopopulism: Toxic waste and the movement for environmental justice*. U of Minnesota Press.

Szasz, A. (1994). *EcoPopulism: Toxic Waste and the Movement for Environmental Justice*. University of Minnesota Press.

Tacks, B. (1977). *Freedom for Myra Hindley?* S.1. E.1. (*Roger Casstles, Dir.). BBC.*

Taylor, T. (2003). *The Clown that Killed*. Prairie Ghosts.

Teasley, M., Schiele, J., Adams, C., & Okilwa, N. (2017). Trayvon Martin: Racial Profiling, Black Male Stigma, and Social Work Practice. *Social Work*, *63*, 1–9. PMID:29136232

Telegram & Gazette. (2014, November 24). Answers to questions about the Ferguson grand jury. *The Worcester Telegram & Gazette*. Retrieved from https://www.telegram.com/story/news/state/2014/11/24/answers-to-questions-about-ferguson/35873516007/

Terrill, W., & Mastrofski, S. D. (2002). Situational and officer-based determinants of police coercion. *Justice Quarterly*, *19*(2), 215–249. doi:10.1080/07418820200095221

Terrill, W., & Reisig, M. D. (2003). Neighborhood context and police use of force. *Journal of Research in Crime and Delinquency*, *40*(3), 291–321. doi:10.1177/0022427803253800

The Guardian. (2021, October 27). Helen's law: killer refused parole for failing to disclose where body hidden. *The Guardian*. https://www.theguardian.com/society/2021/oct/27/helens-law-killer-refused-parole-for-failing-to-disclose-where-body-hidden

The King v Hindmarsh, [1730] 74 ER; [1792] 168 ER 387.

The Myra Hindley Conundrum. (1985, Feb. 7). *The Guardian*, p. 12.

Thomas, A. (2021). *Attitudes Toward the Black & Blue Lives Matter Movements*. https://mcstor.library.milligan.edu/bitstream/handle/11558/5827/Thomas_Alexandria_20210413.pdf?sequence=3&isAllowed=y

Thomas, A. J., & Blackmon, S. M. (2015). The Influence of the Trayvon Martin Shooting on Racial Socialization Practices of African American Parents. *The Journal of Black Psychology*, *41*(1), 75–89. doi:10.1177/0095798414563610

Thomson, G., & Black, S. (2017). Principles of tool mark analysis and evidential best practice. In S. Black, G. Rutty, S. Hainsworth, & G. Thomson (Eds.), *Criminal Dismemberment: Forensic and Investigative Analysis* (pp. 79–96). CRC Press. doi:10.1201/9781315373126-7

Titus, R. M., & Gover, A. R. (2001). Personal fraud: The victims and the scams. *Crime Prevention Studies*, *12*, 133–152.

To, D. (2017). Forensic archaeology survey methods, scene documentation, excavation, and recovery methods. In N. Langley & M. Tersigni-Tarrant (Eds.), *Forensic Anthropology: A Comprehensive Introduction* (pp. 35–56). CRC Press.

Topping, P. (1989). *Topping: The Autobiography of the Police Chief in the Moors Murders Case*. Angus & Robertson Publishers.

Torres, M., Cannito-Coville, M., & Rodriguez, D. (2017). Trayvon Revisited: Race, Fear, and Affect in the Death of Trayvon Martin. *Sociological Forum*, *32*(S1), 1112–1126. doi:10.1111ocf.12369

Towers, T. (2021, May 6). Moors Murderers Ian Brady and Myra Hindley's Chilling Links to Occult and Devil Worship. *Daily Star.*

Ubelaker, D. H., & Wu, Y. (2020). Fragment analysis in forensic anthropology. *Forensic Sciences Research*, *5*(4), 260–265. doi:10.1080/20961790.2020.1811513 PMID:33457044

UK Centre for Ecology and Hydrology. (2022). *Dyfi Bridge 2012*. https://eip.ceh.ac.uk/hydrology/water-resources/#introText

Umoja Noble, S. (2014). Teaching Trayvon. *The Black Scholar*, *44*(1), 12–29. doi:10.1080/00064246.2014.11641209

Valier, C. (2002, June). Cruel Britania. *Counsel*, 14–15.

van Meter, J. G. (1961). Proof of the corpus delicti by circumstantial evidence where the body is never found. *West Virginia Law Review*, *63*(2), 156–161.

Ward, C. V. (2014). Stand your ground and self-defense. *American Journal of Criminal Law*, *42*, 89.

Wattis, L. (2015). Revisiting the Yorkshire ripper murders: Interrogating gender violence, sex work, and justice. *Feminist Criminology*, *12*(1), 3–21. doi:10.1177/1557085115602960

Weichselbaum, S., & Lewis, N. (2020). *Support for defunding the police department is growing. Here's why it's not a silver bullet.* The Marshall Project.

White, B. (1997, Dec. 6). Myra Hindley as Scapegoat. *The Tablet*, p. 15.

White, R. (2012). Land theft as rural eco-crime. *International Journal of Rural Criminology*, *1*(2), 203–217. doi:10.18061/1811/53698

White, R. (2013). Resource extraction leaves something behind: Environmental justice and mining. *International Journal for Crime. Justice and Social Democracy*, *2*(1), 50–64. doi:10.5204/ijcjsd.v2i1.90

Wilson, D. (1972, Sept. 17). Myra Hindley and her Walk. *The Observer*, p. 8.

Worden, R. E. (2015). *The causes of police brutality: Theory and evidence on police use of force*. Routledge.

Yin, K. R. (2008). Case Study Research: Design and Methods (4th ed.). Sage Publications Incorporated.

Yin, R. K. (2009). *Case study research: Design and methods* (Vol. 5). sage.

Yin, R. (2009). *Case Study Research: Design and Methods*. Sage.

Young, A. (1996). *Imagining Crime Textual Outlaws and Criminal Conversations*. Academic Press.

Young, J., Higgins, D., & Austin, J. J. (2021). Soil DNA: Advances in DNA technology offer a powerful new tool for forensic science. *Geological Society of London, Special Publications*, *492*(1), 239–247. doi:10.1144/SP492-2017-351

About the Contributors

Liam James Leonard (BA, M.Phil, PhD), researcher and international academic is based at University of Winchester, UK, formerly at Arden University UK, Manchester UK, Department of Criminology & Criminal Justice, Northern Arizona University, also formerly with California State University, Los Angeles and is also an Associate Professor with West Virginia University, USA. Previously, Liam has been Chair of the Criminology Association of Ireland and former Members Secretary and President of the Sociology Association of Ireland. Dr. Leonard was the Senior Academic and primary instructor on the award winning Custodial Care Prison Studies Program, which trained approx. 1,000 recruits in a humane approach to prison work for the Irish Prison Service. He is the author/editor of over 25 books and numerous journal articles.

* * *

Angelo Brown received his master's at Arizona State University and his Ph.D. Criminal Justice and Criminology at Washington State University. His research and teaching in criminal justice and criminology are primarily on policy and policing from a comparative and intersectional perspective. Dr. Brown is a member of the Academy of Criminal Justice Sciences and a member of the Pullman Police Advisory Board. He is a research associate for the Division of Governmental Studies and Service, analyzing state patrol data. Outside of work, he enjoys mountain biking, martial arts, camping or just about any activity outdoors and in nature, as he spent many years as a camp counselor with the Federated Indians of Graton Rancheria.

Cristie Bussey, after nearly two decades of working in academia, specifically within the discipline of criminal justice, now works as a criminal defense attorney in the state of Alabama. From 2014-2021, she headed the Criminal Justice Department at Judson College, a private four-year Christian college for women. Prior to joining Judson, she taught a variety of undergraduate criminal justice courses at The University of Alabama and at Georgia Southern University. Dr. Bussey has also assisted in myriad research projects: substance abuse histories of arrestees, juvenile participant satisfaction with restorative justice, post-release aspirations of juvenile detainees, case attrition in domestic violence prosecutions, gender construction within jail inmate parenting programs, and creation of "textual outlaws" through Labour's RESPECT initiative. For two years, she worked as an analyst for Indiana Protection of Abused and Trafficked Humans, a task force funded by the Department of Justice's Office for Victims and the Bureau of Justice Assistance, aiding metropolitan police in detecting suspected victims of labor and sexual trafficking. In that capacity, Dr. Bussey tracked investigations of possible forced theft and prostitution operations. Additionally, she interviewed persons arrested while working as escorts or in street prostitution, ascertaining ostensible linkages to pimps or larger criminal syndicates. Dr. Bussey began her career as a Treatment Alternatives to Street Crime case manager in Jefferson County, Alabama, assessing arrestees for substance abuse and dependence, making referrals to social service agencies, and reporting client compliance with program dictates.

Anna Chaussée has consulted in and trained on the use of forensic archaeology in mass fatality incidents, major crime (homicide), suspected no body murder search and civil burial disputes across the UK. Anna is a Senior Lecturer at the University of Winchester and the Director of the university's Cold Case Unit tasked with the investigation of cold cases involving missing persons and unidentified human remains. Anna is a professional member of the Chartered Society of Forensic Sciences and a Senior Fellow of the Higher Education Academy.

Shannon DeBlasio (BSc, MSc, PhD, FHEA) is a Senior Lecturer within the School of Criminal Justice at Arden University. Shannon is a Chartered Psychologist (CPsychol), with an expertise in Forensic and Investigative Psychology. Prior to working in Academia, Shannon spent 10 years supporting men who had become involved with the Criminal Justice System within England and Wales. Some of the roles Shannon engaged with were within Probation, Her Majesty's Prison Services, and community drug and alcohol provisions.

Michelle N. Eliasson is a Ph.D. Candidate in the Department of Sociology and Criminology & Law at the University of Florida. Her research interests are victimology, policing, criminal justice professionals, restorative justice and qualitative methodology and her current research focuses on examining police officers' perceptions of victims.

Shane O'Mahony is a Criminologist whose primary research interests revolve around drug and alcohol policy, criminological theory, and media representations of violent crime. Shane currently serves as a Lecturer in Criminology at the University of Hertfordshire (UK).

Gianna Strube is an Independent Researcher and University Teaching Assistant in Arizona, United States. Gianna is working and researching in the areas of probation, parole and foster care, and has worked in the field and as a researcher in these areas. Gianna is a graduate of Northern Arizona University, US.

Beatrice Ugolini is PhD in "Theories of Law and Politics" and graduated in Philosophy. Honorary Judge of the Surveillance Court in Bologna and Contract Professor in "Occult-esoteric Language" at the University "N. Cusano" of Rome. She collaborates with the Pontifical "Regina Apostolorum" University of Rome and with the G.R.I.S. (Socio-Religious Research and Information Group). Criminologist expert in ritual and symbols used in destructive cults.

Index

A

Abolish the Police 103, 106, 108, 115
Acquittal 94-95, 97, 99-104, 106, 108-109, 115, 122, 128, 134, 136, 141
Aggression 7, 9, 47, 177, 221
Amanda Knox 65, 67, 117-118, 120-123, 126, 132
Analysis 1-2, 4-5, 13, 16, 25, 28, 46-48, 70, 73-74, 79, 84, 88, 91, 112-114, 117-119, 122, 127, 139-140, 146, 148, 150, 164-165, 167-173, 189, 191, 195-197, 201, 204-205, 217, 219, 221

B

Battered Woman Defense 192, 199
Battered Woman Syndrome 192, 194, 199
Black Lives Matter 94-95, 101-102, 106-107, 109-114
Body Concealment 141

C

Case 1-3, 5, 9-10, 13, 15-18, 20, 23-26, 29, 31, 34-35, 37-43, 49, 51, 60, 63-64, 66, 68-70, 73, 75, 77, 81-90, 92, 94, 97-105, 108-109, 111, 117-118, 123-124, 126-128, 130-131, 134-136, 141-142, 145, 147, 149-150, 152-153, 155-160, 162, 169-170, 172, 174, 179-183, 185-188, 192, 196-199, 201-206, 213, 218-221, 224
Chivalry Hypothesis 199
Con-Artist 52
Conspiracy Theories 126, 128, 130-131
Coverage 2, 7, 11, 13, 15, 19-20, 22-26, 30-31, 38, 41-42, 65, 69-71, 73-75, 79, 82-83, 85-86, 88-90, 94-95, 99-101, 103-104, 111, 113, 124, 141, 143, 165, 169-173, 175, 177-178, 181, 211, 223, 225
Crime 1-2, 4-5, 7-10, 22-26, 28, 31, 36, 39, 44-47, 49-51, 58, 65-73, 75, 77-82, 84-85, 87-93, 104-105, 107, 111-115, 117-124, 126-132, 134, 138-139, 161, 165, 168, 172, 186-187, 192-193, 197-199, 201, 218, 220, 222, 226
Criminal Justice 1-2, 4, 7-8, 10, 13, 24, 28, 66, 71, 95-96, 99-110, 112-113, 141-142, 159-162, 166, 169, 188, 193-194, 196-197, 199-200, 203
Criminal Narratives 44-45
Critical Race Theory 170

D

Defund the Police 106, 111-112, 115
Development 3, 6, 28, 166, 196, 201-203, 205, 213-214, 217-220
Dynamics 79, 89, 102-103, 105-106, 109, 111, 130

E

Ecopopulist 201, 204, 211, 218
Environmental Justice 10, 189, 191, 201, 204-205, 218, 220
Ethnonationalism 107, 114-115
Evidence 3-6, 16, 18, 21-22, 34-35, 37-40,

42, 44, 47, 49, 72, 81, 86, 90, 97, 105, 110, 113-114, 122-124, 127, 133-134, 136-137, 139-140, 142-146, 149-152, 156-161, 167, 175, 182, 184, 186-188, 195, 205-206, 210, 215, 224
Evil Woman Hypothesis 200

F

Female Offenders 71-72, 90
Feminist Criminology 93, 193, 200
Ferguson 104, 111, 139, 163, 169-181, 186-190
Forensic Archaeology 140-141, 159, 162-164, 167-168
Forensic Psychology 50
Fraud 7, 36, 52, 58, 61, 67, 152

G

George Zimmerman 94, 96, 113, 115
Grand Jury 169-170, 182-184, 186-187, 189-190, 222
Grand Larceny 52-53, 59-60
Green Criminology 201-203, 220

H

Homicide 46, 51, 71, 92, 97, 134, 139, 141, 145, 153, 157, 160-163, 166, 187, 194, 199, 221, 224

I

Immigration and Customs Enforcement 52, 60
Imperfect Self-defense 195, 200
Implicit Bias 94, 104, 108-109, 112-113, 115

L

Lenore Walker 195, 199
Life Imprisonment 15, 25, 30, 147

M

Media 1-2, 4-11, 17, 20, 22-25, 27, 29-32, 34-35, 37-43, 47-49, 52-54, 61-63, 65-66, 68-75, 78-79, 82-92, 94-95, 99-109, 111-112, 115, 117-118, 121-124, 126-127, 129, 134, 138-139, 143, 145, 154, 157, 160, 165-166, 169-174, 176-177, 180-181, 186-187, 189, 195-196, 198-199, 201, 210-212, 220-222, 225
Media Coverage 1-2, 25, 31, 38, 41-42, 65, 69, 73, 82-83, 85, 88-89, 94-95, 99-100, 103-104, 111, 143, 169, 171, 173, 181, 211, 225
Meredith Kercher 117-118, 127-129, 131-132
Methods 1, 3, 9-10, 123, 140, 144, 151, 155-156, 159-161, 163-164, 167, 195, 199, 205, 220, 224
Metropolitan Police 30, 34
Milly Dowler 31-32, 35, 38-39, 41-43, 48-51
Missing Persons 133, 137-138, 162-163, 165, 168
Mobilization 94, 100, 102, 109, 202, 210-211, 216, 220
Motivation 45, 99-100, 143-144, 221
Murder 2, 6, 13-15, 18, 21-22, 26-27, 30-35, 37-39, 41-42, 44-45, 47-48, 50, 65, 68-69, 71-75, 77, 79-82, 84-85, 87, 89-93, 97-98, 117-118, 121-123, 125, 127-129, 133-139, 141-143, 145-146, 148-150, 152-153, 155-157, 161-163, 166, 170, 199, 221-223, 225
Myra Hindley 11-13, 16-20, 22-29, 154-155

N

Netflix 52-53, 55-56, 60-65, 69, 73-77, 79, 82-86, 91, 126
New Media 7, 9, 68, 70, 73, 75, 78-79, 82-90
Newspaper Coverage 11, 13, 15, 20, 22-23, 26, 74, 83

O

Operation Ruby 38

Operation Yeaddiss 30, 35-36, 38, 40, 43
Overuse of Force 105

P

Perugia 117-119, 121-124, 126, 128-132
Police Brutality 95, 102-107, 109-110, 114-115
Policing 2, 8, 91, 103, 110, 112, 115, 138, 162-164, 169-171, 176, 180-181
Prisoners Act (2020) 133
Professional Narrative Role 47
Psychology 4, 48, 50-51, 91, 114, 139, 141, 163-166, 221
Psychosexual 221
Public Opinion 7, 10-11, 13, 17, 20-21, 26, 92, 118, 129

R

Racial Justice 94-95, 99, 101-102, 106-109, 116
Racial Profiling 94-95, 103-104, 106, 108-114, 116, 190
Raffaele Sollecito 117-118, 120-123
Rudi Guede 118, 120, 122, 124, 129
Rural Community 201, 203, 206, 217
Rural Sentiment 201, 203, 218

S

Self-Defense 94, 97-100, 114, 194-195, 198-200
Sentencing 4, 40-41, 47, 90, 112, 147, 159-160, 193, 225
Serial Killer 23, 32, 34, 40, 51, 53, 64, 163, 192, 194, 221, 226
Serial Killing 23
Social Media 53, 61-63, 65, 68, 94-95, 99-102, 106-107, 109, 129, 171, 201
Sophie Toscan du Plantier 68-69, 74, 76-77, 90, 92-93
Study 1-7, 9-10, 22-23, 45-46, 68-70, 73, 83, 89-91, 104, 111-112, 160, 162-163, 170, 172, 191, 195-197, 199, 201, 203-205, 218-221
Surrey Police 31, 37-38, 48
Systematic Racism 106, 108-109, 116

T

Theft 32, 49, 53, 59-60, 121, 125, 220
Trayvon Martin 94-95, 100, 110-115, 179, 181
Trial 2, 4, 11-12, 14-16, 24, 26-28, 33-34, 37-39, 41-43, 47-49, 52-53, 55, 59-62, 64-65, 74, 90, 92, 95, 97-103, 118, 124, 130, 136, 145-146, 148, 150, 152-153, 156, 161, 165-166, 182-183, 186-187, 195-196, 198, 222-223

V

Violence Against Women 43, 68, 70-73, 82-83, 88-90

W

West Cork 68-69, 73-87, 89-91, 93

www.ingramcontent.com/pod-product-compliance
Lightning Source LLC
LaVergne TN
LVHW061536290926
849162LV00004B/815